PROMISE AND DILEMMA

# PROMISE AND DILEMMA

PERSPECTIVES ON RACIAL DIVERSITY
AND HIGHER EDUCATION

*EUGENE Y. LOWE, JR.*
*EDITOR*

PRINCETON UNIVERSITY PRESS

PRINCETON, NEW JERSEY

*Library of Congress Cataloging-in-Publication Data*

Promise and dilemma : perspectives on racial diversity and higher
    education / Eugene Y. Lowe, Jr., editor.
        p.    cm.
    Includes bibliographical references and index.
    ISBN 0-691-00489-7 (alk. paper)
    1. Minorities — Education (Higher) — United States — Case studies.
    2. Educational equalization — United States — Case studies.
    3. Affirmative action programs — United States — Case studies.
    4. Academic achievement — United States — Case studies.
    5. Educational equalization — South Africa — Case studies.
    6. Universities and colleges — South Africa — Sociological aspects —
    Case studies.   7. Universities and colleges — United States
    — Sociological aspects — Case studies.   I. Lowe, Eugene Y., 1949–        .
    LC3727.P77   1999
    306.43 — dc21                                              98-45778

Publication of this book has been aided by a grant from the
Andrew W. Mellon Foundation

This book has been composed in Sabon

The paper used in this publication meets the minimum requirements of
ANSI/NISO Z39.48-1992(R1997) (*Permanence of Paper*)

http://pup.princeton.edu

Printed in the United States of America

10   9   8   7   6   5   4   3   2   1

# CONTENTS

# FOREWORD

## William G. Bowen and Harold T. Shapiro

WE ARE PLEASED to provide a brief foreword to this important collection of "perspectives on racial diversity and higher education." Not surprisingly, this is a subject on which there are more thoughtful perspectives — moral, constitutional, and practical — than there are contributors to this volume. Nevertheless, the essays and commentaries presented here are a stimulating contribution to the ongoing national debate. They can be grouped under three headings.*

First, there is the broad perspective that can be obtained by careful examination of the complex history of our country's effort to achieve the "promise" of racial diversity while confronting the "dilemma" (or, we would suggest, dilemmas) that are also associated with race in America. Gene Lowe's extensive essay, which is much more than an introduction to the volume, provides this needed historical context. Based on both his considerable personal experience as an educator at universities in the process of becoming more racially inclusive and substantial library and field research, Dr. Lowe's essay reminds us of the ways in which the debate over these policies has changed dramatically over the course of the twentieth century. It also recalls the clarity with which Du Bois and then Myrdal, among others, saw what many chose not to see — then or now.

In addition, Lowe's essay identifies certain recurring phenomena, including the "top-down" nature of much of the impetus for change, at both the governmental level and within educational institutions. It was the federal government (particularly the executive branch), not the states, that took the lead in pushing for affirmative action, and it has generally been presidents and deans, rather than academic departments and faculties, that have articulated, emphasized, and sustained the commitment to diversity within colleges and universities. One result has been ambiguity and even confusion when minority students, in particular, sometimes hear one official message from "on high" and then confront different realities in their day-to-day lives.

A second broad set of perspectives is provided by detailed empirical

---

* These essays all made an important contribution to the Princeton Conference on Higher Education (March 21–23, 1996) held on the occasion of Princeton University's 250th Anniversary.

examination of the extent of the racial disparities in academic preparation and performance and of the factors responsible for these gaps. Scott Miller and Claude Steele's essays represent a welcome blend of tough-minded empirical analysis and candor. Miller summarizes a veritable mountain of data demonstrating the persistence of disparities while Steele presents an intriguing discussion of one very important factor explaining these outcomes—the often deeply debilitating effects of stereotypes. Neither Miller nor Steele has any inclination to gloss over the many remaining problems, and yet both authors also emphasize what can be done to make things better.

Uri Treisman's "practitioner's comment" on these papers is a most useful counterpoint in that he speaks from his own experiences at Berkeley and Texas in constructing model programs that set high standards and then enable minority students to meet these standards through group processes that involve high degrees of faculty involvement. Richard Light brings a statistician's skills to the discussion and reminds readers that when we discuss these issues in the context of colleges where admission is highly competitive we are dealing with "selection at the right tail" of the distribution of measured abilities. All of us concerned with these questions will await with keen interest the results of the Harvard Assessments that Light and his colleagues are now conducting in an effort to understand better how high-scoring students of all races can capitalize more fully on the opportunities afforded them by an undergraduate experience characterized by diversity.

The third set of perspectives is provided by examining racial diversity from a broader societal point of view. Neil Smelser has the advantage of having been an astute student of the national scene for a long time, an active participant at Berkeley in the shaping of events in California, and now an independent observer as director of the Center for Advanced Study in the Behavioral Sciences at Palo Alto. His essay illustrates well the layers of meaning associated with commonplace words, phrases, and concepts; he demonstrates strikingly how both advocates and opponents of affirmative action have emphasized the same cultural value—equality of opportunity. Chang-Lin Tien comments on Smelser's paper from the position of someone who is an outspoken leader of a university (Berkeley) caught up in this debate and who also is an Asian-American. Those of us who were privileged to hear (and not merely read) his account of the social transformations he witnessed will not soon forget the passion that stimulated his decisions and, yes, his acts of courage.

Finally, the volume is enriched greatly, in our opinion, by the inclusion of an essay by Mamphela Ramphele, vice-chancellor of the University of Cape Town. Dr. Ramphele presides today over one of the most important educational institutions on the continent of Africa, in a country that is testing, in "real time," whether it is possible to overcome decades of state-imposed racial exploitation. Her university is dedicated to achieving both "equity and excellence," and she describes eloquently why these goals need to be seen as complementary. She also is candid (as always) in noting that the policies she describes are far from unproblematic and inevitably will be attacked from both ends of the political spectrum.

In commenting on this paper, Randall Kennedy first relates the South African experience to the long history of inequality in our country and then ends by applauding Dr. Ramphele's emphatic commitment to preserving meritocratic ideals while transforming her university. As Kennedy puts it, she thereby provides "an instructive lesson in righting wrongs while preserving what is best in existing institutions." This is, we agree, an important lesson for educators everywhere.

# ACKNOWLEDGMENTS

THIS BOOK, nearly three years in the making, is the product of a stimulating collaboration sponsored by The Andrew W. Mellon Foundation. While the contributors have been together in one place only once—at the March 1996 Princeton Conference on Higher Education (jointly sponsored by Princeton University and Mellon)—we have been in regular communication in order to advance and present this discussion in publishable form. The Foundation has generously supported the process of moving from conference proceedings to published book in more ways than can be counted.

In a formal and personal sense, my thanks go first to William G. Bowen and Harold T. Shapiro, the two Princeton presidents under whom I served as dean of students from 1983 to 1993. Much of the material that has found its way into *Promise and Dilemma* is rooted in what I learned during that decade. As president of The Andrew W. Mellon Foundation, William Bowen has continued to support and encourage this work as well as to urge me to find simpler ways to express my thoughts. My thanks to him and to the Foundation for their patience as I completed this work in the midst of other responsibilities. I wish also to thank my former Princeton colleagues in the Office of the Dean of Students and the Office of the Dean of the College in whose company I initially explored many of the questions that underlie this book.

Jennifer Hochschild, Sheldon Hackney, and a reader for Princeton University Press critically reviewed the manuscript and recommended its publication while also making important suggestions for improving it. My long-time friend and colleague, Nancy Weiss Malkiel, Dean of the College and professor of history, gave Part I a very careful reading.

In the preparation of the manuscript and in the coordination of communication among the contributors, I have been helped from the beginning by Dorothy Westgate of the Princeton office of The Andrew W. Mellon Foundation. My Northwestern-based assistant, Mary Bucholtz, also provided invaluable assistance in the latter stages of manuscript revision.

The initial planning for this project took place as I was completing a term of service at Princeton's Department of Religion and preparing to move to Northwestern. I am grateful for the support of colleagues at what was my academic base for twelve years. This project moved with me to Northwestern University a few months before the Princeton Conference. The bulk of the work, therefore, has been completed in Evanston, where I have enjoyed the support of, and learned from, a new group of administrative and faculty colleagues. I wish to convey my particular thanks to Henry Bienen, president of Northwestern, and Lawrence Dumas, provost of Northwestern, for their encouragement of this work.

I am also indebted to Princeton University Press, particularly to Walter Lippincott and Peter Dougherty, for their counsel and support during the review process. Karen Fortgang of bookworks has provided critical energy and focus in the final stages of manuscript preparation.

I wish finally to thank my wife, Jane Pataky Henderson, who has been a patient believer that this project would one day be complete, and our children for their abiding tolerance of my divided attention.

Eugene Y. Lowe, Jr.
Evanston, Illinois
Thanksgiving 1998

# CONTRIBUTORS

**Randall Kennedy**, professor at Harvard Law School, teaches courses on contracts, freedom of expression, and the regulation of race relations. He has written numerous articles for scholarly journals and magazines for the general public and is the author of the recently published book *Race, Crime, and the Law* (1997). A former Rhodes Scholar, he also served as law clerk for Judge J. Skelly Wright of the United States Court of Appeals and for Justice Thurgood Marshall of the United States Supreme Court. He is also a member of the American Law Institute, a member of the editorial boards of *The Nation*, *Dissent*, and *The American Prospect*, and a Princeton University trustee.

**Richard J. Light** is professor of education and public policy at the John F. Kennedy School of Government, Harvard University. He is author or co-author of six books, including *By Design* (with Judy Singer and John Willett [1990]), a study of modern methods for assessing educational effectiveness. He also is director of the Harvard Assessment Seminar, a consortium bringing together faculty and administrators from twenty-four colleges and universities. He has served as president of the American Evaluation Association and on the boards of the American Association for Higher Education and the Fund for the Improvement of Postsecondary Education. He is a past recipient of the Paul Lazarsfeld Award for distinguished contributions to scientific practice.

**Eugene Y. Lowe, Jr.** is associate provost and senior lecturer in religion at Northwestern University. From 1983–1993 he served as dean of students at Princeton University and as a member of the department of religion. His research on diversity in higher education has been supported by the Andrew W. Mellon Foundation. An Episcopal priest and historian of American religion, his writings on the social gospel, progressivism, and race in American history have been published in a number of volumes. He is a member of a number of boards, including Berea College and Seabury-Western Theological Seminary.

**L. Scott Miller** is director of the National Task Force on Minority High Achievement of The College Board. Previously he served as senior program officer of the Exxon Education Foundation and as senior vice president of the Council for Aid to Education. His book, *An American Imperative: Accelerating Minority Educational Advancement* (1995), has won two awards: the American Educational Research Association's Outstanding Book of the Year for 1997 and the 1998 Grawemeyer Award in Education of the University of Louisville.

**Mamphela Aletta Ramphele,** a physician and anthropologist, is the vice-chancellor of the University of Cape Town, one of South Africa's major research universities. She holds the distinction of being the first black and the first woman vice-chancellor of the University of Cape Town. Known for her research on life in migrant workers' hostels of the western Cape, she has published several important studies including *A Bed Called Home: Life in the Migrant Labour Hostels of Cape Town* (1993) and *Restoring the Land—Environment and Change in Post-Apartheid South Africa* (1992). Her autobiography, *Mamphela Ramphele: A Life*, was published in 1995 in Cape Town and in 1996 in New York with the title *Across Boundaries: The Journey of a South African Woman Leader.*

**Neil J. Smelser** is director of the Center for Advanced Study in the Behavioral Sciences, Stanford, CA. Also University Professor Emeritus of Sociology at the University of California, Berkeley, he is author of a number of major works including *Comparative Methods in the Social Sciences* (1976) and *The Changing Academic Market* (with Robin Content [1980]), as well as *Problematics of Sociology* (1997). A former Rhodes Scholar and Junior Fellow in the Society of Fellows at Harvard University, he was elected to the National Academy of Sciences in 1993.

**Claude M. Steele** is professor of psychology and chair of the Department of Psychology at Stanford University. A social psychologist, his work has focused on self-evaluative processing, addictive behaviors, and the role of stereotypes in shaping intellectual identity and performance. His research has been supported by the National Institutes of Health, the Russell Sage Foundation, and the James Irvine Foundation. His work has been published in *The American Psychologist, The Atlantic Monthly*, and the *Journal of Personality and Psychology.* He is a member of the board of directors of the American Psychological Society and has served as president of the Western Psychological Association.

**Chang-Lin Tien** is NEC Distinguished Professor of Engineering and former chancellor of the University of California at Berkeley. As chancellor from 1990 to 1997, he was the first Asian-American to head a major research university in the United States. Internationally recognized for his research in the field of heat transfer technology, he was elected to the National Academy of Engineering in 1976. He is the author of one book and more than 300 research journal and monograph articles and has edited fifteen volumes.

**Philip Uri Treisman** is professor of mathematics and the director of the Charles A. Dana Center at the University of Texas at Austin, as well as executive director of the Texas Statewide Systemic Initiative. He is a member of the management team of the National Institute for Science Education and of the National Research Council's Center for Mathematics, Science, and Engineering Education; he is also president of the board of the Consortium for Mathematics and Its Applications. In July 1992, he was named a MacArthur Fellow. For his work in developing programs that have helped minority and other underserved student populations to excel in mathematics, he was named by *Newsweek* magazine as one of three American educators "on the leading edge of innovation." For his studies of the dynamics of black student performance in calculus at the University of California at Berkeley, he received the 1987 Charles A. Dana Award for Pioneering Achievement in American Higher Education.

*PART I*

## One

# PROMISE AND DILEMMA

*INCORPORATING RACIAL DIVERSITY IN SELECTIVE*

*HIGHER EDUCATION*

Eugene Y. Lowe, Jr.

CELEBRATING the value of racial and ethnic diversity has become routine in educational circles. The idea is deeply consonant with shaping ideals of the American ethos, the conviction that out of many origins and backgrounds, a new people is formed; out of divergent "manyness," new opportunity is created. A similar-sounding theme is struck about the missions of colleges and universities and about the centrality of the interplay of different viewpoints and experiences — the robust exchange of ideas — in the search for new interpretations of experience. The practice of teaching and research, so the argument goes, is strengthened by the engagement of intellectual and cultural diversity.

Whether support for the value of diversity is grounded in an interpretation of the national motto, *e pluribus unum*, or in an appreciation of the purposes and requirements of a learning community, diversity exercises strong appeal socially and intellectually. The fusion of this two-sided appeal reinforces prevailing patterns of belief about the promise of education as a process of transformation and growth. To be sure, while colleges and universities have distinctive purposes in teaching, research, and service, their legitimacy, their capacity to evoke the most durable support from constituencies, derives from their role as agents of change and opportunity for individuals.

While, then, the value of diversity is consistently affirmed, there is also considerable contemporary evidence of ambivalence and opposition to institutional strategies designed to enhance diversity. In higher education, many such concerns focus on admissions policies in professional and undergraduate education. The point of tension and friction is aggravated under conditions of scarcity when racial preference affects the allocation of a sought-after, but finite good, such as an acceptance to a law or medical school or to a selective undergraduate program. The scarcer the good, the greater the pressure on the allocation mechanism. Under such conditions, the process used to enhance demographic diversity is fundamentally an individual meritocratic evaluation procedure in which individual cases are considered in some systematic fashion. When opportunity is allocated from one individual to another for reasons having to do with factors other than an evaluation of the merits of the applicants, questions do arise. Recent experience in the United States strongly suggests that under such circumstances, appeals about unfairness to individuals that result from institutional commitments to diversity will pit civil rights arguments on behalf of individuals against diversity rationales adopted by institutions. In such situations, the consensus about diversity as a value is challenged. Put another way, when the "price" of diversity is represented in a way that raises questions about fairness, a "crisis" of belief develops about the relationship of means and ends, and the cost and value of diversity.

Affirmative action is certainly a case in point. When this concept is understood as facilitating diversity by providing opportunity to those who have unfairly been denied opportunity, for example, by providing opportunities for people to gain the skills needed for successful competition, or by insisting on search processes that cast the net more widely in the search for job candidates, support for such action tends to be strong. On the other hand, if, in a particular case, an institution chooses to accept or to hire someone and race becomes a "tipping" factor in the decision, suspicions are aroused and the legitimacy of the decision can become problematic for both the institution and the individual selected. Of course, the degree of suspicion is directly related to how much benefit is accrued to one party, and how great the loss sustained by the other, based on the racial plus factor (see, e.g., Steeh and Krysan 1996). We find ourselves in a difficult quandary, valuing diversity but eschewing preference. It is one manifestation of America's continuing dilemma about race. The tension between these values has been difficult to resolve because of the complex ways in which a historical legacy of inequality continues to be reflected in our experience, particularly in the ways in which we evaluate intellectual competence and merit.

Originally a federally sanctioned policy to provide access and opportunity for blacks in employment and contracting, affirmative action was extended in the period following 1965 to encompass college and university admissions as well. In this latter area the tensions between American traditions valuing individualism and traditions supporting egalitarianism are most apparent. Affirmative action was conceived to address, and to redress, exclusion experienced by black Americans. The black/white relationship that shapes American history and sensibility retains an unresolved centrality even as affirmative action efforts have been extended to focus on other groups who have also experienced discrimination. Peter Schrag, former associate editor of the *Sacramento Bee*, has offered a thoughtful reflection about this permutation and expansion of the meaning of "minority." Affirmative action, he observes, which was "originally designed to remedy the effects of slavery and Jim Crow," has "been broadened to include a host of other minority groups, many of which can make no equivalent claims to a history of discrimination" (*Sacramento Bee* 14 August 1996). In California, a state that has played a central role in depicting the changing racial composition of the United States, the danger is, as Schrag sees it, that affirmative action is no longer understood in a specific historical context. As such it becomes highly vulnerable to becoming delegitimated in the public mind. While the binary pattern of black and white no longer describes the country's racial demography, the problem of the "color line," as W.E.B. Du Bois predicted nearly a century ago, continues to constrain at the conclusion of the twentieth century, as it did at its beginning, the resolution of America's struggle with racial issues. At the century's end, however, we seemed to have learned to make diversity a value, while remaining divided about the means to achieve it. This underlying ambivalence conditions public and private discourse and experience in important ways.

Until rather recently, it has not been common to express reservations publicly about affirmative action in elite colleges and universities. Many would undoubtedly identify with the sentiment expressed by a Berkeley faculty member that an "unwritten compact" precluded such discussion (Hollinger 1997). The reasons for this probably included such factors as a deeply shared recognition by members of the academic community about the historical injustices visited on blacks and other minorities, the hope that special measures put into effect to advance minority participation would be temporary, the belief that diversity made educational sense, and, finally, a fear of being branded as racist (a fear rather widely felt among many white college and university administrators).

It is not easy to assess the impact of this last inhibition. A combination of factors have enabled educators as well as the broader public to diffuse focus on a problem that emerged very early in the affirmative action debate: the measurable performance differentials characterizing members of different ethnic groups who present themselves as candidates in competitive admission processes (Klitgaard 1995). Measured qualifications are, as many have persuasively argued, not the only qualifications that matter, or the only objectives institutions seek to maximize through admissions policies and practices (Fetter 1995). They are, however, understood as important and helpful indicators about the capacity to use the verbal and mathematical languages of the academy, and the prospects for academic success in environments that take for granted a certain level of proficiency in the use of those "languages" as a precondition for such success. The formidable limiting factor here has been the small number of non-Asian minorities whose measured academic qualifications are comparable to the much larger number of Asian-American and white candidates for admission at selective institutions (College Entrance Examination Board 1992). These imbalances in the applicant pools have created a new scarcity, which institutions have worked to address: a shortage of black and Hispanic students who can thrive in elite institutions. The small numbers problem combined with an institutional commitment to diversity has aggravated the unsettled relationship between the value of diversity and the value of individual fairness in meritocratic evaluation procedures.

The essays in this volume presuppose that a critical examination of empirical data about and experience with diversity is important. First, and perhaps most important, there is a shared concern that racial diversity is a positive development for educational as well as other reasons in higher education; at the same time, those involved in this project also believe that it is time for a more candid discussion than takes place in many venues about the kinds of strategies and institutional programs that have promoted diversity on college and university campuses. The long-term interests of educational institutions and the many kinds of students they help to train are not well served by avoiding critical analysis of strategies that may be well intentioned in their origins, but that serve students and institutions less well than they might. We are, in short, committed to the proposition that we can become wiser teachers and administrators if we take stock of what we have done, learn from our experience, and aim to do better.

Second, the various contributors recognize that it is important to understand that this progress continues to be affected by the legacy of the past. It takes a long time and careful thought and action to overcome a long history of inequality. To be responsible to the present and the future entails a deep appreciation of the impact of what has come before.

Third, in ways that are particularly the concern of this introductory essay, the appropriation of change in patterns of access has affected the responsibilities of institutional leaders — presidents and senior administrators — in distinctive ways. This group, in contrast to faculty members and students, has been responsible for mediating and articulating institutional purposes for a number of critical constituencies, including the general public and the courts. As a consequence, public opinion and judicial decisions have had profound and shaping influence on the ways in which colleges and universities have understood and executed their responsibilities in affirmative action and diversity.

Finally, it should be noted that we emphasize empirical experience and its assessment. In ways that this volume will make clear, equity and excellence are not easy partners to align in institutional policy and practice. We need to recognize this, learn more about the constraints we face, and improve institutional practice, particularly in highly selective colleges and universities.

Over the last third of the twentieth century, educational institutions have mediated the persisting tensions between individualistically oriented values about fairness and opportunity provision and the shared social values of diversity and pluralism. Debates about diversity have chiefly been debates about who goes to what schools and what and how those schools teach. As mediating institutions in society, schools of all sorts will incorporate tensions on unresolved dilemmas of their communities. Under such circumstances, educational leadership entails important responsibility for mediating, searching for consensus, and navigating through conflicts.

The group of essays collected here reflect what I have characterized as the *promise and dilemma* of selective higher education principally in the United States. Both the United States and South Africa—the subject of one essay in this volume—share a historical ideology based on the Biblical idea of the promise. Both have secularized in very different contexts the motif of exodus. In both cases, as indeed in the Biblical story itself, the realization of the "promise" for one group has been profoundly compromised by the cultural subjugation of others. This cultural subjugation—based on race—has had long-lasting political, institutional, and ideological consequences in both situations.

The dilemma faced by educational institutions is that they are inextricably bound up in the history that roots them, while, at the same time, they seek to transform individuals and serve their host communities. Their dilemma is that "transformation" cannot be sustained unless its value is endorsed by its constituencies.

*Promise and Dilemma* represents an assessment of what we have learned about the workings of an influential category of educational institutions involving issues of racial diversity. The introductory essay, comprising Part I, focuses on the mediating responsibilities of institutional leaders during a period of shifting public and judicial norms. In Part II, the focus shifts to fundamental questions having to do with the continued small numbers of high-achieving black and Hispanic students and the ways in which stereotypes continue to constrain the promise of intellectual equality. The implications of the research summarized in Part II for admissions, teaching, and learning in selective higher education are profound. Presently available evidence suggests that an "achievement" gap between whites and Asian-Americans, on the one hand, and blacks and Latinos on the other, will persist for some time to come. What is understood and, just as importantly, what is believed about this will have important consequences in both public policy and in patterns of instruction.

In Part III, as in Part I, the focus is on a more qualitative, macroscopic analysis of the institutional and cultural dimensions of affirmative action in California and South Africa. Both in California and South Africa, public institutions of higher education find themselves in a crossfire of community expectations. Mamphela Ramphele describes the tension of equity and excellence where pent-up demands of a fully enfranchised black majority for opportunity and inclusion, no longer subjugated by the policy of apartheid, must be balanced in relation to the objectives of a world-class African research university. Like California, the new South Africa has invested heavily in the development of a state-sponsored system of higher education, designed to increase opportunity and to advance research. While *Promise and Dilemma* is essentially oriented toward the United States, the juxtaposition of California and South Africa provides a useful reminder about the "cross-national" dilemmas associated with overcoming histories of discrimination.

The incorporation of the promise of diversity in the life of institutions and communities has raised expectations on many fronts that the legacy of a burdened and prejudiced history can be overcome by a new ideology of inclusion and transformation. The dilemma societies with histories of discrimination face is that history has consequences, consequences that persist beyond the discrediting of the ideologies they reflect. However, reckoning responsibly with those consequences requires something more than the promulgation of a different ideology. It requires the development of patterns of institutional action, both administrative and pedagogical, that validate in practice what is professed as ideal.

In sum, this volume might usefully be viewed as a collection of reflections about the interplay of academic values, educational practice, and community beliefs. The tension between the values of diversity and meritocracy are not new: The ways in which the pressure between them has been concentrated in elite educational institutions are increasingly experienced as a conundrum. Sorting out what we know, what we have learned, and what we can do is a critical responsibility as we prepare for the challenges of a new century. The resolutions of the dilemma must emphasize the development and assessment of more effective practices as we continue to grapple with the underlying ideological and cultural tensions that characterize the discussions about affirmative action.

*Promise and Dilemma* provides a "thick description" of the status of racial diversity at this critical juncture. To begin, it is important to describe the historical and policy backdrop that conditions the ways in which we all approach this question.

## THE CONTINUING BURDEN OF RACE IN AMERICAN EXPERIENCE

The debate about affirmative action and racial preferences — a "wedge" issue for many pundits — constitutes another painful chapter in a long history. Unlike earlier controversies, the present unsettlement is not about rights, or whether segregation or integration is permissible. The contemporary discussion is focused on fairness, in light of a history of unfairness that has not yet released its grip on the present. What makes this debate difficult to ajudicate is not that Americans fundamentally disagree about the formal terms of equality, or that the heritage of the past regarding racial separation must be repudiated. The points of continuing divisiveness are about how to move forward with responsible cognizance about the impact of the past. More specifically, if the grip of the past continues to aggravate the social injury of racism, how does a society, a community, or an institution sustain procedures of allocation or choice that distribute opportunity fairly? How do communities make progress in the distribution of opportunity if they believe that the grip of the past social injury continues to compromise the capacities of different groups of individuals to demonstrate their qualifications and talents? What is the nature of the interest that a community has in making certain that its procedures assuring fairness work in the aggregate to be inclusive of individuals of different ethnic or racial groups? And, bluntly, how much special consideration is enough? How does a community decide when to stop making such provisions?

The long-standing antagonism between American ideals about equality of opportunity and American habits of racial separation and division is a subject of deep historical irresolution. The 1896 decision of the Supreme Court in *Plessy v. Ferguson*, declaring that segregation was constitutional, sealed the legacy for the twentieth century to which Du Bois referred. The states were obligated to provide "equal" facilities and accommodations for all, but the development of such opportunities could be pursued separately if local jurisdictions preferred to provide segregated arrangements. Since political equality and racial separatism were compatible, the idea of "separate but equal" set the tone for the new century. "Separated" equality was, of course, stigmatized equality, a problem Du Bois clearly recognized. Writing just after the turn of the twentieth century, two generations after Appomattox, Du Bois understood clearly that the continuing legacy of the Civil War would not include a stable consensus about civil rights and social inclusion for blacks and that the relationship between blacks and whites would remain unsettled. Reconstruction had come to a close with a reunited nation tacitly agreeing that unity was paramount and that local customs and mores would prevail in the interpretation of the equal protection clause of the Fourteenth Amendment. The problems of implementing formal equality would be deferred until another time.

Nearly a half-century later, in 1944, when the Swedish economist Gunnar Myrdal published *An American Dilemma: The Negro Problem and Modern Democracy*, the United States was enmeshed in an international conflict, waging with a segregated military a war cast as a crusade for freedom. Following the logic of *Plessy v. Ferguson*, segregation did not compromise equal protection under the law. Myrdal, who had been invited several years earlier to undertake a study of race relations in the United States because his Carnegie Foundation sponsors believed he could view the situation without preconceptions, found the contradiction between what the United States professed about universal equality and the maintenance of segregation in public and private life impossible to understand. "Separate but equal," in his estimation, effectively created and condoned a caste system in American life that compromised profoundly the principal tenets of the American creed of opportunity and equality. In Myrdal's interpretation of American experience, this contradiction could not endure. The instability of the relationship between ideals and practice constituted the crux of the American dilemma (Myrdal 1972).

Myrdal's work catalyzed many parts of the culture and the academy. In policy terms, it helped prepare the ground for the development of government-sanctioned civil rights initiatives, beginning with President Truman's 1948 executive order to integrate the armed services. It also anticipated the development of social science that focused on intergroup relations, including such important works as Gordon Allport's 1954 study, *The Nature of Prejudice*. Perhaps most important, *An American Dilemma* helped set the stage for the reversal of *Plessy* in 1954 in *Brown v. Board of Education*, when the Supreme Court unanimously declared, in a case about school segregation in Topeka, Kansas, that "separate but equal is inherently unequal."

Myrdal's strong emphasis on the importance of modifying institutional arrangements to alleviate injustice established a pattern of institutional reform and practice. His work was oriented by a sense that social science could serve both an educational and an ameliorative purpose, that by pointing out in what ways the American experience fell short of American ideals, the collective will could be mustered and a way to change could be devised. This tradition of social science with origins in

Wisconsin Progressivism was rooted deeply in a sensibility about the relationship between the pursuit of truth and advancing the social good. Its spirit was deeply consonant with a sensibility that would emerge in the 1960s around the challenges of race: that institutional adjustments would effectively reshape personal beliefs. Understanding the relationship between this kind of social scientific analysis and the impulse to improve social conditions that characterized *An American Dilemma* helps provide a context for appreciating the ways in which an activist federal sector became a catalyst for further racial reform. The federal government became the dominant institution in American life in the redefinition of race relations.

## THE FEDERAL GOVERNMENT AS PATRON OF EQUALITY AND DIVERSITY

The formal repudiation of racial discrimination in American public life stimulated a new optimism about the possibilities of integration in American experience. The Civil Rights Act of 1964 and the Voting Rights Act of 1965 represented a decisive enlargement of the meaning of pluralism in American life and, as such, constitute one of the most important developments in the second half of this century. Abruptly, it came to symbolize the end of the tradition of according a privileged status to white Americans. While segregation has deeply affected the status of black Americans, it has also affected other groups as well. For example, immigration policies long favored migration from Europe rather than Asia or Africa, a reflection of pervasive tendencies in American culture favoring whites over people of color. Less noted, the Immigration Act of 1965, somewhat unintentionally, has had a complementary impact on the meaning of pluralism in American experience, particularly as it facilitated immigration from Asia, India, and Pakistan. This law, as Peter Schrag has written, has had "enormous consequences," and by eliminating the national origins quota system, has facilitated a massive increase of legal immigration, bringing to the United States more than 15 million people who qualified for minority group preferences (Schrag 1995).

While significant progress has been achieved toward the goal of integration in many sectors of American society, movement has occurred chiefly in the agencies of government, the workplace, higher education, and, to a significantly lesser extent, in K–12 schools. Indeed, one of the paradoxes about this development has been the simultaneous embrace of integration as a public value and the intensification of racial division in residential settings and in other situations defined, like neighborhoods, by patterns of voluntary association.

Federal action and occasionally federal intervention helped catalyze a broad social consensus against racial discrimination. Each of the three branches of the national government — but particularly the executive and judicial — has, at different moments, served as impetus to the process through which the country changed its laws and habits. This association of civil rights progress with federal power had, however, another consequence. From its beginnings, the strong identification of civil rights with an activist federal sector provided a basis for resistance to these changes because of a view about the division of authority between states and central government. States' rights became a proxy for resistance to racial change. The emphasis in the civil rights tradition on the importance of law and government obscured somewhat the continuing persistence of more informal and voluntary patterns of association that maintained segregated patterns of association. The civil rights tradition in law and policy emphasized the working of positive state action as an instrument of social change.

Not surprisingly, one of the most successful institutions in American society in dealing with racial integration has been the United States Army (see, e.g., Moskos and Butler 1996). At the other extreme, its religious institutions and primary schools are among the most segregated associations in the country. Where voluntary choice is given freer rein, the dominant patterns of life effectively continue to be segregated. In more hierarchical situations, to different degrees, the impact of individual freedom of choice is constrained, as in the Army or, also interestingly, in many Roman Catholic schools. In these institutions the social distance between members of different ethnic groups decreases in the context of an overarching ideological commitment that emphasizes the good of the community as a whole. (In addition, there is evidence in such environments that the kinds of achievement differentials between whites and blacks that characterize so many schooling situations are decreased. See Bryk et al. [1993] for a fascinating analysis about the role of parochial schools in advancing academic achievement for underrepresented minority students.)

On the other hand, as Anthony Lukas' prize-winning account of the struggle over the integration of the Boston public schools, *Common Ground*, makes clear, public schools have also become lightning rods for community conflict. The federal court order to bus school children across neighborhood boundaries to achieve racial balance in schools precipitated an extended community crisis with far-reaching consequences for the evolving patterns of race relations. The Boston school crisis of the 1970s dramatically exemplified the social and perceptual distances between the races and even between individuals who shared the goal of a genuinely integrated school system (Lukas 1985). That experience clearly taught the country how formidable an obstacle community sensibilities and beliefs pose for judicial mandates. Public schools, particularly at the primary level, comprise the first node of connection between the patterns of private or voluntary association that define neighborhoods and the more encompassing body politic. While they are agencies of local government, they also illustrate the tensions "revealed preferences" manifested in local patterns of voluntary association that shape neighborhoods and the public imperative not to discriminate and to be inclusive. These conflicts have regularly forced a recognition of the tension between voluntary associational habits and public values.

The commitment to ethnic diversity, appealing at the level of principle, is a difficult social condition to create and sustain. It is not a condition to which very many people commit themselves voluntarily, as the persistent complaints about social engineering in higher education seem to suggest. Despite nearly a quarter century of civil rights legislation, residential patterns do not suggest that the nation's neighborhoods are less segregated. In fact, a 1993 study conducted at Harvard University found that nearly two-thirds of the black students in public schools in the 1991–92 school year attended schools that were predominantly minority (*The New York Times* 10 April 1994, p. 1; Orfield 1993). Other research suggests that the country has remained more segregated in those parts of life that allow the greatest degree of personal choice: where one lives, what kinds of affiliations one makes with voluntary associations, what one does with private time and private thoughts, and by extension what one is free to say (Milburn and Bowman 1991; Massey and Denton 1993). These kinds of patterns strongly suggest that the difference between legislating nondiscrimination and legitimating diversity must be understood.

The Civil Rights movement helped to change the ways in which private as well as public institutions of higher education conceived of their responsibilities regarding the recruitment and admission of students. Colleges and universities developed organized programs to identify and attract minority students, a category that was initially interpreted to encompass black Americans. During and after that time, in colleges and universities across the nation, the task of facilitating access for black students — the population excluded most pervasively and consistently — became a special project in higher education administration.

Frequently catalyzed by extraordinary events like urban riots and campus demonstrations, the duty to care about these questions tended to settle in central administrative functions. To be sure, during the late 1960s and early 1970s, the impetus to undertake such efforts came from many faculty and students, often following a campus crisis or sit-in. At that point the objectives of campus protestors focused on ending discrimination against blacks and other minorities. This change has deeply affected the ways in which colleges and universities manage processes of recruitment and admission both for baccalaureate and postbaccalaureate degree programs. The civil rights "revolution" of the 1960s, succeeding urban riots in cities outside the South, and the assassination of Martin Luther King, Jr. in April 1968 provided the immediate backdrop for a decisive shift in the ways that colleges and universities thought about admissions. Cognizant of a heritage of exclusion caused by — in the term used by President Lyndon Johnson's advisory committee on civil disorders, the Kerner Commission — "white racism" (United States Kerner Commission 1968), institutions devised policies and procedures to increase the representation of black students on their campuses.

It was characteristic during this early period to introduce special academic enrichment and social support for minority (dominantly black) students. Virtually all of these programs were premised on the idea that minority students lacked something necessary for full participation and success in elite institutions. The impact of this deficit-based institutional response — conceived to bring more people into the system — remains ambiguous. Clearly, the numbers of students increased dramatically. It is more difficult to evaluate their relative levels of academic success.

As with the change in the country as a whole, these developments on campus tended to be sponsored by central responsibility units in the administration of the college or university. Admissions and financial aid — responsibility areas that dealt with access — and, frequently, the office of the president or of a senior administrator with ability to respond directly and immediately to the imperatives and opportunities that diversity presented became the focal points for institutional response. A review of a number of institutional histories suggests that the pattern of institutional engagement in this area did not evolve systematically; rather these institutional responses were opportunistic forms of crisis management, undertaken in the hope that the assimilation of minority populations would follow historical patterns that had characterized other outsider groups. While these responses by colleges and universities were endorsed by what emerged as strongly supportive campus consensus, they were from the beginning fundamentally administrative actions, initiatives shaped in the context of a crisis about access and fairness. By eliminating barriers to access, it was hoped that these actions would resolve a problem threatening to undermine the ability of American higher education to make good one of its fundamental claims to legitimacy.

What emerges from this review as one of the pervasive quandaries about the status of racial pluralism in higher education is the relationship between centrally expressed values and activities promoting diversity that emanate from the leaders of colleges and universities and the more ambivalent patterns of acceptance and validation that developed among the various constituents of these communities. This distinction became more apparent as the crisis about inclusion was resolved, and institutions began to face charges about "reverse" discrimination that limited opportunity for whites. In a decentralized institution that cultivates a high degree of freedom of thought, leverage over people's opinions and beliefs is, and should be, limited. The freedom of choice and thought that characterizes such places includes the freedom not to engage and even to shun the human differences represented in a diversely populated residential college or university. Yet opinions and beliefs are a crucial component of the educational environment. If these sensibilities are not consistent with the public values of the institution regarding diversity, these patterns, or "mores," as Tocqueville would have described them, can become a medium of questioning and even rejection.[1] If the opinions and beliefs of institutional constituents do not corroborate the expressed values about pluralism of the institution itself, the academic environment will be hospitable. The college or university has few effective defenses against the reluctance or ambivalence of its constituents regarding institutional commitments in the area of diversity.

Thus, while colleges and universities have been at the forefront of institutions encouraging access to opportunity and social pluralism, these institutions have other characteristics that can make it hard to stimulate the kinds of voluntary consensual approbation that maintain cohesion about purposes and goals. The college or university has characteristics that reflect both the ethos of the centrally driven and regulated organization and of a voluntary association or guild. It is corporation and academy. An important consequence of this institutional characteristic is a de facto division between the administrative and academic sectors of educational institutions. Administrators, whose language and belief about diversity have been conditioned by judicial decisions, tend to speak about and understand the issue of diversity in ways that reflect and support the leadership of their presidents.

It is also true that, at least initially, the argument about the beneficial effect of diversity was based on the character of community life that resulted from a diverse population. This argument, therefore, was more appropriately put forward by these who had responsibility for the life of the community (presidents, deans of students, and other central administrators), since the educational benefit being discussed was not based on formal classroom teaching. In short, administrators have been called upon to represent the "interests" of the extracurricular as faculty roles have become more exclusively focused on formal teaching responsibility.

On the other hand, faculty and students, who are influenced by these institutional "tone-setters," tend to bring additional kinds of experience to this question, experience that more sharply highlights the tension between diversity goals and equity aspirations. Faculty and student cultures, which in different ways are more voluntaristic, seem to experience in more complicated ways the trade-offs involved between equity and excellence. This contrasting pattern of intra-institutional experience of diversity between the administrative and voluntary sectors of institutional life is a critical dimension of a persisting dilemma. Maintaining alignment between central institutional values and individual opinions and sensibilities about pluralism and diversity becomes more difficult when the question posed is diversity as an educational value rather than nondiscrimination.

Because pluralism of racial association is such an unusual condition, colleges and universities have to stretch themselves to achieve the kinds of demographic diversity that unregulated patterns of social interaction do not tend to generate. The debates about speech codes on many college campuses (University of Michigan, Stanford, University of Pennsylvania, Tufts, University of Wisconsin) during the late 1980s and early 1990s signaled the fragility of the campus equilibrium about race. At the same time, they also manifested the vulnerability of minority students to unwelcoming or hostile campus climates. Arguably, a significant measure of the uncertainty gripping those who worry about this issue and feel somewhat stalemated about what to do next results from an underestimation of the degree of difficulty and the consequences of the task to which the higher education community committed itself during the late 1960s in the heyday of enthusiasm and hope about the Civil Rights movement.

## ACADEMIC LEADERSHIP AND VALUES MEDIATION

Universities and colleges are in one sense open systems whose interacting human agents vie in relationship to one another and to the surrounding environment for recognition and support of their interests. They are dynamic institutions that thrive on their ideological commitments to skepticism and change. In another sense, however, they are subject to a certain conservatism, a cautiousness resulting from resource constraints, decentralized patterns of decision-making, and the highly deliberative processes demanded for changing academic priorities. So, colleges and universities have shouldered distinctive responsibilities both as catalysts and conservators. As catalysts, they have been expected to be provocative about the tenets of conventional wisdom and to extend the borders of knowledge. As conservators, these institutions have — like the religious foundations from which many of them arose — been regarded as guardians of core values like the pursuit of truth and service to community. If the community consensus supporting an institution concurs in the kinds of judgments being made about these different values, the leaders of the institution can attend to the prickly issues of resource allocation. If the community consensus is divided and basic values contested, then the resource battle can take on an ideological cast as well. Either way, there will be friction of interests.

Colleges and universities are artifacts of the society that creates them. They thrive in symbiotic relationships with their "worlds," expecting that, in exchange for various forms of support, they will do something important for the communities that depend on them. The constituencies of colleges and universities have come to expect that, in addition to these broadly conceived cultural roles, these institutions provide opportunity for individuals to make better lives for themselves. Their existence is also justified by practical ends, like training a student to get into a good graduate or professional school, or to become an employee of a highly regarded firm. As the capacity to provide opportunity becomes constrained, those institutions in which demand for the opportunities they can provide exceeds the supply develop mechanisms to distribute their scarce goods. High quality and high selectivity are correlated; so also are institutional quality and quality of postcollegiate outcomes. It becomes a difficult moral and educational calculus to justify how to distribute a scarce and desired good when it is clear that, for example, an admissions decision at age 17 or 18 can have a tangible, life-long impact.

During this same period in which the value of diversity has been professed, it has become even more important to leaders of academic institutions, and to the academic profession as a whole, to continue to enhance the quality of institutions, demanding still higher standards of achievement. Such aspirations have, as it were, built up still more pressure in a system (i.e., the college or university) already "heated up" by the interplay of interests and expectations bouncing against one another within the confines of a finite institutional resource base, further testing the relationship between equity concerns and excellence concerns in the institutional value consensus.

Academic culture is driven by a peculiar combination of individualism and social purpose. On the one hand, it exalts a kind of maximization of individual development and choice; on the other, it appropriately justifies its efforts in a discourse based on public mission and the common good. Market analogies stressing the benign workings of an invisible "mind" rather than a hand help illuminate the relationship between individualism and the common good. The convergence of individual "maximization" and public purpose was reflected in the ethos of what Clark Kerr characterized as a "federal era" of higher education, roughly the 40-year period starting with the "G. I. Bill" during World War II and lasting into the mid-1980s. Two themes predominated. First, benefit support was directed to individuals, who would carry their benefits and use them at the institution where they could maximize their own opportunities. Second, following the successful 1957 Sputnik launch by America's cold-war antagonist, the Union of Soviet Socialist Republics, federal support of education stimulated emphasis on the roles of science, technology, and the underpinnings of foreign policy in a geopolitical competition with the Soviet Union. The escalating influence of government in higher education supported the mix of individualistic maximization and social purpose that has become characteristic of the ethos of American higher education. Arguably, it also contributed to a frame of mind that overestimated institutional capacities to solve social problems (Kerr 1995).

More recently, a number of college and university leaders have advanced the argument that the connections between equity and excellence are deeper and more fundamental, bearing directly on the teaching and research missions of the institutions themselves. One of these in the United States is the highly regarded former chancellor of the University of California, Berkeley, Chang-Lin Tien. Also a contributor to this volume, Tien is a distinguished engineer and scientist, and a product of the era of strong federal support for university research. An immigrant whose family fled China during the 1949 revolution, he has become a public symbol of the ways in which California and the United States are changing. His personal story is a gripping account of the power of determination and belief in education. As the first Asian-American to lead a University of California campus, he exemplifies much of the complexity of California in the 1990s. His public disagreement with the California Board of Regents about affirmative action put him at odds with many members of the Asian-American community. As chancellor he enjoyed observing that his transition from engineering to administration had not been so difficult as many might have thought because his specialty had been the analysis of the dynamics of heat transfer. With a characteristically effective use of humor, he struck a chord that resonates with a wide range of academic leaders.[2]

As college presidents have become representative spokespersons, mediating among the various constituents of the college community, they may also have obscured from external view some of the conflicts that exist within their institutions. In the case of race, for example, the relatively consistent ways in which these leaders have embraced the principle that equity and academic excellence are inextricably interrelated has tended to present a more unified conviction about this than the more diverse views of its constituents may support. Academic institutions, even while their leaders attest to the importance of diversity as a public and institutional value, do not coerce the beliefs of other members of the institution because of intellectual freedom. The beliefs of those outside the administration matter for the success of diversity as an institutional goal. Indeed, their questions or ambivalences can shape the experience of those who represent the new populations of the institution.

The commitment to racial inclusion in higher education was both consistent with national ideals and unprecedented in national experience. It emerged during a time when resources supporting higher education had facilitated a sense of optimism and boldness about the future. Unfortunately, this optimism was soon mitigated by the intense social division regarding the country's role in the Vietnam War and by campus unrest about the relationship of educational institutions to the government prosecuting that war. Just as it seemed that the most important breakthrough in civil rights in a century was being realized, the country seemed to be falling apart for other reasons. The civil rights revolution was, thus, part of a broad social shift affecting the terms of consensus about the relationships of individuals, common values, and the role of institutions in American life. This was the context in which many colleges and universities undertook to justify new approaches to racial inclusion.

Access, however, turned out to be only part of the challenge facing these same institutions. Despite, in many cases, well-articulated programs to aid in academic and social transition, particularly to undergraduate life, significant numbers of minority students experienced academic difficulty, and their graduation rates were lower than for majority students. These early experiences — at that time more focused on black students than any other group — shaped the sensibilities of individuals and institutions about the tension between the values of equity and excellence. Colleges and universities struggled with the challenges embedded in this tension, which was more widely recognized than discussed. It was hoped that most measures adopted to facilitate access that modified academic standards would be interim adjustments only. More than a generation later, that same struggle continues because the number of high-achieving underrepresented minority students continues to be small (see also Miller 1995). At the same time, academic programs based on principles of remediation are being questioned.

A double dilemma has emerged. First, among the most competitive undergraduate and professional schools, there continues to be a scarcity of opportunities compared to the number of applicants. Second, there is a scarcity of minority students available to meet "institutionally based" demand for their presence on these campuses. Dealing with the double problem of scarcity — too few slots in relation to overall demand and too few non-Asian minority applicants who are competitive — has become part of the normal work of college and university administrators. Increasingly, in mediating this dilemma, they have relied on the assistance of their lawyers and the guidance of the judicial system, because of the recurring pattern in which questions of individual rights and educational policy interpenetrate. This is the empirical manifestation of the value conflict between the goals of diversity and meritocratic evaluation. The outstanding example of this pattern, the 1978 *Bakke* decision of the Supreme Court, is discussed further below.

For many reasons, college and university leaders frequently have found themselves in the line of fire since the 1960s. They came to be perceived as public symbols embodying the stress of social and cultural change. As educators and administrators, "captains of erudition" in Thorstein Veblen's phrase, college presidents and their administrative colleagues are regularly engaged in a balancing act mediating the frequently divergent expectations of students, faculty, community, and their governing boards. Their task: to weigh the demands of the present against the needs of the future. Dependent on the support and good will of diverse constituencies, successful academic leaders rely on a capacity to instill in students, faculty, staff, and their governing boards a desire for and enjoyment of being part of something larger than any particular individual or group interest. At the same time, they are charged to take responsibility for the future, supervising the deployment of resources for the long-term best interests of the institution's purposes to advance teaching, scholarship, and service.

The equity theme played itself out on campuses in other ways as well. For more than a generation, for example, the question of college and university endowment relationships to the apartheid regime in South Africa was a continuing source of campus discussion and campus activism. It is, perhaps, only coincidental that, following the release of Nelson Mandela from prison in 1990 as campus activism about South African investments subsided, affirmative action in the United States became more controversial.

The equity theme has also stimulated many academic disciplines to emphasize cultural, gender, and ethnic studies. The results, particularly manifested in the humanities, in history, and in many of the social sciences, have deepened our understanding of the human condition, bringing into focus previously unobserved or unappreciated perspectives on human experience. The debates about the "canon" and the curriculum that raged on many campuses, even though they gave rise to much ideological ventilation, were a manifestation of this important reorientation, which, at a minimum, forced consideration of the role of social location or context for the formulation and maintenance of intellectual and civic values.

As the former dean of undergraduate admission at Stanford, Jean Fetter, has observed, changing demographics and increased diversity in student bodies leads inevitably to questions about curriculum (Fetter 1995, p. 243). In a carefully phrased reflection about the roles of "classical" texts in the curriculum, Stanford professor W. B. Carnochan corroborated this, observing that "liberal education remains a belief system that survives not so much through institutional self-understanding as through continued acts of faith," which form the basis of a consensus. He continued:

> In the United States, which is unlike European nations in this respect, these acts of faith rest most deeply on the sense of social obligation that has come naturally to a nation of immigrants (a sense of obligation, not extended until recently to the nation's indigenous peoples). We expect "liberal education" to provide something more than compensation for the professional and commercial ways of the world—though we believe that a sense of social obligation corrects for limitations of the professional and commercial. We also expect something more from "great books" than aesthetic rewards—though we believe that aesthetic sensibilities contribute in their way to the fulfilling of civic responsibilities. And, whether we favor the multicultural curriculum or not, we argue our case by referring to societal needs, to the claims of diversity, or alternatively, to the value of the melting pot. But the crucial fact, which is a crucial problem, is this: the tradition of "Western Civilization" arose out of ideas, practices, attitudes so deeply ingrained as to have precluded serious inquiry into the relationship between social ends and curricular means, between civic and liberal education. (Carnochan 1993)

The "belief system" that will sustain the evolving consensus taking shape in American higher education remains a delicate construction, one that seeks to accommodate an interplay of forces that remain in unresolved tension. The complex relationship between a changing intellectual climate in which traditional articles of faith are regularly criticized as being culturally limited, and the arguments of college and university leaders about the educational benefits of diversity, is an important characteristic of the contemporary academy.

In his 1993–1995 *President's Report* (p. 20), Neil Rudenstine attempted to address this deficiency by putting forward a historical reflection about the educational significance of diversity. Reaching back in Harvard's history to a point before the contemporary focus on race developed, Rudenstine cited the recollection of a member of Harvard's Class of 1910, John Reed (who later covered the 1917 Bolshevik revolution in *Ten Days that Shook the World*) acknowledging that "a diverse community can lead to pain, isolation of separateness, as well as to intellectual exhilaration, greater self-knowledge, and moment of human reconciliation." Yet it is also the case that this undeniable progress has been accompanied by tension and uncertainty.[3]

The relationship between quality and diversity is a difficult value to measure in a way that might convince someone who believes differently. While it is demonstrable that higher status institutions have incorporated this value in their missions, these same institutions have been under pressure to maintain and enhance their own quality and reputations. This pressure has pushed them to emphasize other values that are not easy to align but that have critical consequences for the pursuit of diversity objectives. This is reflected, for example, in the way in which undergraduate admissions deans describe the results of their labors, emphasizing — frequently with a disclaimer — the improvement in SAT (Scholastic Assessment Test) scores from one year to the next as the proxy for quality, and then talking about the diversity of the class using some combination of numbers and percentages. The distribution of SAT scores across the different racial populations is such that whenever such a report is given, underrepresented minority students will be classified within the peer reference group as below average in quality. The implications of this recognition are not widely appreciated and, therefore, it is not surprising that few institutions are addressing the implications of racially bifurcated patterns of measurable academic quality in the high status institutions that have been most aggressive in diversifying their student populations.

In recent years, domestic and global politics have been regularly characterized by what Charles Taylor has characterized as a "politics of recognition."[4] This works in two ways: First, through the recognition of injustice and exclusion, it can stimulate those who have been disadvantaged to a new appreciation of their identities and roles in a continuing human saga; second, it provides a rationale for constructing institutional arrangements that redress the inequities of the past. The arena of higher education has provided an important space in American culture for the engagement of the tensions that follow this kind of politics. The Civil Rights movement, an expanding view of the meaning of racial minority, changes in the patterns of immigration, a shifting consensus about the roles of women and men, as well as re-formed views about gender and sexuality, comprise a context of changed circumstances and presuppositions in personal and institutional experience. The campus has become the archetypal space in American life where these pluralistic and highly energized impulses are mediated culturally, educationally, and politically.

Du Bois explicitly anticipated the debate about race, which became a paradigm for the other liberation movements stimulated by its moral and political force. The debate about affirmative action and racial preferences in California and Texas during the mid-1990s — like the debate about open admissions in the City University of New York in the 1970s — exemplifies the tension between ideals and practice (Traub 1994). In a more formal way, public institutions have been forced to face squarely the relationship between objectives and strategies that maximize access and those that maximize excellence. Much more recently, following the transition to black majority rule in 1994, South Africa — which, like California, relies heavily on a public system of higher education — has begun to face a similar dilemma: the problem of qualification and performance measures and their inequitable distribution across different racial groups. Thus, in both California and South Africa, social fairness and qualifications evaluation have become contentious matters of public debate.[5]

What is argued about in these cases, whether in public or private systems, is the character of institutional response to skewed patterns of qualification across different racial groups, patterns that tend in the United States to manifest themselves in lower levels of academic success for African-Americans and Hispanics, and in South Africa for blacks. Institutions of higher education have focused principally on issues of access in executing their affirmative action policies, while asserting — on the basis of belief — that diversity and quality are mutually reinforcing goals. The dilemma that institutions face, given these skewed patterns of qualification, is how to pursue excellence and equity while maintaining requisite levels of internal and external support when painful trade-offs become necessary. One strategy has been focused on developing a better understanding of the relationship between standardized preadmission testing and academic performance at the undergraduate level. An implication of such a line of inquiry is that the tests themselves might be "biased" toward some kinds of people and not toward others. A second strategy has been to find better ways to improve the academic preparation for those who need such assistance.

The mediation of these various aspirations and disagreements has become part of the practice of college administration. Because administrators are entrusted with the responsibility to see the institution "whole," they can find themselves perched rather precariously in a position to see and often to comprehend, but often not able to be influential in areas that may resist changes. In areas like admissions, student affairs, and nonfaculty personnel matters, the leverage can be more direct. In other matters having to do with faculty and curriculum, administrative leverage is limited to issues of process, a constraint not widely appreciated outside the academy where there is a tendency to impute more power to administrators than they, in fact, are able to exercise.

Thus, colleges and universities have become a crucible in which these continuing dilemmas and aspirations vie with one another as the institutions proceed to incorporate a historically unprecedented measure of human diversity. At the same time, the ambivalence and vulnerability that mark the human condition and are exhibited throughout civil polity and our voluntary associations have not been absent during this time of profound cultural redefinition. Institutions of higher education are people-intensive organizations. The continuing viability of the enterprise of higher education and the status of affirmative action efforts within it will depend on what people believe, and on whether those whose cooperation cannot be mandated support the view that the kind of inclusion affirmative action encourages is good for everyone.

Higher education has advanced considerably the mission of providing access; this progress notwithstanding, it has also become the crucible in which the unresolved dilemmas of a complicated racial history continue to be tested. Those charged to administer — to care for and manage — our colleges and universities do indeed live out this vocation in the heat of conflicting aspirations.

## AFFIRMATIVE ACTION AND INSTITUTIONAL EXCELLENCE: CIVIL RIGHTS AND ACADEMIC FREEDOM

During the period following the Civil Rights movement of the 1960s, the active practice of inclusiveness in the provision of opportunity and access, which came to be known as "affirmative action," has been accepted as a responsibility by institutions in both the private and the public sectors of American life. College, university, and professional school admissions practices have reflected an initial concern for facilitating access for black students. The numbers of minority persons admitted to or hired by institutions that previously would not have welcomed them increased dramatically. By the early 1970s, women as well as other underrepresented minorities joined blacks as designated target groups for affirmative action efforts, a step that led to more complex and not necessarily overlapping patterns of minority group interests. In California, for example, the initial target group for affirmative action, blacks, comprised less than 10% of the population. By the early 1990s, the expanded target group of "underrepresented" minorities — not including women — comprised more than 40% of the population, according to Berkeley sociologist Troy Duster. In a *San Francisco Chronicle* interview (10 April 1992), Duster, who has been a member of the Berkeley faculty for more than 25 years, observed that "we are up to a point where 8 out of 10 people" are claiming a status that brings some form of special consideration. "There is," he noted, an "unraveling of interest group conflict over scarce resources" (see also Fetter 1995, pp. 136 ff).

The commitment to expand opportunity and participation has now in many circles been joined to a reformulation of the meaning of excellence. It is better to be inclusive of a range of experiences and backgrounds represented to be homogeneous not only because of a responsibility to educate a broad representation of future citizens and leaders, but also because, it is argued, the condition of social diversity is believed to be a better educational medium for all students. Thus, the themes of equal opportunity and enhancement of quality have been yoked to a view about the relationship of pluralism to educational excellence as well as to social progress.

The relationship between what could be characterized as the "civil rights justification" for diversity and an "academic freedom justification" for diversity is important to appreciate because it represents a significant shift in the kinds of institutional arguments that were employed to support inclusion. In this area, the judiciary has increasingly become the arbiter of the shift from arguments based on equity, rooted in the civil rights law, to arguments based on diversity, rooted in a view about academic freedom. This development emerges from the landmark 1978 Supreme Court decision, *Bakke v. Regents of the University of California*. A revisiting of the legal context will help make this clear.

## THE *BAKKE* CASE

Alan Bakke, a 38-year-old engineer who had been rejected for admission to the University of California at Davis Medical School, sued the University of California on the grounds that a disadvantaged-minorities-only program in effect in 1973 at the medical school on the Davis campus had accepted candidates less qualified than he. Bakke had argued that because the minorities-only program set aside medical school slots for which he could not be considered, he had been deprived of his right to equal protection. When the case was finally decided by the United States Supreme Court in 1978, the Court ruled that the practice of setting aside a specific number of places for disadvantaged minority students in the California medical school was not constitutional. Therefore, the Court prohibited the use of quotas. However, the Court did sanction the use of race as a "plus" factor in admissions decisions if racial diversity supported the educational mission of the school. The Court also ordered that Bakke be admitted to the Davis medical school, agreeing with his contention that he had been denied his right to equal protection.

The judgment that race could be considered in the context of an admission decision, but that numerical quotas that set aside a given number of the spaces were unconstitutional, provided a new rationale for colleges and universities to continue their efforts in recruiting and admitting underrepresented students. On this matter the Supreme Court divided in a 5–4 vote, with Justice Lewis Powell casting the decisive vote in favor of the Regents of the University of California, who were the defendants in the lawsuit. Six of the nine justices issued opinions about the case. This divided judgment set the framework within which affirmative action would continue to develop in succeeding years. Even though five of the nine justices of the Court had joined in the decision, the character of their concurrence signaled profound ambivalence about concrete measures undertaken by colleges and universities to implement the goal of equality of opportunity. Justice Powell's view that the achievement of a diverse student body was a legitimate educational objective that could be pursued through an admission policy that took race into consideration was widely adopted by colleges and universities as a rationale for admission policies that continued to consider race. This was, however, his view only; no other justice joined in this specific interpretation. Thus, the *Bakke* decision divided the Court almost down the middle and the five concurring justices were not able to agree on a justification for the actions being endorsed.

As a practical matter, the *Bakke* outcome provided a Supreme Court-sanctioned method to continue to admit significant numbers of underrepresented minorities as long as there was no set quota. Colleges and universities could insist, as most did, that they did not use quotas as rigid admissions targets, but that they evaluated each individual in the context of his or her talents, life experiences, and potential. To meet the equal protection test for all applicants, the Court stipulated it was essential that all candidates be considered in a common process and that they be evaluated together. Institutions, through their admission offices, were free to use race as a plus factor as long as these procedural norms were respected.

The practical consequences of this ambivalent resolution were such that admission offices could continue to act as they had before and that some people with stronger measured qualifications could be rejected in favor of others above a threshold, but less strong in measured qualifications. In the context of a "whole-person" admission evaluation, as long as every candidate was considered in the same process, undergraduate and professional schools could admit students with lower qualifications than others they might reject if the presence of these students helped them to meet institutional objectives in diversity. That is to say, an institution could reasonably and responsibly preserve an option — in considering applicants above the threshold for academic success — to take into consideration a broader range of capacities and contributions than a calculus based solely on maximizing academic measures would yield.

This mutual support and compatibility of nondiscriminatory inclusiveness and an expanded view of educational value have become part of the conventional rhetorical patterns of institutional life. It is thoughtfully argued that a more diverse student body challenges faculty as well as students, expanding the range of questions considered and helping to recognize the important ways in which different life experiences shape ways in which questions are posed and answers rendered. The claim that diversity was educationally beneficial moved the discussion into territory where academic institutions have been accorded the responsibility for self-regulation. The status of this claim and its justification as a value, as Uri Treisman and Richard Light suggest, have not been fully analyzed. It was a plausible claim and provided a measure of breathing space. It was a belief and represented a hope. Although the context of the *Bakke* and the *Hopwood* cases (discussed below) was admission to a professional school, the predominant focus and use of the court-sanctioned argument has been to justify diversity in undergraduate education.

There has been far greater consensus about the broad goal of diversity than about the measures that should be undertaken to achieve it. While there is broad consensus about nondiscrimination, there is considerable difference of view about the pursuit of diversity as a positive good when actions and policies follow from that pursuit that are in tension with other institutional values or goods, such as meritocratic evaluations of individuals. While a nondiscriminatory inclusiveness about access represents a minimum policy and ethical standard, actions and policies to promote diversity beyond this minimum are intended to take into account other values that are subject to intense and, frequently, divisive debate. This debate could be said to chart the contours of a new "American dilemma" about the level and duration of responsibility for past discrimination and oppression or, to cast the quandary in different terms, the "cost" of providing a community in which such diversity can flourish.

Two important developments in 1996 illustrate America's continuing quandary about race: the decision of the Fifth Circuit Court of Appeals in *Hopwood v. University of Texas* and the Civil Rights Initiative on the 1996 California ballot. These two events illustrated the painful and confusing difficulties Americans continue to experience seeking to balance claims based on historic and persistent patterns of racial discrimination and claims based on individual merit. Each of these events can reasonably be viewed as part of the continuing struggle to become a color-blind society. Yet, also through these two events, the divided mind of the country about the way to achieve that goal is manifested in a divisive debate about the role and consequences of racial preference in American experience.

## *Hopwood et al. v. Texas:* The Limits of Judicial Approaches to Affirmative Action

In 1996, a century after *Plessy v. Ferguson,* the Fifth Circuit Court of Appeals in *Hopwood v. Texas* struck down a University of Texas Law School admissions process that sought to guarantee that set percentages of Mexican-American and black students would be represented in law school classes. The unsuccessful petition by the University of Texas for United States Supreme Court review of the Fifth Circuit Court rejection of its admissions policies left the university and the country in a state of uncertainty about the status of affirmative action in college and university admissions decisions. The fact that a number of state supported institutions in the region covered by the Fifth Circuit (in Louisiana and Mississippi) continued under federal court-ordered desegregation mandates made it clear that the judiciary would enforce desegregation mandates when there have been clear patterns of de jure discrimination. Absent such a record, the Fifth Circuit Court argued that race should not be considered in admissions decisions, thus not addressing — or assuming that the problem was beyond the scope of law — how to move the country toward a future in which the heritage of discrimination, de facto as well as de jure, would be overcome.

At issue here were conflicting visions on how to advance widely shared principles about civil rights: How and under what circumstances should race be taken into account in the allocation of opportunities when the goal is to achieve a color-blind society? The tension between group-based policies — whether they were intended to be remedial or directed toward the educational goal of diversity — and individual rights to equal protection manifested itself in this dispute. At what point do practices aimed at overcoming the effects of past discrimination against one group become discriminatory against individuals in another group? The tension between achieving equity and acting in a manner that is color-blind represents the most difficult dilemma in the ethics of civil rights.

The specific facts upon which Cheryl Hopwood, an unsuccessful applicant to the University of Texas Law School in 1992, based her case about reverse discrimination provided the three judges of the Circuit Court an opportunity to engage the jurisprudence underlying the 1978 *Bakke* decision; two of them chose to take on the matter directly and challenge the use of race under any circumstances. Hopwood, who is white, was at the time a 32-year-old Air Force veteran raising a severely handicapped child as a single mother. As such she represented a non-traditional candidate for admission who, it was argued, would bring important and different life experiences to the law school and its student body. The crux of the lawsuit turned on a critical procedural matter that set admission practices of the University of Texas outside the framework delineated in the *Bakke* case for ensuring fairness. In 1991, the admissions committee, after testing a number of alternatives, formed a subcommittee to review the files of minority students and to recommend a large enough number to achieve a class that was 5% black and 10% Mexican-American. For more than a decade after the *Bakke* decision, those responsible for the University of Texas Law School admissions process had to deal with the need for a class that was representative of the state and reckoned with the scarcity of qualified black and Hispanic applicants (*Synfax Weekly Reports* 5 September 1994, p. 264). An important objective of this process was to focus the admissions effort in a way that could evaluate black and Chicano candidates differently, since so few of them would be competitive based on the "Texas Index" score, a combination of the Law School Admission Test score and the college grade-point average that the law school used to evaluate applicants. The fact that this procedure had the effect of limiting opportunities potentially available to the plaintiffs was the ground upon which they pressed their claim about denial of equal protection. Since the University of Texas Law School had virtually reverted to pre-*Bakke* modes of decision making, the law school had created a very vulnerable target for plaintiffs to attack. Finding that the practice in which majority and minority students were considered in separate tracks was unconstitutional, the Fifth Circuit Court in a 2–1 decision, addressed not only the procedural problem that triggered the suit, but went further and effectively reversed the judgment of the Supreme Court that race could be taken into account at all, even if, as Justice Powell had insisted, proper procedural safeguards were respected.

In 1992, the year that Cheryl Hopwood had been denied admission, admissions practice in the University of Texas Law School utilized separate committees to consider majority and minority applicants. This had the effective result, according to Hopwood and the other plaintiffs, of denying their equal opportunity for admission because the minority admissions committee was able to admit blacks and Mexican-Americans with lower scores on the Texas Index than Hopwood and the others had achieved. On its own, the law school had modified its admissions procedures the following year so that all applicants would be considered by the same process. Because Hopwood's complaint was based on the process in effect at the time her application had been considered, the law school and the university were constrained to defend their affirmative action policies in the context of an administrative practice that had been abandoned.

Although the case had been based on a different set of circumstances than what law school policies dictated at the time of the 1996 Fifth Circuit Court of Appeals decision, the judgment of that court that race could not be taken into account in admissions decisions effectively repudiated the compromise embedded in the *Bakke* decision. By declaring that diversity was not a valid justification for race-sensitive admissions policies, this Court directly challenged a cardinal tenet in the development of selective admissions in the post-*Bakke* period. The Fifth Circuit essentially held that diversity was not a sufficiently compelling interest to justify the kinds of individual unfairness that the Texas decision-making process produced.

The tendencies reflected in judicial decision making now suggest that courts will endorse short-term rectifications of specific institutional practices that have been discriminatory but will be far more cautious about programs that aim to rectify racial imbalances for which there is no obvious responsible party. Thus, the courts have endorsed efforts to cure the effects of past discrimination at a particular institution, but have not looked favorably on the use of race as a consideration in hiring in order to provide role models for public school students. Therefore, decisions in affirmative action cases have turned on judgments about particular situations in their contexts. The case-oriented evolution of legal thinking about this subject has not advanced resolution of the persisting dilemma of how to deal with the burden of past decisions for which responsible parties are impossible to identify. Nor does it appear that the courts will provide much assistance to those who seek to redress broader issues of representation that reflect historic or cultural patterns of underrepresentation.

The pattern of interpretation and judgment manifested in this approach reflects the uncertainty that many continue to share about the unsettled ground of affirmative action. The decisions of the courts continue to reflect the divergent understandings and beliefs about what a responsible approach should entail. The increasing tendency of the court has been to sanction narrowly tailored remedies and serve a pressing government interest. Thus, courts seem more prepared to endorse minimum conditions for the avoidance and correction of specific patterns of discrimination than to prescribe how colleges and universities should carry out their educational missions by taking responsibility for diversity.

Thus, affirmative action has developed to encompass two distinguishable goals: First, it has focused on, and continues to target, issues of access for members of underrepresented groups; second, it has become an institutional policy mechanism to ensure the representation of diversity for educational purposes. When the composition of the student body and the representation of different kinds of life experience within it are understood as educationally relevant variables, the processes and actions that colleges and universities undertake to secure this goal are, arguably, activities for which an academic institution can expect some degree of protection from outside interference. When, however, the pursuit of that objective is enmeshed in evaluation processes to distribute scarce, and in the case of state-sponsored institutions, publicly supported resources, these processes cannot be entirely protected as an expression of institutional academic sovereignty. Private institutions have more "freedom" to assert a prerogative to pursue the goal of educational diversity, but very few institutions are really "private" enough to be secure about escaping scrutiny for claims about the violation of individual rights.

In July 1996 the Supreme Court of the United States declined to review and, therefore, let stand the decision of the Fifth Circuit in *Hopwood*. In so doing, the Supreme Court did not resolve the dilemma, a conundrum reflective of the ambiguity and uncertainty about the status of race in admissions decision making. In a comment about the Supreme Court action, Justice Ruth Bader Ginsburg suggested that the Supreme Court's review of the Texas Law School case was not necessary because the law school changed its procedures in 1994, observing that "we must await a final judgment on a program genuinely in controversy before addressing the important questions raised in this petition."

The suggestion that the "important questions" raised in the *Hopwood* case remained unresolved may seem to understate the matter. Similar concerns underlay the public debate raised in the California Civil Rights Initiative, where again a commitment to diversity and the aspiration to be color blind conflict with each other. Stimulated by the discussion of the University of California Regents about admissions policies, there has been a mounting concern that the commitment to diversity and the search for quality are in unresolvable tension with one another.

The connection between racial preference and the advancement of civil rights remains unsettled. At best, one might say that Americans have settled for an ambivalent accommodation of this strategy that takes race into consideration in the distribution of opportunity. Polling data about the Civil Rights Initiative was consistent with findings that most Americans continue to believe that racial preferences constitute reverse discrimination (*Los Angeles Times* 31 December 1995, p. 1; Jencks 1992). To offer preference as a means for achieving diversity as an educational value, when that preference has the effect of skewing processes based on meritocratic judgments about individuals toward outcomes that are different than they would have been were it not for the preference policy, can have deleterious consequences for all concerned.

## The 1996 California Civil Rights Initiative

In November 1996, California voters endorsed the following proposition: "Neither the state of California, nor any of its political subdivisions or agents shall use race, sex, color, ethnicity or national origin as a criterion for either discriminating against, or granting preferential treatment to, any individual or group in the operation of the state's system of public employment, public education or public contracting." The Civil Rights Initiative, supported by 54% of the electorate, after several challenges has become the new law in California.

Following in the wake of the divisive political battle about Proposition 187 on the 1994 ballot, a resolution designed to constrain the claims that illegal immigrants could make on public resources, and the decision of the California Board of Regents in July 1995 to abandon the use of race as a criterion for preferment, the Civil Rights Initiative of 1996 confirmed California's status as a bellwether for a national debate about affirmative action. California became the scene of conflict between the ethics and politics of nondiscrimination on the one hand, and the ethics and politics of an evolved realism about inclusion and fairness on the other. This was not, however, a debate about abstracted values. Proponents and opponents argued their case on the basis of fairness. The argument and the conditions leading up to it pierced directly into the heart of a new American dilemma. The question of the adequacy of nondiscrimination as a basis of affirmative action was counterpoised to a view about the role of the state as a catalyst for expanding opportunity for underrepresented minorities.

The terms of the argument about fairness are illustrated in the divergent observations of Deval Patrick, assistant attorney general for civil rights in the Clinton Administration, and Representative Charles T. Canady, a Florida Republican, who had been a principal sponsor of congressional legislation to ban most federal affirmative action efforts. In response to Patrick's argument that "there is only one tool by which government, business and schools, mostly voluntary, have really taken on the business of trying to integrate" their populations and "that is affirmative action," Canady rejoined that "the system of preferences" currently in place "is inherently racially divisive" (*Los Angeles Times* 31 December 1995, p. 1).

The July 1995 decision of the Board of Regents of the University of California to ban racial preferences in hiring, admissions, and contracting was a prelude to Proposition 209, which was conceived to apply the ban on preferences to all aspects of state government. While the governor of California expressed strong support for Proposition 209, the effective leadership in the Regents' discussion fell on the shoulders of Ward Connerly, a Sacramento-based African-American business executive, whose own experience caused him to worry about the ways in which programs based on racial preference become sources of unfairness and stigma. Connerly's protest about the destructive impact of preferences on minorities converged with views shared by many others about preferences: namely, that they undermine fundamental fairness in the allocation of scarce opportunities. Thus, from two vantages, he argued that preferences jeopardize the social fabric: in the one case by compromising the capacity of underrepresented minorities to believe that they are capable of achieving at high levels, and in the other because the use of preferences based on membership in a certain group compromises the capacity to evaluate merit on an individual basis. The campaign supporting Proposition 209, as well as the wording of the proposition itself, emphasized the problem of preferences, the most controversial interpretation of affirmative action.

The president of the University of California, Jack Peltason, as well as its two most visible campus chancellors, Chang-Lin Tien of Berkeley and Charles Young of UCLA, reacted strongly in defense of the kinds of admissions policies used on their campuses that made race a "plus" factor above a certain academic threshold. As Chancellor Tien observes in his comment below, without such a policy, the student population of the university could not come close to being representative of the population of the state, given the distribution patterns of academic eligibility in California in which the top 12.5% of high school graduates are eligible for admission to one of the campuses of the University of California. Under this policy, 32% of Asian-American high school graduates, 13%

of white high school graduates, and only 5% of blacks and 4% of Chicano-Latinos were eligible for admission to the university in 1990. In this same year the percentage of high school graduates by race was Asian-American 17%, Caucasian 55%, African-American 9%, and Hispanic 35% (University of California 1997). The administration and academic leadership of the university argued that other considerations in addition to the academic index merited review in the evaluation of applicants if the university was to serve all the people of the state, and that student diversity was itself an important educational resource. The arguments of the University of California leadership effectively joined the civil rights and the academic freedom rationales for diversity. These arguments seem not to have addressed the kinds of concerns that animated the proponents of Proposition 209, concerns that Berkeley sociologist Troy Duster and colleagues had discovered based on data gathered for the *Diversity Project* report (1991) in which respondents expressed concerns about preferences benefiting *middle class* blacks and Hispanic students.

Ward Connerly, who took over the leadership of the petition drive placing the Civil Rights Initiative on the ballot, argued — invoking a phrase from Martin Luther King's 1963 "I have a dream" address — that a ban on racial preferences would "insure that every man, woman, and child in California" would be "judged by the content of their character" (*Chronicle of Higher Education* 1 March 1996, A34). On the other hand, UCLA Chancellor Charles Young argued for candor about acknowledging the disparity in academic credentials of African-American and Latino applicants who, without some form of preference, would be represented in much smaller numbers in the university: "We won't convince everyone that we're right, but some may say 'What they're doing isn't as bad as we thought.'" In this latter observation, Young voiced a long-standing concern about the lack of public understanding about the small-numbers problem.

## THE PROBLEM OF SMALL NUMBERS

Thus, the lines were drawn between competing visions of the American promise and contrasting interpretations of the relationship of individual achievement and the responsibility to provide opportunity to all. While the principal context for this debate in California has been the responsibility of the public university, the issues raised in that discussion represent questions that all selective institutions — private or public — face as they seek to sustain missions that combine commitments to academic excellence and seek to be inclusive. California's eligibility patterns are still distinctive, in large measure because of the extraordinary increase in the numbers of Asian-Americans who have settled in the state over the last generation. However, the social bifurcation of measured high achievement that would allow institutions like the University of California virtually to fill their student bodies with white and Asian-American students is a pattern that affects any selective college or university with admissions policies based on thresholds like those in use at the University of California. There continues to be, despite the many kinds of efforts that have been made over the last 30 years, a significant "supply" problem in the numbers of high-achieving black and Latino students prepared to undertake study in our leading academic institutions. The persistence of this shortage of human capital, as L. Scott Miller argues below, remains a fundamental constraint in the situation confronting not only the University of California campuses, but, indeed, all of selective higher education. The ways in which institutions adjust to and compensate for this constraint become the foci of arguments about individual merit, social fairness, and the relationship of race and class. Whether acknowledged or not, this shortage of comparably qualified underrepresented minority students, a shortage that has persisted for more than a generation, has placed enormous pressures on elite institutions, which themselves have also sought to enhance quality, to explain and justify their admission practices internally among their many constituencies.

The dilemma of too few who are comparably qualified and the consequent need to think differently about the evaluation of qualifications persists, as difficult as it is for many to acknowledge. The distinction between "comparably qualified" and meeting a basic threshold qualification is important, because there is a larger supply of underrepresented minorities who meet the basic threshold for admission to a selective institution than there is of the same group who remain as academically competitive as the threshold rises. Put another way, there is simply a far larger supply of white and Asian-American candidates above the basic threshold with stronger academic qualifications than the above-the-threshold group of black and Latino candidates. The difficulty institutions face is not a result of admitting people who are not qualified, but the degree of selectivity that is possible above the basic threshold. Competitive institutions are able to continue to be very selective above their basic qualifications threshold for white and Asian-American students, but they are not able to do this for black and Latino students because the numbers of this latter group are so much smaller and their relative qualifications not as strong. In the case of the University of California, for example, access policy has been guided by the 1960 Master Plan for Higher Education, under which the top 12.5% of high school graduates would be eligible for admission to the university. The problem of comparable qualifications materializes above a threshold, so that Berkeley and UCLA, the campuses with the most competitive admissions within the University of California, could easily fill their undergraduate classes with the most highly qualified of the eligible candidate group, and in so doing skew their campus populations further toward more predominant representations of Asian-American and white students.

On the other hand, interinstitutional competition tends not to be nearly as vigorous for the white and Asian-American students whose academic credentials above the basic threshold are superior to the more sought-after underrepresented minorities whose qualifications, though less strong, are still above threshold. These kinds of dilemmas confront the admission and recruitment staffs of elite institutions on a daily basis. These are the dilemmas of the "right tail" of the distribution that Richard Light describes. The distinction between qualified above threshold and comparably qualified can become consequential if peers, mentors, or others who help shape campus climate come to believe that standardized measures of ability are determinative. This kind of institutional inhospitality, as Uri Treisman observes, can have serious academic consequences. This is an important area where impulses about quality maximization, social fairness, and a supportive educational climate come into play. The reluctance of most institutions to engage this tension directly has not helped their own constituencies or the general public understand the problem of scarcity of high-achieving minorities or the important role diversity can play in higher education.

The 1996 California Civil Rights Initiative, the successor debate to the 1995 Regents' decision to abolish preferences, was a public debate on the subject that had often been held in private settings. The difficulty of this discussion is a function of the discomfort involved in talking about different levels of academic attainment by race. It is one of those subjects about which many people have knowledge, but for which safe settings to discuss the problem are hard to find. The introduction of the use of the adjective "underrepresented" to qualify the noun "minority" represented an adjustment in language designed to refocus on the problem that the expanding compass of affirmative action had begun to obscure. In important respects, affirmative action could be declared a success. Since many expected that the time would come when it would no longer be necessary to sustain such a program, the ways in which it had succeeded were welcomed in the hope that the country could move on and put its legacy of racism and other forms of exclusion behind it. Such a mindset, conditioned by the hope of progress, and by the obvious success of two of the important targeted groups, was certainly consistent with the increasing questioning of affirmative action that characterized much of the political discourse of the 1980s.

In selective colleges and universities, the persistent discomfort surrounding communication about differential academic attainment may have been accommodated by increasing tendencies toward specialization and separation of admissions offices — as an administrative function — from other parts of the institution. Those responsible for administering selective admissions policies have deep appreciation about the academic characteristics of different ethnic groups. Such offices with responsibilities to maximize "quality" as well as diversity have experienced the brunt of the tension between egalitarian and meritocratic objectives in admissions decision making. The isolation of this process from other academic and administrative units has made it difficult for people outside of admissions to understand how difficult it is, given the characteristics of applicant pools, to satisfy diversity objectives.

This discomfort surrounding communication about race is also reflected in other patterns of campus experience, including debates about restraining speech that is racially offensive, concerns about patterns of in-group segregation, and an increasing sense that there is a difference between what institutions publicly profess and what many faculty and students privately believe about race.

## The Dilemmas of Pluralism

The papers and comments in this book are based on materials initially prepared for the Princeton Conference on Higher Education convened at Princeton University in March 1996. This meeting, sponsored by the university and The Andrew W. Mellon Foundation, focused on a number of important subjects facing American higher education at the beginning of a new century. Importantly, two full sessions of the conference were devoted to a consideration of the subjects of diversity and affirmative action. These themes and terms have come to symbolize the extraordinary progress and change marking the final third of the twentieth century. At the same time they stimulate a profound and unresolved ambivalence about the relationship between the belief in equality of opportunity and the sobering recognition of the persistence of measurable academic achievement differences between different racial groups. The methods institutions have devised to enhance opportunity and access to higher education have been the focus of pointed criticism and attack in a wide variety of private and public colleges and universities. The tensions between "democratic" and "meritocratic" impulses have been particularly acute in higher education where values based in a commitment to diversity and those based in a commitment to high standards are commonly experienced to be in tension with one another.

Thus, it should be no great surprise that this subject has generated interest among many constituencies inside and outside the academic community. In both private and public institutions, this issue continues to raise fundamental questions about mission and purpose. At its starkest, the tensions in the debate are represented as a collision of values between merit and fairness, between excellence and justice, between claims of individuals and the ability of educational institutions to manage their affairs and pursue their mission. In some measure, the situation confronting us arises as a result of the remarkable progress that has been made in bringing about higher levels of social diversity than has been heretofore contained in single institutions.

This volume has been conceived as part of a needed discussion and assessment about what has been accomplished and what remains to be understood about racial diversity in higher education. Colleges and universities have become intellectual and cultural battlegrounds in which debates about access, empowerment, fairness, and merit have dominated the attention of faculty, administrators, students, and the general public. While these institutions have devoted significant attention to many dimensions of the challenges posed by racial pluralism, there are also a number of questions that have been less carefully explored. In general terms, the response to racial pluralism has emphasized administrative and co-curricular patterns of adjustment to the presence of minority students. Less attention has been focused on patterns of educational development and achievement, or the curriculum. The focus on numbers of students has led necessarily to a concentration on enrollment patterns. The quality of success has tended to be evaluated by citing retention and graduation statistics, measures that do not tell us as much as we might like to know about highly selective institutions where the admissions decision virtually assures graduation.

The quality of academic experience achieved by underrepresented minority students in such institutions is a function of a web of relationships that validates or undermines their academic confidence. Addressing this scarcity at the "right tail" of the distribution will require persistence and patience as well as political savvy. L. Scott Miller has provided an exceptionally complete summary of the available data describing the present situation, particularly the dearth of high-achieving non-Asian minority students and, in aggregate terms, their comparative statistical relationships to white and Asian-American students. This study, which carries forward an analysis fully set forth in Miller's award-winning book, *An American Imperative*, is a sobering assessment combined with a number of useful ideas about ways in which this scarcity might be overcome. Despite their abilities, black and Hispanic students in elite institutions will generally find themselves relatively overmatched in terms of conventional admissions measures because the supply of higher achieving whites and Asian-Americans is so much larger. Thus, relative positions and perceptions about ability can take on a greater significance. In the most competitive environments, high-achieving, underrepresented minority students can be subject to stereotyping, which can cause them to "disidentify" with academic achievement. In highly selective institutions this phenomenon can be easy to miss because students will graduate at impressive rates and still advance to positions of accomplishment in subsequent professional life.

Claude Steele, the Stanford University psychologist, has put forward an elegant description of the force of stereotyping in a controlled experiment demonstrating how stereotype threat can depress academic performance. The implications of this research based on the experience of women and the experience of African-Americans are substantial because institutional practices need to be cognizant of race, but must avoid stigmatizing those prone to stereotyping. The policy implications of Miller and Steele's analyses are substantial because it is common practice among elite institutions to target and give special consideration to underrepresented minorities based on race. This practice and other institutional efforts that follow from it simultaneously embrace students who represent diversity and, potentially, activate academic vulnerability by emphasizing their racial background and their need for remedial assistance. The roots of the commonly reported syndrome by black and Latino students that they often feel "used" by institutions that have recruited them, or that they feel that they are responsible to "teach" others about diversity, can doubtless be located in the habits of mind that are associated with special efforts. Joining Steele's argument with Miller's analysis of small numbers raises questions about unintentional stigma in selective institutions and the problem of being at or above an academic threshold for admission, but still below average in relation to peers. This is the challenge of what Steele calls "wise" educational practices. Addressing the small numbers dilemma without activating the deficit or remedial orientation about black and Hispanic students represents a formidable challenge for faculty and administrators.

The second area of focus is the public context in which commitments to diversity and pluralism are generated and sustained. In this section, a provocative contrast is developed between California and South Africa, two jurisdictions that have experienced high rates of change and that rely heavily on the public sector for higher education. Sociologist Neil Smelser, Director of the Center for Advanced Study in the Behavioral

Sciences, provides a careful framing of California's recent experience in the context of the so-called "Civil Rights Initiative." His observation about the different ways in which success can be understood, and his careful distinction between "institutional" and "political" success, are reminders of how social conflict and social change frequently accompany one another. Progress does not necessarily lead to equilibrium. Smelser's sense of the "problematic" of affirmative action contrasts Chang-Lin Tien's exhortation that diversity is an opportunity for all, because it reflects the promise and the distinctiveness of California and, indeed, of the nation as a whole.

Mamphela Ramphele's concern about maintaining a long-term focus on quality for the University of Cape Town in the face of pent-up pressures for equity and access to opportunity is a poignant reminder of the need to recognize trade-offs and to communicate with candor about them. With courage and clarity, she describes a course of development where high standards and social justice must be held together as goals in which an impatient and needy community can believe. Like Chang-Lin Tien, she has a fascinating life story. A physician and anthropologist, as well as a former member of the Black Consciousness movement led by Steven Biko, she has devoted her life to advancement of social equity and educational excellence. Her recent election as Vice Chancellor of the University of Cape Town culminates an extraordinary journey, which she characterizes as a process of transformation based on "the transgression of social boundaries [that] stand in the way of creative responses to a changing environment" (*Mamphela Ramphele* 1995). Her essay also provokes consideration of the implications of the ways in which we measure quality and merit, and the impact those assumptions have in situations where there is the kind of history of stigmatization that she confronts in South Africa at one of that country's leading research universities. Both Smelser and Ramphele help to clarify the roles and the diverging interests of the many constituencies of public education during a time of social transition. Of particular concern, both in California and in South Africa, is the question of how a forward-looking community develops a consensus about the continuing responsibility to deal with the consequences of past discrimination as pressures mount to adopt strategies that are color-blind in their application, and provide the strongest foundation for the continuing strength of higher education.

## A RECONSTITUTION OF BELIEF

One president of a New England liberal arts college has observed that his role through such times of questioning was to be the "chief believer" in the community about the importance of diversity, based on the impact discrimination had at his college and in the United States. He candidly acknowledged that his college continued to manifest characteristics of an unconscious institutional racism expressed in the form of a hegemonic assumption and shared belief about the "normalness" of the social and intellectual traditions of the place. With respect to issues of diversity, this sensibility reflected itself, he suggested, in the unconscious assumption that those who came to college would change and be reformed in the image of those college norms, not that the college would itself be changed.

Beliefs form the basis of consensus. When the experiences of the community corroborate the beliefs of its leadership about issues of change, a transformed environment embodies a new spirit of openness toward what is new. When the community of "believers" is ambivalent or uncertain about their beliefs or about the "head believer," the environment becomes much more difficult to navigate for those whose presence signifies change and difference. In this latter case, a situation occurring on many campuses, the predicament develops in which the signals are mixed and the institution is experienced as "speaking" with inconsistent voice and conviction about change. The very capaciousness of the academic community to encourage diverse points of view contributes to this possibility.

The hope underlying this volume is that this capaciousness will be a resource as we look toward a new century with the problem of the "color lines" and the social and educational challenges they present clearly within our gaze. Progress toward more inclusiveness has been impressive, but much hard work remains. Some of that work must be devoted to a serious assessment of what we have accomplished and what we must learn to do better. Some other portion of that work involves what we are prepared to believe is of value for ourselves and for those who follow. We remain ensnared by this dilemma — the gap between belief and practice. We have re-formed the dilemma as we have progressed toward unprecedented levels of inclusiveness in our colleges and universities, but we have not escaped it. Our best hope, as Randall Kennedy wisely suggests, is that we engage the truth, even when the truth describes a reality that is not what we want to face. We are not yet free of the burden of a discriminatory past.

On the other hand, we should not encumber the pursuit of the promise of diversity with a lack of will to be critical about what has been done to correct the inequities that follow from that history. We can be responsibly cognizant about the burdens of the past, and constructively critical about strategies and programs that have developed to redress those injustices. This double orientation, a commitment to cognizance and to criticism, offers a basis for moving beyond the dilemma into a deeper appreciation — and belief about — the promise of diversity in our institutions of higher education and in our lives together.

## NOTES

1. De Tocqueville's understanding about the difference between law and mores is nicely illustrated in this comment in which he anticipated many of the complexities that would follow when slavery was abolished: "A natural prejudice leads a man to scorn anybody who has been his inferior, long after he has become his equal; the real inequality, due to fortune or law, is always followed by a imagined inequality rooted in mores." In antiquity the most difficult thing was to change the law; in the modern world the hard thing is to alter mores, and our difficulty begins where theirs ended (Mayer 1969).

2. The heat analysis comparison has some historical salience in the California context. Clark Kerr, who served as Berkeley Chancellor (1952–1958) and subsequently as President of the University of California (1958–1967), has quipped on a number of occasions that he ended the latter assignment as he had begun it, "fired with enthusiasm!" Acceding to the wishes of incoming Governor Ronald Reagan, the California Board of Regents forced Kerr to resign in 1967.

3. Rudenstine's sense about the extent to which diversity emphasis can lead to tension is corroborated by research undertaken by Alexander Aston and colleagues (1993).

4. Taylor introduces an important essay, "The Politics of Recognition," with the following observation: "A number of strands in contemporary politics turn on the need, sometimes the demand for *recognition*. This need, it can be argued, is one of the driving forces behind nationalist movements in politics. And the demand comes to fore in a number of ways in today's politics, on behalf of minority . . . groups, in some forms of feminism and in what is today called the politics of multiculturalism" (Taylor 1994).

5. The comparison between California and South Africa has been developed in a useful study by the former Vice Chancellor of the University of Cape Town, S. J. Saunders (1992).

## REFERENCES

Aston, Alexander, et al. 1993. "Diversity and Multiculturalism on the Campus: How Are Students Affected?" *Change* March/April: 44–8.
Bryk, Anthony S., Valerie E. Lee, and Peter B. Holland. 1996. *Catholic Schools and the Common Good.* Cambridge, MA: Harvard University Press.
Carnochan, W. B. 1993. *The Battleground of the Curriculum: Liberal Education and American Experience.* Stanford, CA: Stanford University Press, 117–8.
College Entrance Examination Board. 1992. *Profiles, College-Bound Sen-*

*iors . . .* , *and College-Bound Seniors: 1992 Profile of SAT and Achievement Test Takers.*

Fetter, Jean. 1995. *Questions and Admissions: Reflections on 100,000 Admissions Decisions at Stanford.* Stanford, CA: Stanford University Press.

Hollinger, David. 1997. Quoted in Barry Bearak, "Questions of Race Run Deep for Foe of Preferences." *The New York Times*, 27 July 1997, 1.

Institute for the Study of Social Change. 1991. *The Diversity Project: Final Report.* Berkeley: University of California, Berkeley, 60–1.

Jencks, Christopher. 1992. *Rethinking Social Policy.* Cambridge, MA: Harvard University Press.

Kerr, Clark. 1995. *The Uses of the University*, 4th ed. Cambridge, MA: Harvard University Press, 35–63, 150–4.

Klitgaard, Robert. 1995. *Choosing Elites.* New York: Basic Books.

Lukas, J. Anthony. 1985. *Common Ground: A Turbulent Decade in the Lives of Three American Families.* New York: Knopf.

*Mamphela Ramphele: A Life.* 1995. Cape Town: David Phillip, 201.

Massey, Douglas S., and Nancy A. Denton. 1993. *American Apartheid.* Cambridge, MA: Harvard University Press.

Mayer, J. P. 1969. In J. P. Mayer, ed. *Democracy in America.* New York: Harper & Row, 341.

Milburn, Norweeta G., and Philip J. Bowman. 1991. "Neighborhood Life." In *Life in Black America*, James S. Jackson, ed. Newbury Park, CA: Sage, 31–45.

Miller, Scott. 1995. *An American Imperative: Accelerating Minority Educational Advancement.* New Haven, CT: Yale University Press.

Moskos, Charles C., and John Sibley Butler. 1996. *All That We Can Be: Black Leadership and Racial Integration: The Army Way.* New York: Basic Books.

Myrdal, Gunnar. 1972. *An American Dilemma: The Negro Problem and Modern Democracy.* New York: Pantheon, 3–25.

Orfield, Gary. 1993. *The Growth of Segregation in American Schools.* Alexandria, VA: National School Boards Association.

Saunders, S. J. 1992. "Access to and Quality in Higher Education: A Comparative Study with Some Thoughts on the Future of Higher Education in South Africa." Unpublished, Cape Town.

Schrag, Peter. 1995. "So You Want to be Color-Blind: Alternative Principles for Affirmative Action." *The American Prospect* Summer: 41.

Steeh, Charlotte, and Maria Krysan. 1996. "The Polls—Trends: Affirmative Action and the Public, 1970–1995." *Public Opinion Quarterly* 60(1): 129–58.

Taylor, Charles. 1994. *Multiculturalism: Examining the Politics of Recognition*, Amy Gutmann, ed. Princeton, NJ: Princeton University Press, 25.

Traub, James. 1994. *City on a Hill: Testing the American Dream at City College.* Reading, MA: Addison-Wesley.

United States Kerner Commission. 1968. *Report of the National Advisory Commission on Civil Disorders.* Washington, DC: U.S. Government Printing Office.

University of California. 1997. "The University of California Responds to: UC Regents' Resolution SP-1 and California Proposition 209." 24 February 1997, internal document, Department of Student Academic Services.

*PART II*

# Two

## PROMOTING HIGH ACADEMIC ACHIEVEMENT AMONG NON-ASIAN MINORITIES

### L. Scott Miller

WHEN ONE reviews skill and academic achievement data for both adults and children in the United States, it is clear that, despite considerable educational progress over the past few decades, there are still very large human capital gaps among racial/ethnic groups in our society at all age levels. For example, Asian-American and non-Hispanic white adults have much higher literacy skills, on average, than African-Americans, Latino-Americans, and Native Americans; and, these group differences are largest in the "tails" of the literacy skills distribution (Kirsch et al. 1993). Similarly, within the under-18 population, African-American, Hispanic, and American Indian students are heavily over represented among low achievers and severely underrepresented among high achievers, while the reverse is true for Asians and whites (Campbell et al. 1997).

The consequences of these patterns are profoundly important. With much larger proportions of top performing high school students, whites and Asians are significantly better positioned than non-Asian minorities to enter and to perform very well at selective colleges and universities (Owings et al. 1995; Elliott et al. 1995). As a result, they also are better positioned on graduation to secure desirable entry-level professional jobs — jobs that offer career avenues to a wide variety of executive and other leadership positions in our society. At the same time, much higher proportions of low achieving students, blacks, Latinos, and Native Americans continue to be much more likely than whites and Asians to experience unemployment and to have low-paying jobs as adults (O'Neill 1990; Ferguson 1995; Raudenbush and Kasim 1998).

With the continuing reality of these divergent educational and career trajectories as a backdrop, in this analysis I will (1) describe the size of the high achievement gaps among racial/ethnic groups, (2) review some of the reasons why these gaps persist, and (3) suggest some steps that our society can take to make more rapid progress toward eliminating them.

## HIGH ACHIEVEMENT GAPS AMONG RACIAL/ETHNIC GROUPS

Some of the most important ways in which we measure academic achievement are school grades, class rank, and standardized test scores. There is a large body of research indicating that, using these traditional measures of academic performance, non-Asian minorities are underrepresented among high achievers, from the primary grades through graduate school (Miller 1995). Moreover, although there continues to be concern in some quarters about the potential for cultural bias in standardized testing or in the grading processes of some teachers, available evidence indicates that these traditional measures of academic achievement are generally valid and reliable in a very important way: They tend to be reasonably good aggregate predictors of future performance in school and in the labor market for most groups (Ramist et al. 1994; Wagner 1997; Raudenbush and Kasim 1998).

It must be noted, however, that one of the difficulties in assessing groups' progress is that few sources of academic achievement trend data, broken down by race/ethnicity, go back very far in time. Our best single source may be the federal government's National Assessment of Educational Progress (NAEP) testing program, which has been administering subject area tests to nationally representative samples of elementary and secondary students for about three decades.

The genuinely positive news from NAEP is that in the 1970s and 1980s both African-Americans and Latinos made substantial gains on NAEP reading and math tests and, consequently, closed much of the score gaps with whites on these tests. For example, in the mid-1990s, the gaps in average NAEP reading and math scores between black and white 17-year-olds were 45 and 33% smaller, respectively, than they were in the early 1970s; and they were 35 and 28% smaller, respectively, between Hispanics and whites than in the mid-1970s (Campbell et al. 1997).

Much of the improvement in NAEP math and reading scores of blacks and Hispanics is the result of having many fewer students from these groups score at the lowest levels than was the case a generation ago. Encouragingly, substantial gains also have been made at middle performance rungs, along with some gains at top levels as well. A generation ago, for African-Americans in particular, top scorers on NAEP reading and math tests among these groups were relatively rare. That is no longer the case, although both blacks and Latinos remain very much underrepresented among top scorers on all NAEP tests. Table 1 illustrates these points using NAEP reading trend data for 17-year-olds.

Another encouraging aspect of the NAEP math and reading score

TABLE 1

National Assessment of Educational Progress Reading Score Trends for Age 17, by Race/Ethnicity

| | 1971 | 1975 | 1980 | 1984 | 1988 | 1990 | 1992 | 1994 | 1996 |
|---|---|---|---|---|---|---|---|---|---|
| *Average scores for each group* | | | | | | | | | |
| White | 291 | 293 | 293 | 295 | 295 | 297 | 297 | 296 | 294 |
| Black | 239 | 241 | 243 | 264 | 274 | 267 | 261 | 266 | 265 |
| Hispanic | NA | 252 | 261 | 268 | 271 | 275 | 271 | 263 | 265 |
| *% of each group scoring 200+* | | | | | | | | | |
| White | 98 | 99 | 99 | 99 | 99 | 99 | 99 | 98 | 99 |
| Black | 82 | 82 | 86 | 96 | 98 | 96 | 92 | 93 | 95 |
| Hispanic | NA | 89 | 93 | 96 | 96 | 96 | 93 | 91 | 94 |
| *% of each group scoring 250+* | | | | | | | | | |
| White | 84 | 86 | 87 | 88 | 89 | 88 | 88 | 86 | 87 |
| Black | 40 | 43 | 44 | 66 | 76 | 69 | 61 | 66 | 67 |
| Hispanic | NA | 53 | 62 | 68 | 72 | 75 | 69 | 63 | 64 |
| *% of each group scoring 300+* | | | | | | | | | |
| White | 43 | 44 | 43 | 46 | 45 | 48 | 50 | 48 | 45 |
| Black | 8 | 8 | 7 | 16 | 25 | 20 | 17 | 22 | 18 |
| Hispanic | NA | 13 | 17 | 21 | 23 | 27 | 27 | 20 | 20 |
| *% of each group scoring 350+* | | | | | | | | | |
| White | 7.7 | 7.2 | 6.2 | 6.9 | 5.5 | 8.7 | 8.3 | 8.8 | 8.0 |
| Black | 0.4 | 0.4 | 0.2 | 0.9 | 1.4 | 1.5 | 1.6 | 2.3 | 1.7 |
| Hispanic | NA | 1.2 | 1.3 | 2.0 | 1.3 | 2.4 | 2.3 | 1.9 | 1.6 |

Source: J. R. Campbell et al. 1997. *NAEP 1996 Trends in Academic Progress: Achievement of U.S. Students in Science, 1969 to 1996; Mathematics, 1973 to 1996; Reading, 1971 to 1996; and Writing, 1984 to 1996.* Washington, DC: Educational Testing Service/U.S. Department of Education, U.S. Government Printing Office.

gains made by African-Americans and Latino-Americans in the 1970s and 1980s is that they evidently occurred in several different social class segments for both groups. Analyses of changes in scores for 9- and 13-year-olds in this period found gains made by black and Hispanic students who had no parent with a high school diploma, those with parents who had graduated from high school, and those with one or more parents who had at least some postsecondary education (Anderson 1990, 1991).

Unfortunately, Table 1 also illustrates another important point: Progress for non-Asian minorities on NAEP tests has slowed over the past decade. In fact, average reading scores for black and Hispanic 17-year-olds in 1996 were about the same as they had been in the mid-1980s,

TABLE 2

Percentages of 1992 College-Bound Seniors Who Were Academically Prepared for Selective Colleges and Universities, by Race/Ethnicity

|  | 3.5+ GPA | 1100+ SAT |
|---|---|---|
| Asian | 29.3 | 27.7 |
| Hispanic | 10.3 | 8.0 |
| Black | 4.1 | 2.6 |
| White | 20.9 | 25.0 |
| American Indian/ Alaskan Native | 5.3 | 2.2 |

*Source:* J. Owings et al. 1995. "Making the Cut: Who Meets Highly Selective College Entrance Criteria." In *Statistics in Brief.* Washington, DC: U.S. Department of Education.

although some math score gains have been made in the 1990s (Campbell et al. 1997). At this juncture, it is not clear why NAEP test score progress by African-Americans and Latinos has tailed off in the 1990s, but identifying the sources of this pattern should be a high priority for researchers and policymakers. Examples of questions that should be raised are: Is this trend centered more among low, middle, or high SES (socioeconomic status) black or Hispanic children? Is it related in part to growing segregation of African-American and Latino students in high poverty concentration schools? Is it related in any way to the growing number of children of immigrants who have little formal education?

Because NAEP tests represent only one source of information on minority academic achievement, it is important to look at data from other sources as well. Since the focus of this chapter is on promoting high academic achievement among non-Asian minority students, it is appropriate to review the findings of a federal report on academically very well prepared college-bound high school seniors in 1992 (Owings et al. 1995). The report's data are from the National Education Longitudinal Study of 1988 (NELS:88), which began tracking a large sample of young people when they were in the eighth grade.

Table 2 shows that fully 29% of the Asian and 21% of the white college-bound students in this sample had high school GPAs (grade point averages) of 3.5 or higher (on a four-point scale), while this was the case for only 10% of the Latinos, 5% of the Native Americans, and 4% of African-Americans. And, 28% of the Asians and 25% of the whites had a combined verbal and math score of at least 1100 out of 1600 on the SAT (Scholastic Assessment Test)—using the old SAT scoring norms—or they had an equivalent score on the ACT (American College Test), while just 8% of the Hispanics, 3% of the blacks, and 2% of the American Indians scored 1100 or more.

TABLE 3
Number of High SAT Math Scorers Nationally in 1981 and 1995,
by Race/Ethnicity

| | Number 600+ | | Number 750+ | |
|---|---|---|---|---|
| | 1981 | 1995 | 1981 | 1995 |
| American Indian/Alaskan Native | 329 | 1,109 | 8 | 36 |
| Asian/Pacific Islander | 7,946 | 31,102 | 633 | 3,827 |
| Black | 1,541 | 4,758 | 24 | 107 |
| Mexican-American | 770 | 3,161 | 24 | 86 |
| Puerto Rican | 350 | 923 | 9 | 32 |
| Other Hispanic | NA | 3,643 | NA | 144 |
| White | 117,000 | 160,337 | 5,077 | 9,519 |
| Other | 2,433 | 5,859 | 140 | 424 |
| Ethnicity unknown | 13,197 | 18,821 | 655 | 1,737 |

Source: Leonard Ramist and Solomon Arbeiter. 1982. *Profiles of College-Bound Seniors, 1981.* New York: College Entrance Examination Board; College Entrance Examination Board. 1995. *1995 College-Bound Seniors: Ethnic and Gender Profile of SAT and Achievement Test Takers for the Nation.* New York: College Entrance Examination Board.

Since the 3.5 GPA and 1100 SAT thresholds are not as high as those typically employed by the nation's most selective colleges and universities, they cannot be used to assess fully the degree to which non-Asian minorities are underrepresented among top college-bound seniors. For this reason, Table 3 presents information on the absolute number of students nationally, by race/ethnicity, who scored at least 600 and at least 750 out of 800 (also using the old SAT norms) on the math section of the SAT in 1981 and 1995. Those who score 750 or more tend to represent some of the (mathematically) very best prepared college-bound students in the nation, while those who score at least 600 are close to the math performance threshold implicit in the 1100 combined SAT score used in the previously mentioned federal study. (Prior to the recent renorming of the SAT, a math score of 570–580 and a verbal score of 520–530 would have been a common way to score 1100, as test takers tended to average 50+ points higher on the math section than on the verbal section.)

As Table 3 shows, there were very large overall increases in the 1981–95 period in the number of test takers who scored 600+ and 750+ on the SAT math section, and each of the racial/ethnic groups shared in these gains to varying degrees. However, because the gains made by non-Asian minorities were usually from very low bases, their numbers were still relatively small in 1995, especially at the 750 threshold. Col-

TABLE 4

Percentage of SAT Test Takers Nationally with High Math Section Scores in 1981 and 1995, by Race/Ethnicity

| | %600+ | | %750+ | |
|---|---|---|---|---|
| | 1981 | 1995 | 1981 | 1995 |
| American Indian/Alaskan Native | 7.1 | 12.4 | 0.2 | 0.4 |
| Asian/Pacific Islander | 26.7 | 38.2 | 2.1 | 4.7 |
| Black | 2.0 | 4.6 | 0.0 | 0.1 |
| Mexican-American | 5.3 | 8.7 | 0.2 | 0.2 |
| Puerto Rican | 5.0 | 7.1 | 0.1 | 0.2 |
| Other Hispanic | NA | 11.9 | NA | 0.5 |
| White | 16.3 | 23.8 | 0.7 | 1.4 |
| Other | 13.1 | 23.3 | 0.8 | 1.8 |
| Ethnicity unknown | 10.6 | 20.0 | 0.5 | 1.8 |

Source: Leonard Ramist and Solomon Arbeiter. 1982. *Profiles of College-Bound Seniors, 1981.* New York: College Entrance Examination Board; College Entrance Examination Board. 1995. *1995 College-Bound Seniors: Ethnic and Gender Profile of SAT and Achievement Test Takers for the Nation.* New York: College Entrance Examination Board.

lectively, only 405 blacks, Mexican-Americans, Puerto Ricans, other Hispanics, and Native Americans scored at least 750 on the SAT math section that year. In contrast, 9519 whites, along with a very impressive 3827 Asians, were able to do so.

To put this in perspective demographically, non-Asian minorities made up only about 3% of the "750 club" in 1995, even though they currently represent about 30% of the under-18 population. In contrast, Asians alone made up 24% of these top scorers, despite representing just 3–4% of this population segment.

The situation was better for non-Asian minorities who reached the 600 threshold in 1995, yet African-American, Hispanic, and Native American test takers were still only 6% of this group. And, by themselves, Asians outnumbered non-Asians minorities at the 600 line by more than two to one.

As dramatic as these absolute figures are, Table 4 demonstrates that the underrepresentation of non-Asian minorities may be even more extreme when viewed from the vantage point of the percentages of each group that score 750 or more on the SAT math section. For example, only 0.1% of African-American and 0.2% of the Mexican-American test takers reached the 750 threshold in 1995, but 1.4% of the whites did so, along with an extraordinary 4.7% of the Asians.

Very large differences in percentages were recorded at the 600 level as

TABLE 5

Selected Information on 1995 SAT Test Takers with a Combined Verbal and Math Score of 1200+ and 1400+, by Race/Ethnicity

| | 1200+ Test Takers | | | 1400+ Test Takers | | |
|---|---|---|---|---|---|---|
| | Number | Avg. No. Math Courses | Avg. Math GPA | Number | Avg. No. Math Courses | Avg. Math GPA |
| American Indian/Alaskan Native | 536 | 3.68 | 3.61 | 39 | 3.72 | 3.69 |
| Asian/Pacific Islander | 14,485 | 3.71 | 3.80 | 2,504 | 3.76 | 3.94 |
| Black | 2,031 | 3.66 | 3.57 | 115 | 3.70 | 3.83 |
| Mexican-American | 1,253 | 3.77 | 3.67 | 81 | 3.88 | 3.85 |
| Puerto Rican | 406 | 3.71 | 3.69 | 27 | 3.85 | 3.81 |
| Other Hispanic | 1,708 | 3.74 | 3.66 | 164 | 3.82 | 3.85 |
| White | 90,469 | 3.76 | 3.69 | 10,258 | 3.84 | 3.87 |
| Other | 3,540 | 3.71 | 3.65 | 432 | 3.83 | 3.85 |
| Total | 114,428 | | | 13,620 | | |

Source: Unpublished analysis of 1995 National SAT Data Tape by Marian E. Brazziel for L. Scott Miller.

well. With 38%, Asians had the highest percentage of test takers at this level, while, at 5%, African-Americans had the lowest.

This same general pattern is found on the verbal section of the SAT. In 1995, for instance, Asians had the highest percentage of test takers who scored at least 700 on the verbal section, 1.8%, followed by whites with 1.1%. In contrast, only 0.2% of the blacks, 0.3% of the Mexican-Americans and Puerto Ricans, and 0.5% of the other Hispanics and Native Americans reached the 700 level on the verbal section (see College Entrance Examination Board 1995d).

Table 5 shows the results of such patterns on a combined verbal and math SAT score basis. African-Americans, Latinos, and Native Americans constituted only 3% of the test takers in 1995 who had a combined score of 1400+ and only 5% of those scoring 1200+. These data help explain why it is so difficult for non-Asian minorities to become well represented at the nation's most selective colleges and universities.

One way to interpret the 1981 and 1995 SAT math data is that the American educational system is getting more competitive from a high achievement standpoint—in no small measure due to the rapid increase in the number of top Asian-American students — at a time when it is very important that non-Asian minority representation among high achievers be greatly expanded. Of course, this conclusion might not be drawn if the SAT was a poor predictor of academic performance in college. But this is not the case. A number of studies over the past two decades have found that SAT scores, along with high school grades and high school class rank, tell a great deal about the likely performance of students in college. For example, Warren Willingham (1985) found that, together, high school class rank and SAT scores were very accurate predictors of which students would graduate with honors at a group of several private liberal arts colleges. Students in the top quarter of their entering freshman classes in terms of high school class rank and SAT scores had excellent chances of graduating with honors, while this was a rare event for students in the bottom quarter by these measures of academic preparation.

A College Board study by Leonard Ramist, Charles Lewis, and Laura McCamley-Jenkins (1994) offers one of the most sophisticated analyses to date of predictors of academic performance in higher education. Using a large sample of institutions and students, Ramist et al. found that high school grades and SAT scores are good predictors of both freshman GPA and individual freshman course grades, especially after adjusting for the selectivity of colleges and universities that students attend as well as for the comparability of the courses that they take.

Nonetheless, there is an important caveat to these general findings. The study by Ramist et al., as well as those by several others (e.g., Klitgaard 1985, Nettles et al. 1986, and Pennock-Roman 1990) has found that SAT scores tend to overpredict the grades of blacks and Hispanics in many cases. That is to say, students from these groups often do not do as well in college as their SAT scores would suggest (compared to white or Asians students with similar SAT scores).

Definitive explanations of the overprediction phenomenon are not yet available. Nonetheless, the study by Ramist et al. found that overprediction for African-Americans and Latino-Americans is most common and largest in magnitude in quantitative courses. At selective colleges and universities, these are courses that tend to be extremely competitive in terms of students' academic preparation and very demanding in terms of the rate at which new material is introduced; the grading also is often quite strict and the building block nature of math and science means that failure to master concepts and techniques at one point can undermine performance later (Elliott et al. 1995). In these circumstances, various interfering forces, ranging from campus climate issues to the need to work to pay college expenses, could be contributing to the underperformance of a number of minority students. Whatever the reasons, the research clearly suggests that, not only is the supply of academically very well prepared non-Asian minority college-bound seniors still relatively small, these students' prospects for performing at the highest levels academically in college are, on average, less promising than those of similarly prepared whites and Asians.

Before examining several underlying factors that appear to be contributing to differences in the proportions of high academic achievers among groups, it is important to review three other dimensions of this issue. The first is the reality that there are both large between- and within-social-class differences in academic achievement among racial/ethnic groups in America. The second is that there are still significant regional variations in academic achievement within most groups. And the third is that recent immigration to the United States has been educationally bimodal — with many immigrants having a great deal of formal education and many having very little — and this bimodal pattern has racial/ethnic dimensions.

## BETWEEN- AND WITHIN-SOCIAL-CLASS
## ACADEMIC ACHIEVEMENT GAPS

When thinking about academic achievement differences among racial/ethnic groups, there is a tendency to focus on the low achievement patterns of disadvantaged students. This makes a great deal of sense, since black, Hispanic, and Native American youngsters are heavily overrepresented among the most disadvantaged children in our society, including those who experience long-term poverty, those who grow up in communities that have high concentrations of poor families, those who have parents with little formal education, and those who attend schools that serve heavily disadvantaged student clienteles (Kennedy et al. 1986; Wilson 1987; Miller 1995; Puma et al. 1997).

Certainly, a large body of research and data supports the conclusion that disadvantaged/low-SES students do much less well academically than high-SES students. We can turn again to the National Education Longitudinal Study of 1988 for data on this point. When the students in the sample were in the eighth grade, collectively all of those with no parent with a high school diploma had a 51% chance of being in the lowest achievement quartile (on a battery of standardized tests) and only a 5% chance of being in the highest quartile, while those with at least one parent with a graduate or professional degree had a 7% chance of being in the lowest quartile and a 56% chance of being in the top quartile. Moreover, non-Asian minorities in the NELS:88 sample were heavily overrepresented among students who had parents with little formal schooling and quite underrepresented among those who had parents with a great deal of formal education (see Hafner et al. 1990 and Miller 1995).

Nonetheless, research on between-social-class achievement patterns offers only a partial (descriptive) explanation for differences in academic performance among racial/ethnic groups. A great deal of standardized test data suggest that differences in overall academic achievement patterns among racial/ethnic groups have significant within-social-class dimensions as well. In fact, these data suggest that some of the largest within-social-class differences are among high SES segments of the groups. This has important implications for the underrepresentation of some racial/ethnic groups among high academic achievers in school, because high achievers are drawn disproportionately from high-SES population segments.

Probably the earliest national data on within-social-class differences in achievement are from *Equality of Educational Opportunity*, the seminal study in the mid-1960s undertaken by a team headed by the late sociologist James S. Coleman, which first documented systematically that there were large differences in academic achievement among racial/ethnic groups in the United States (Coleman et al. 1966). Secondary analysis of data from the "Coleman Report" found that in the sixth, ninth, and twelfth grades there were large differences in achievement among racial/ethnic groups at high, medium, and low SES levels, with SES defined in terms of the education of both parents and the occupations of fathers (Okada et al. 1972). For example, white and Asian students at each SES level generally had higher verbal test score averages than their African-American, Mexican-American, Puerto Rican, and American Indian counterparts. In several cases, these within-social-class differences were quite large — the equivalent of two to three grade levels.

Table 6 illustrates the current magnitude of both between- and within-social-class gaps among a large proportion of the nation's college-bound seniors, using average math, verbal, and combined SAT scores for 1995 for test takers who had at least one parent with a graduate or professional degree and for those who had no parent with a high school diploma. Consistent with the findings of many studies (e.g., White 1982; Hafner et al. 1990; Campbell et al. 1997), data in Table 6 show that, generally, high-SES youngsters achieve academically at much higher levels than low-SES youngsters. Indeed, (using the old SAT norms) the average verbal and math scores for all test takers on the 1995 SAT with at least one parent with a graduate or professional degree were 143 and 135 points higher, respectively, than for all test takers with no parent with a high school diploma. This general pattern also held within each

TABLE 6
1995 Average Verbal, Math, and Combined SAT Scores for Test Takers
Nationally, by Race/Ethnicity and Selected Parent Education Levels

| | No Parent Has High School Degree | | | At Least One Parent Has Graduate Degree | | |
|---|---|---|---|---|---|---|
| | Verbal | Math | Combined | Verbal | Math | Combined |
| American Indian/Alaskan Native | 344 | 390 | 734 | 449 | 495 | 944 |
| Asian/Pacific Islander | 338 | 478 | 816 | 482 | 592 | 1074 |
| Black | 308 | 347 | 655 | 406 | 438 | 844 |
| Mexican-American | 331 | 389 | 720 | 430 | 479 | 909 |
| Puerto Rican | 317 | 355 | 672 | 412 | 461 | 873 |
| Other Hispanic | 327 | 375 | 702 | 433 | 494 | 927 |
| White | 374 | 418 | 792 | 490 | 545 | 1035 |
| Other | 338 | 402 | 740 | 485 | 545 | 1030 |
| All | 338 | 405 | 743 | 481 | 540 | 1021 |

*Source:* College Entrance Examination Board. 1995. *1995 College-Bound Seniors: Ethnic and Gender Profile of SAT and Achievement Test Takers for the Nation.* New York: College Entrance Examination Board.

racial/ethnic category. For most of the groups, the differences in average verbal and math scores between the high and low parent-education segments were about one standard deviation (College Entrance Examination Board 1995d).

Nevertheless, as Table 6 also shows, there were very large differences among the groups within each of the parent education categories, with the largest gaps generally among those with at least one parent with a graduate or professional degree. Compared to the combined averages of 1074 and 1035 for Asians and whites with at least one parent with a graduate or professional degree, African-Americans in this category were at the greatest disadvantage, as they had a combined average of only 844. With combined averages of 873 and 909, respectively, Puerto Ricans and Mexican-Americans also were experiencing large gaps in this parent education segment.

All other things equal, with these sizable differences in average scores, non-Asian minorities with at least one parent with a graduate or professional degree would be expected to have much smaller proportions of high achievers than their white and Asian counterparts. For example, the standard deviation on the math section was 110 for all Puerto Rican

TABLE 7

1994 Average NAEP Reading Scores for 12th Graders, by Race/Ethnicity and
Parent Education Level

|  | Parent Education Level | | | |
|---|---|---|---|---|
|  | Less Than High School | Graduated from High School | Some Education Beyond High School | Graduated from College |
| White | 274 | 283 | 294 | 302 |
| Black | 258 | 258 | 271 | 272 |
| Hispanic | 260 | 265 | 279 | 283 |
| White − Black = | 16 | 25 | 23 | 30 |
| White − Hispanic = | 14 | 17 | 15 | 19 |

Note: Differences in white and black scores and white and Hispanic scores were calculated before rounding.

Source: Jay R. Campbell et al. 1996. NAEP 1994 Reading Report Card for the Nation and the States: Findings From the National Assessment of Educational Progress and Trial State Assessments. Washington, DC: U.S. Department of Education.

SAT test takers in 1995, while it was 120 for whites that year (College Entrance Examination Board 1995d). Going out two standard deviations (on the high side) from the 461 math mean for Puerto Rican test takers with at least one parent with a graduate or professional degree (see Table 6), we get an estimated score of 681 for the 98th percentile. In contrast, going out only one standard deviation from the 545 math mean for whites with a parent with a graduate or professional degree, we get an estimated score of 665 for the 68th percentile. This, of course, is only 15 points lower than the estimated 98th percentile score for Puerto Ricans, which clearly illustrates why the large within-social-class differences in SAT scores among racial/ethnic groups are important contributors to the underrepresentation of non-Asian minorities among high achievers.

The 1994 NAEP reading test produced results that are quite similar to those of the 1995 SAT. As Table 7 shows, African-Americans and Latinos in a nationally representative sample of high school seniors had much lower average reading scores than their white counterparts at each parent education level, and the gaps were largest for students who had at least one parent with a college degree. Importantly, black twelfth graders with a parent with a college degree had a lower average score than the white students who had no parent with a high school diploma.

## REGIONAL VARIATIONS IN ACADEMIC ACHIEVEMENT

Another important finding of the Coleman Report was that there were some large regional variations in academic achievement among students from all ethnic groups. Possibly the most notable finding of this kind was that students in the South lagged well behind students in the North and some other regions of the country (Coleman et al. 1966).

Trend data over the past quarter-century from NAEP reading, math, and other subject area tests suggest that there continue to be regional differences in academic achievement (Campbell et al. 1997). Since 1990, several NAEP tests designed specifically to allow interstate comparisons of student achievement also have found some important differences at the state level. For instance, consistent with the Coleman Report, students in some southern states have scored considerably lower on NAEP interstate math tests than students in several states in the upper middle west and elsewhere in the country (Mullis et al. 1993).

There also are sizable interstate differences in scores on the SAT, some of which may have important implications for the underrepresentation of non-Asian minorities among high academic achievers. For example, black test takers in Texas with at least one parent with a graduate or professional degree had a combined verbal and math score average of 805 in 1995 (using the old SAT norms), which was 39 points lower than the 844 national average for African-Americans in this segment, and 34 and 29 points, respectively, lower than the 839 and 834 averages for this segment in New York and California (College Entrance Examination Board 1995a–d).

These differences in scoring patterns among regions of the country stand alongside another set of geographic variations in achievement — those that exist among urban, suburban, and rural areas (Campbell et al. 1997). Students in suburban public schools tend to perform considerably better, on average, than their counterparts in rural and, especially, central city public schools. Much of this advantage reflects the de facto extensive segregation by social class as well as race/ethnicity that now exists in urban and suburban areas in much of the country (Massey and Denton 1993). Many suburban public school systems serve disproportionate numbers of white students from middle and professional class families, which is associated with much if not most of their academic performance advantage over central city and rural school systems. Although there is some evidence that disadvantaged and minority children may fare somewhat better academically in suburban schools, it is also clear that they typically do not enjoy anything close to the academic success of their middle class white counterparts (Rosenbaum et al. 1987; Levine and Eubanks 1990; College Entrance Examination Board 1995d). Moreover, as some suburban school districts have seen their minority and disadvantaged student populations grow to substantial levels, they are now experiencing many of the concerns and debates over low minority student achievement, measured by grades and standardized test scores, that have characterized the nation's central city school systems for the past several decades (Dumenigo 1997; Tinsley 1997).

## EDUCATIONALLY BIMODAL NATURE OF IMMIGRATION TO AMERICA

The racial/ethnic composition of the United States has been changing rapidly for several decades and seems likely to continue to do so for the foreseeable future. As recently as 1950, non-Hispanic whites constituted nearly nine-tenths of the American population and African-Americans were the primary minority group, making up about a tenth of the population. Collectively, Hispanics, Asians, and Native Americans represented a very small fraction of the population — only a few percent — at that point. However, by 1990, the non-Hispanic white share of the American population had fallen to about three-quarters. Moreover, not only had the minority component of the population doubled, its composition had changed dramatically as well. While blacks had reached 12% of the population by 1990, Latinos had grown to 9% and demographic forecasts suggest that they will become the nation's largest minority segment early in the next century. The Asian share of the population had reached 3% by 1990, up from less than 1% in 1950, while the Native American share had doubled to about 1% in the interval (see Miller 1995).

The demographic shift has been even more rapid among the young than among the American population as a whole. Minorities had reached 31% of the under-18 population by 1990, and by 1995 — only five years later — they were 34% of this age segment (Population Reference Bureau 1992; Day 1996). By 2030, the non-Hispanic white share of the under-18 population is forecast to fall to 51%, while the African-American, Latino-American, Asian-American, and Native American shares are projected to be 16, 25, 7, and 1%, respectively (Day 1996).

The demographic shift has been in part the result of a large drop in the white majority's birth rate, which occurred in the middle 1960s. But it has also been driven by a sustained upsurge in immigration, especially from Asia and Latin America, that began after the nation's immigration laws were liberalized in the mid-1960s (Glazer 1985; Fuchs 1990).

A central feature of the current period of immigration is its educational bimodality. Among recent immigrants over age 25, about 21% have had at least a bachelor's degree, compared to 15% of the U.S. population in this age segment, while 36% have had less than a high school education, compared to 17% in this age group for the nation as a whole (Holmes 1995). Crucially, this bimodal educational quality of current immigration has a strong racial/ethnic dimension. Asian nations have been the source of a disproportionate number of immigrants with a college education, while Latin America has been a primary source of immigrants with less than a high school degree. For example, during the 1990–94 period, 61% of the immigrants from India over 25 years old had a bachelor's or graduate or professional degree, while only 20% had less than a high school diploma; and the comparable percentages for Korean immigrants were 32 and 8%. In contrast, only 8% of the Mexican immigrants over 25 had a bachelor's degree, while fully 70% had not completed high school; and the comparable percentages for El Salvadorian immigrants were 10 and 58% (see Bureau of Census 1995).

The consequences of this interaction of race/ethnicity and educational attainment in America's immigrant stream can be seen in parent education profiles of the student-age population and, therefore, in the differences in academic achievement patterns among groups. Certainly, immigration can be viewed as an important factor in both the over-representation of Asians among top students and the underrepresentation of non-Asian minorities among these students, along with the latter's overrepresentation among low achievers as well.

The previously mentioned National Educational Longitudinal Study of 1988 provides an excellent example of the large differences in parent education patterns that now exist for students in the United States. For the eighth graders originally sampled in 1988, 45% of the Asian students and 30% of the white students had at least one parent with a bachelor's or graduate or professional degree, but only 17% of the Native Americans, 14% of the blacks, and 13% of the Hispanics had a parent with a bachelor's or graduate or professional degree. At the same time, for fully 33% of the Latinos in the sample, along with 16% of the African-Americans and 15% of the Native Americans, neither of their parents had finished high school. In contrast, only 6% of the white students and 9% of the Asian students were in this position (see Hafner et al. 1990).

These kinds of differences also can currently be seen in the composition of the students who take the SAT. In 1995, 58% of the Asian test takers had at least one parent with a bachelor's or a graduate or profes-

TABLE 8
Percentage of SAT Test Takers in California with High Math Section Scores
from Each Racial/Ethnic Group in 1995

| | % of Those Scoring 600+ | % of Those Scoring 750+ |
|---|---|---|
| American Indian/Alaskan Native | 0.8 | 0.4 |
| Asian/Pacific Islander | 30.4 | 45.9 |
| Black | 1.3 | 0.3 |
| Mexican-American | 4.1 | 1.2 |
| Puerto Rican | 0.2 | 0.1 |
| Other Hispanic | 2.2 | 1.3 |
| White | 49.3 | 38.9 |
| Other | 4.9 | 4.2 |
| Ethnicity unknown | 6.7 | 7.6 |

*Note:* Columns may not add to 100% due to rounding.

*Source:* College Entrance Examination Board. 1995. *1995 College-Bound Seniors: Ethnic and Gender Profile of SAT and Achievement Test Takers for California.* New York: College Entrance Examination Board.

sional degree, along with 57% of the whites; but the percentages for blacks, Mexican-Americans, Puerto Ricans, other Hispanics, and Native Americans were 34, 25, 38, 40, and 42%, respectively (College Entrance Examination Board 1995d). Thus, although large percentages of non-Asian minority test takers have at least one parent with a great deal of formal education, they are much smaller proportions than those of Asians and whites.

Regarding SAT test takers with no parent with a high school diploma, unsurprisingly Latino groups tend to have the highest percentages in this category. For example, the highest by far on the 1995 SAT was the 28% of Mexican-American test takers who had no parent with a high school degree; the other Hispanic category was second with 17%, followed by Puerto Ricans and Asians with 11% each, 6% for African-Americans, 4% for Native Americans, and 1% for whites (College Entrance Examination Board 1995d). Consistent with the fact that many immigrants from Mexico over the past few decades have had very little formal schooling, about one-sixth of the 1995 Mexican-American seniors nationally who had taken the SAT had no parent who had gone beyond elementary school (College Entrance Examination Board 1997).

California offers a glimpse of what that future could be like from a high academic achievement perspective in America in a few decades, should substantial levels of immigration (especially from Latin America and Asia) continue as projected and large achievement gaps among groups persist as well. In 1990, the under-18 population in California was 47% white, 34% Hispanic, 10% Asian, 8% African-American, and 1% Native American (Population Reference Bureau 1992). As Table 8 shows, whites and Asians, together, made up 85% of the California students in 1995 who scored 750 or more on the SAT math section and 80% of those who scored at least 600 on it (using the old SAT norms). By themselves, Asians made up a remarkable 46% of the SAT test takers in the state who scored 750 on the math section and 30% of those who reached the 600 threshold. But, the three Latino groups (Mexican-Americans, Puerto Ricans, and other Hispanics), along with blacks and Native Americans, made up only 3 and 9%, respectively, of those who scored at least 750 and 600 on the math section.

The story was similar on the verbal section, with whites and Asians accounting for 79% of those who scored at least 700 and Asians alone constituting 25% of the total. The non-Asian minorities accounted for only 4% of those who reached 700 on the verbal section (see College Entrance Examination Board 1995a).

## SOURCES OF MINORITY UNDERREPRESENTATION AMONG HIGH ACHIEVERS

I would now like to turn to a discussion of five factors that contribute in an important way to the underrepresentation of non-Asian minorities among high academic achieving students: (1) racial/ethnic prejudice and discrimination; (2) differences among racial/ethnic groups in average human capital levels possessed by parents at essentially all social class levels; (3) cultural differences among the groups; (4) differences in economic resources among the groups; and (5) the almost inevitably limited capacity of schools, by themselves, to produce substantial achievement gains consistently and rapidly for large numbers of disadvantaged youngsters, especially when they are highly diverse as well.

### Racial/Ethnic Prejudice and Discrimination

Although racial/ethnic prejudice and discrimination are obviously not unique to the United States, there are two features of our homegrown varieties that have made them quite virulent from a minority educational advancement standpoint. The first is that at the core of America's approach to discrimination for most of the nation's history was a government-enforced, rigidly adhered to caste system that blocked African-Americans and, in varying degrees, Hispanics and other minorities from getting a good education or making full use of their schooling for purposes of economic, political, or social advancement (Weinberg 1977; Acuna 1988; Anderson 1988). The second is that our caste system came to be supported by a theory that held that blacks were innately inferior intellectually to whites and that blacks, Latinos, and Native Americans were culturally inferior in ways that made education problematic for them (Fredrickson 1988).

Fortunately, not only was our caste system swept away a few decades ago by the Civil Rights movement, the proportion of whites who embrace innate or cultural theories of minority intellectual inferiority also has declined substantially over the past half-century. Nonetheless, from its grave, the caste system is still exerting a negative influence in several ways on the academic performance of African-Americans and some other minorities. And sufficient numbers of whites still believe that blacks, Hispanics, or some other groups are intellectually inferior for innate or cultural reasons for these notions also to be having negative impacts. The publication of *The Bell Curve* (Herrnstein and Murray 1994) offers a reminder of how powerful such ideas continue to be.

Although very hard to quantify, the notions of innate and cultural inferiority seem to be having negative influences on minority achievement both through the behaviors of some teachers and through those of some minority students themselves. For some teachers, these ideas may contribute to lower academic expectations for minority students that can be manifested, for example, in the form of limiting minority students' access to intellectually demanding courses or course conduct (Oakes 1985, 1990) or through interactions in the classroom that are not positive from an academic development standpoint (Dusek and Joseph 1986; Irvine 1990).

Over a decade ago, Jeff Howard and Ray Hammond pointed out that "rumors of inferiority" still seemed to be leading many African-American students — both poor and middle class — to avoid academic competition out of a fear that, should they not do well, it would tend to confirm the white stereotype of blacks as intellectual inferiors (Howard and Hammond 1985). Although there has been little empirical evidence on this point, psychologist Claude Steele has recently developed a formal (psychological) theory of how this process might work. He and some colleagues also have conducted experiments with students at a highly selective university, which offer tentative support for his theory (see Steele and Aronson 1995; Steele 1997).

Based on these experiments, Steele argues that the threat of the negative intellectual stereotype to African-Americans is probably having two impacts. First, fear of confirming this negative stereotype may lead a number of African-American students to underperform in high-stakes academic settings, such as when taking a difficult test (Steele 1997). In essence, if replications and extensions of this research confirm the initial experiments, "stereotype threat" may be a de facto source of test bias for a number of black and possibly other minority students, including some of the most academically well-developed individuals.

Second, Steele suggests that, over the course of their academic careers, many black and possibly other minority students may "disidentify" with academic achievement as a means of avoiding the negative intellectual stereotype altogether. Steele hypothesizes that these students may simply learn to avoid the negative stereotype by shifting their energies from academic achievement to other pursuits. This reduction of effort would result in less academic development and lower achievement over time (see Steele 1997).

Anthropologist John Ogbu has conducted illuminating research on the legacy of America's caste system that in important respects dovetails with the work of Claude Steele. Ogbu believes that African-Americans, Native Americans, and (to some extent) the Latino community share a history of having been incorporated into the United States on an involuntary basis and then being blocked in varying degrees from becoming full participants in the society. In his view, this combination of factors has led some members of these groups to develop an oppositional orientation to the white majority as well as to aspects of American society that they view as "white." For some minority students, this may include viewing high academic achievement as a white attribute, which should be avoided (see Ogbu 1988, 1990, 1992).

Using this framework, extremely disadvantaged minority youngsters who perceive that they have few opportunities seem likely to be most vulnerable to disidentifying with academic achievement. But Ogbu and a colleague, Signithia Fordham, have found that even academically successful black students may experience strong antiacademic peer pressure, which may lead them to hide or to downplay their academic interests (Fordham and Ogbu 1986; Fordham 1990).

Another feature of racism in America is the desire of some whites and others to avoid living near significant numbers of blacks or certain other minorities, which contributes to residential and school segregation (Denton and Massey 1989; Smith 1990). To the degree that this helps to produce much heavier concentrations of extremely disadvantaged minority students in some schools than would otherwise be the case, it also helps to create severe mismatches between school resources and students' needs.

Of great significance from a social policy standpoint, researchers have found evidence that negative racial/ethnic attitudes are an important factor in opposition among some whites to a wide variety of policies, from welfare spending to school busing to affirmative action (Sears et al. 1997), with opposition heightened when social policies are targeted to African-Americans rather than to poor and disadvantaged groups as a whole (Bobo and Kluegel 1993). Negative racial/ethnic views also seem to contribute to doubts among some whites about the capacity of society (and government) to help improve the fortunes of some minority groups (Kluegel 1990).

We also must understand that negative views of one or another racial/ethnic group are not confined to whites, but seemingly are held by members of a number of groups, including recent immigrants (Tomas Rivera Policy Institute 1997). They even can be held by members of particular groups about other members of their own group (Smith 1990). This almost certainly dynamic set of negative attitudes and beliefs may be one of the most complex and challenging features of our increasingly diverse society.

## Parenting-Related Human Capital Differences among Groups

Access to formal education changes the way people think and behave — they acquire skills, habits of mind, and information that are important for functioning effectively in the modern world. A hallmark of schools is that they offer a structured means of acquiring knowledge (such as mathematics) that would be hard for most people to come by though informal learning processes.

It is unsurprising that access to formal education influences the behavior of individuals in their role as parents. In fact, the more schooling that people have, the greater these behavioral changes appear to be. For example, researchers have found that formal education is related to how much time parents spend with their children in education-related activities, how they pursue the role of parent as teacher, what parenting styles they tend to use, and how they interact with school personnel with regard to their children (Miller 1995). For example, compared to parents with little formal schooling, parents with a college degree tend to spend more time with their children in such education-related activities such as reading (Leibowitz 1977; Hill and Stafford 1980) and to work more with school professionals in response to their children's academic problems and needs (Baker and Stevenson 1986; Stevenson and Baker 1987; Gamoran 1991).

Because white parents have more schooling, on average, than non-Asian minority parents, they have substantial human capital advantages, including some of those relevant to parenting for high levels of school success. In essence, they have greater quantities of intergenerationally accumulated human or "school" capital to invest in their children. Moreover, it is extremely difficult for schools to compensate for this advantage within a single generation of students.

Whites with college degrees seem to have human capital advantages not only over minority (and majority) parents with little formal education, but also with regard to a number of minority parents who themselves have college degrees. The latter seems to be a related to the fact that, historically in the United States, minorities have had much less educational opportunity than whites (Weinberg 1977; Jaynes and Williams 1989). This suggests that, in general, the current generation of African-American, Latino, and Native American parents with college degrees would have had less combined home/school human capital invested in them when they were children than was invested in the present generation of white parents.

On the school side, many of the current generation of minority parents with college degrees may have attended relatively undemanding or underresourced elementary and secondary schools in urban or rural areas, while many of their white counterparts may have attended excellent suburban schools. Since tracking was undoubtedly an even greater problem a decade or two ago than it is now, many current minority parents would not have had the benefit of strong college prep programs. And relatively few would have attended selective colleges and universities or majored in quantitative fields. On the home side, few of the minority parents' parents would have gone to college and many may not have completed high school. And, in the latter's generation, a lot of the schools were seriously underresourced institutions in the Jim Crow South (Smith and Welch 1986; Anderson 1988).

The conclusion that there are large average differences in human capital among parents from several racial/ethnic groups in the United States tends to be supported by recent research on adult literacy. In a major study based on a nationally representative sample of adults, not only were large literacy skill differences found among racial/ethnic groups, but these gaps existed on a within-social-class (educational attainment level) basis as well. At virtually all levels of educational attainment, white adults had a literacy skill advantage over minorities (see Kirsch et al. 1993).

## Education-Relevant Cultural Differences among Groups

Human capital differences, of course, can be viewed as cultural differences among groups that have been generated through different degrees of access to formal schooling, particularly over the course of the twentieth century, as ever larger amounts of formal education have become widely available in the United States and many other nations. However, other cultural differences — language, religion, etc. — reach much further back in time and may have few or no linkages to formal schooling.

During the past quarter-century, an extensive amount of research has been undertaken directed at the question of how cultural differences contribute to variations in academic performance among racial/ethnic groups in the United States. There also is a rapidly growing body of cross-cultural education research of a transnational nature — research that makes comparisons between societies. Both the U.S.-oriented and transnational research have focused on a wide variety of school, home, community, and society-wide cultural dimensions that bear on academic achievement (e.g., Scribner and Cole 1973; Boykin 1982; Heath 1982; Tharp 1989; Stevenson and Stigler 1992; Cummings and Altbach 1995).

Much of the U.S.-oriented research has been concerned with improving the educational prospects of blacks, Latinos, American Indians, and other minority groups, such as Native Hawaiians, that have been doing much less well in school than the white majority. As a result, a great deal of this research has been directly or indirectly concerned with helping educators change pedagogical, curricular, and other aspects of schooling to make it more compatible with minority groups' learning styles, primary languages, and other culture-specific attributes and needs (Greenbaum and Greenbaum 1983; Shade 1989; Tharp and Gallimore 1989; Ramirez et al. 1990; Solorzano and Solorzano 1995).

Using cross-cultural research to help guide school-improvement and adaptation efforts on behalf of black, Hispanic, and Native American children is extremely important, especially if we are concerned with increasing the number of high achieving students from these groups. In the years ahead, however, there are several reasons also to expand the use of such research to help strengthen the *out-of-school* educational experiences of minority youngsters. First, cross-cultural research is continuing to find that out-of-school experiences are of great importance academically, including with regard to high achievement. For example, differences are being found in the strength of the academic orientations of student peer networks that follow racial/ethnic lines, and these differences are associated with variations in the groups' academic achievement levels (Moore 1987; Steinberg et al. 1992). In one major study of high school students, Asian-American students were the most likely to have high GPAs, followed by whites, while Latino and black students were heavily underrepresented among students who earned high grades. Differences in the academic-orientation and achievement levels of the groups' peer networks were associated with these differences, with Asian students having the strongest academic peer groups (see Steinberg 1996).

Second, by giving so much attention to school reform since the early 1980s (editors of *Education Week* 1993 and 1997), we may have been putting too little effort into promoting high minority achievement through home and community strategies that draw in part on the cultural research base. For instance, the latter could conceivably be used to improve the quality of community-based supplementary education programs available to African-American, Latino-American, and Native American students.

And third, a growing body of research is now available on immigrant and nonimmigrant students and families of East and Southeast Asian origin (e.g., Chinese, Japanese, Korean, and Vietnamese). They are of growing interest, because of the generally high levels of academic achievement of Asian-American students, especially those of East Asian origin. Factors found to be associated with Asian-American students' high academic performance include working harder and longer on their studies, placing a high value on school achievement, viewing education as the route to life success, and spending more time on education-related activities, e.g., receiving private tutoring, participating in after-school study groups, and taking music lessons (Chao 1998).

With patterns such as these, researchers are giving a great deal of attention to Asian parents' child-rearing values and strategies. They are finding that much of Asian students' academic success is grounded in what the parents do, beginning when their children are very young (Farver et al. 1995). Being concerned with helping their children do their best and develop their individual talents, emphasizing effort as the basis of school success, emphasizing training their children for success in school, and structuring their children's time to maximize their opportunity for development are evidently practices of many parents of East Asian origin (Chao 1998). Regarding training, research suggests that many Asian parents focus on helping their children develop attributes that support school success, such as willingness to work hard, diligence, perseverance, thoroughness, and self-discipline (Matute-Bianchi 1986; Chao 1998). Regarding the structuring of time, a number of Asian American parents evidently begin providing formal and informal educational opportunities outside the school while their children are young, including access to demanding after-school programs in some instances (Schneider and Lee 1990; Dunn 1995). Many Asian parents also help their children learn to work on their school assignments via group efforts, which may involve siblings, beginning in the children's initial years of school (Caplan et al. 1992). The latter may contribute to the previously noted strong peer learning networks that have been found among Asian-American high school students.

These findings for Asian-Americans are echoed in transnational research that includes students from various East Asian nations (Hess and Azuma 1990; Chen and Stevenson 1995; Fuligani and Stevenson 1995). For example, in the recent Third Mathematics and Science Study, Japanese eighth graders were found to be very likely to attend after-school programs in math or science (U.S. Department of Education 1997; Stevenson 1998).

Some of the findings on how Asian children are acculturated by their parents to learn are particularly informative when juxtaposed with research on other groups, including some research that had very different starting points, such as the previously discussed question of how racial prejudice may undermine the academic performance of many African-American students. While we now have reason to believe that the propensity of many Asian-American students to place academics at the center of much of their peer socializing may be grounded partly in family acculturation processes, we also have reason to believe that the tendency of many black students to study alone may be associated with avoidance of antiacademic peer pressure that is partly a legacy of America's historic racial caste system (Fordham and Ogbu 1986; Steinberg et al. 1992). This suggests that taking full advantage of the cultural difference research base in the development of strategies for expanding educational opportunity for non-Asian minorities almost certainly will also require taking the research base on racial/ethnic prejudice into account.

## Economic Sources of Achievement Differences among Groups

Having a lot of money can be educationally beneficial in many ways. For starters, parents with high incomes can buy homes in communities with very well-resourced public schools or send their children to excellent private schools. But in many respects, money counts most not when parents have an enormous amount to spend on their children's education and general well-being, but when they have very little money available for this purpose. Children who experience intense, long-term poverty are very likely to be exposed to several risks, such as serious health problems, like lead poisoning, which can undermine learning (Newman and Buka 1990); high family/school mobility rates (Miller et al. 1992; General Accounting Office 1994); and living in high-poverty neighborhoods in which there are relatively few educated, regularly employed adults with strong ties to the mainstream of society and where the schools serve almost exclusively (extremely) disadvantaged student populations (Wacquant and Wilson 1989).

Unfortunately, African-American, Latino, and Native American children are much more likely to experience intense, long-term poverty of the kind that produces multiple-risk-factor environments (Kennedy et al. 1986; Hafner 1990). Until we substantially reduce the number of minority youngsters growing up in such circumstances, it is unrealistic to expect that all or even most of the differences in academic performance between whites and non-Asian minorities will — or can — be eliminated. Certainly, it seems very unrealistic to expect that the currently large high achievement gaps will disappear.

## Limits of Schools as Educational Institutions

It has been over three decades since the Federal Government began to fund programs to improve educational opportunities for educationally at-risk youngsters on an extensive basis, via Head Start (early childhood education) and Title I (academic support primarily at the elementary level). It also has been about the same amount of time since school reformers began to design school improvement strategies focused on raising achievement levels of disadvantaged and minority youngsters. For instance, the School Development Program, with its emphasis on establishing high-quality relationships among school staff and parents with the objective of promoting the academic development and social competence of disadvantaged urban students, was initiated by James Comer and his colleagues at Yale University in 1968 (Haynes et al. 1998).

Over the past 15 years, there has been a significant expansion of school reform efforts. Virtually no aspect of K–12 education has been spared the scrutiny of reformers, and school improvement efforts have been launched in numerous directions. Examples of the many reform agendas that either have been or are being pursued include (1) establishing higher secondary school graduation standards, for example, requiring more college-prep math and science courses; (2) achieving curricular reform in virtually every subject — English, social studies, math, science, etc.; (3) creating alternative assessment systems; (4) reducing ability grouping and tracking; (5) promoting school-based management and school "restructuring"; (6) establishing small schools or schools within schools; (7) providing extensive school choice; and (8) achieving teacher preparation reform. While reformers have been interested in raising academic performance for all students, they have placed considerable emphasis on improving educational outcomes for the disadvantaged and minorities (e.g., Carnegie Forum on Education and the Economy 1986; Carnegie Foundation for the Advancement of Teaching 1988; Quality Education for Minorities Project 1990).

These three decades of work have begun to bear fruit. There are now a number of research-demonstrated school reform or improvement strategies available to raise the academic performance of low-achieving student segments, including disadvantaged black, Hispanic, and Native American children (Stringfield et al. 1997; Fashola and Slavin 1997).

For example, in addition to the School Development Program, another promising strategy is Success for All, which offers students an articulated preschool, kindergarten, and primary grade experience designed to ensure that each youngster is reading at grade level by the end of the third grade (Slavin et al. 1996).

Nonetheless, the nation's current portfolio of promising strategies has several limitations. One of the most important for purposes of this discussion is that even the best programs have been able to close only a portion of the achievement gap between advantaged and disadvantaged students — and between minority and majority students. Moreover, most of the documented achievement gains have been in the form of fewer students achieving at very low levels (Stringfield 1997). It is not yet clear what the capacity of these strategies is to increase the number of high-achieving non-Asian minority students, since evaluations of them have not tended to look at this question. In fact, increasing the representation of non-Asian minorities among high-achieving students has not yet become an explicit, major objective of the school reform movement.

Another important limitation is that it is proving very difficult to implement most reform strategies on a widespread basis, while at the same time maintaining the quality and productivity demonstrated by the prototypes. Among the obstacles being encountered are several that may be virtually inherent in an institutional sector as large as the nation's K–12 "system." Some of the more important of these obstacles are inflexibility of state and school district rules and regulations for operating schools, differences in educational philosophy among district administrators and among principals and teachers; lack of adequate amounts of appropriate technical assistance and training for those who must implement reforms (especially at the school level); and the long hours required over time to implement change (Muncey and McQuillan 1996; Bodilly 1996; Stringfield 1997; Fashola and Slavin 1997).

In addition, there are important societal forces that impede successful reform, which are largely outside the control of educators. Some of the most important of these are the economic duress and associated instability of many disadvantaged communities and, therefore, of the schools that serve them. The previously noted high mobility rates among disadvantaged students are often mirrored by high turnover of principals and teachers in their schools. In these circumstances, it can be difficult to implement ambitious reforms, because the professional cadres change too much (Lewis 1993; Useem et al. 1997). Even if reforms are successfully implemented in a school, highly mobile students will not be able to attend it long enough for the school to make a difference for them. Unfortunately, high student mobility is a problem at both the elementary and secondary levels (White et al. 1996; Kerbow 1996).

It is reasonable to believe that the reform movement can gradually produce genuinely valuable improvements in a great many schools across the country, including many that serve large numbers of non-Asian minority students. But, as in the case of virtually all institutional sectors, school quality will remain uneven and probably will be most uneven in disadvantaged communities where school resources are often scarce. Moreover, as suggested in the previous section, school reform may be of secondary importance for many of our most disadvantaged students, at least until their economic circumstances improve significantly. For example, for many of these children and youth, increasing the supply of adequately paying jobs for their low-skilled parents may be more pressing than school improvement. Yet, the shortage of these jobs has persisted for several decades. Similarly, providing high-quality childcare/early education during infancy and toddlerhood also may be of more pressing importance in many disadvantaged communities, but the nation is not yet close to providing universal preschool for 3- and 4-year-olds (Committee for Economic Development 1993; General Accounting Office 1995). And elementary and secondary schools typically do not operate during the summer months, even though research shows that summer learning loss is a major factor in the achievement gaps that open up for disadvantaged students in the primary grades (Heynes 1987; Entwisle and Alexander 1992). We are far from providing sufficient summer educational opportunities to counter the summer learning loss problem.

All of this suggests that a much more broadly conceived educational and social reform agenda may be required to respond effectively to the needs of our increasingly diverse student population and its most disadvantaged segments. Although this is not a new insight it remains true, including for the elimination over time of the underrepresentation of non-Asian minorities among high academic achievers.

## SOME RECOMMENDATIONS FOR INCREASING THE PROPORTION OF NON-ASIAN MINORITY HIGH ACADEMIC ACHIEVERS

I would like to suggest three principles to help guide efforts to increase non-Asian minority representation among high-achieving students substantially. First, it is essential that we take a long-term, several-generation perspective. Historically, group advancement has fundamentally been an intergenerational process in the United States (and elsewhere).

For groups that begin with little formal education, it may take three, four, or more generations before they enjoy a level of educational success that approaches that of the mainstream population, even under relatively favorable circumstances (Hauser and Featherman 1976; Neidert and Farley 1985; Husen and Tuijnman 1991; Borjas 1993). This is a particularly important perspective to take for non-Asian minorities, because it has been less than two generations since the Civil Rights movement eliminated the legal basis for America's race-based caste system and the current period of immigration is bringing large numbers of newcomers with little formal education into our society each year. Moreover, as we have seen, poverty and racial prejudice continue to take a toll on non-Asian minorities. As a result, we should expect that even good, well-executed minority educational advancement strategies will take a long time to produce all the desired results.

Second, to maximize the rate of intergenerational advancement for non-Asian minorities, we must be prepared to address both common and distinctive needs and opportunities for several minority segments that are at different stages of the intergenerational advancement process. The existence of both large between- and within-social-class differences in academic achievement among racial/ethnic groups in our society underlines just how important it may be to undertake a (partially) segmented approach. Indeed, these circumstances make a strong prima facie case for aggressively addressing needs of black, Hispanic, and Native American students and their families, from all social class levels, to ensure robust intergenerational educational advancement for these groups.

And, third, as long as there is extreme underrepresentation of non-Asian minorities among high academic achievers, it is especially important to ensure that as many of the top students from these groups as possible perform at very high levels academically throughout their school careers. If non-Asian groups are to become even modestly better represented in a wide range of professional and leadership tracks in the next couple of decades, these students must be fully competitive with their much more numerous white and Asian counterparts. The fact that top African-American and Latino students may not be performing as well as top Asian and white students adds urgency to this issue. Certainly, it suggests that this group of non-Asian minority students should be targeted in ways designed to ensure their ongoing academic success.

There is not space in this chapter to offer a detailed description of a segmented minority educational advancement strategy that addresses both similar and distinctive needs of low-, medium-, and high-SES non-Asian minority students at all levels of the educational system, as well as those of non-Asian minority students who are well prepared for college. Certainly, there is not space to discuss some of the broad social policy responses alluded to earlier that seem required, if the most disadvantaged students are to maximize their rate of educational advancement. Thus, my suggestions here are concerned primarily with a few broad educational strategies. And there will be some emphasis on minority segments, such as the middle and professional classes, that have historically not received much attention from educational reformers and policy makers, and are now getting even less attention in some quarters as obstacles to affirmative action in higher education have grown in states such as California and Texas in recent years. Yet, from a high-achievement perspective, these are very important population segments, because they are reasonably well positioned to provide large numbers of additional high-achieving black, Hispanic, and Native American students over the medium term. As we have seen, their average level of academic performance is much higher than that of very low-SES non-Asian minority students. Their numbers are also significantly larger than a generation ago and some of their parents have a considerable amount of resources to invest in them (Welniak and Littman 1990). The latter is especially important, because it means that a wide range of privately initiated and funded educational efforts could be pursued on these students' behalf, even if a much larger publicly financed minority education effort, centered on the most disadvantaged students, does not materialize for many years.

From a public education standpoint, one thing that could be done with modest resources would be to encourage more suburban school districts to engage the minority high-achievement issue as part of the school reform efforts that they may be making. Growing numbers of stable working class, middle class, and professional class non-Asian minority children and youth are attending suburban schools, but many educators in these districts may not yet fully recognize the special responsibilities that they have for maximizing the performance of these students. One way to heighten awareness, and to share knowledge and experience, would be to create a network of suburban districts with an interest in this issue. The network could develop a clearinghouse and technical assistance service to promote effective strategies as they emerge. This is the kind of endeavor that could reasonably be housed at a major university.

Such an initiative might yield even greater dividends if a simultaneous effort was made to add minority high achievement to the list of primary objectives for the national school reform movement. Such an effort might add much needed legitimacy to work by school- and district-level administrators who are concerned with increasing the number of high-achieving black, Latino, and Native American students.

It also is clearly timely to begin to evaluate a number of national reform efforts from the perspective of whether they can help more minority students achieve at very high levels. Evaluations of this kind would potentially have the most immediate benefits for low-SES minority students, because schools serving large numbers of these students have been the focus of so much reform work over the years. Encouragingly, an initial look at this question, suggests that exemplary versions of some elementary reform approaches may be able to help increase the number of high-achieving minority students (Borman et al. 1998).

In a related vein, educators who have been developing reform strategies directed at very disadvantaged, mostly low-achieving students should be encouraged to extend or modify their approaches in ways that might be more beneficial to youngsters who are not low achievers. Even in schools serving mostly extremely disadvantaged students, there are often a number of children who are doing well academically by traditional measures. For instance, there may be several second graders who are above-average-to-excellent readers, using national norms. How to provide these youngsters with more expansive educational opportunities in schools in which a great deal of effort must be made to ensure that the many very low-achieving youngsters move toward grade-level academic performance is an important challenge for reformers. There are examples of demanding curriculum and instruction reform approaches that may be able to meet simultaneously the developmental needs of many low-, middle-, and high-achieving disadvantaged students, but implementing such strategies at a high level of quality and consistency over time can be very difficult in schools with high rates of student mobility and severe resource constraints—two all too common conditions (McHugh and Spath 1997).

To the extent that there are school reform strategies that show signs of having the capacity to help promote more above-average to high achievement in schools serving extremely disadvantaged student clienteles, there is also reason to encourage experimentation with these strategies in settings in which the minority student populations are not primarily from low-SES circumstances. These may often be schools in suburban areas that have substantial working, middle, and/or professional class minority student segments.

Turning to the potential for private action, it has long been recognized that additional educational opportunities outside traditional elementary and secondary education are necessary—and extremely valuable—for disadvantaged and minority students. The early childhood education movement has been based in part on that model. Summer and Saturday programs for the disadvantaged are consistent with it as well, as are similar programs for academically promising students, such as those for minority high school students interested in engineering and science. Summer bridge programs operated for incoming minority college freshman interested in the sciences and engineering are a variation on this approach.

There are now many reasons to consider increasing the use and scope of non-school-based programs for low-, medium-, and high-SES minority students. The academic trajectories of most youngsters from all racial/ethnic groups are generally established at the elementary school level, frequently in the primary grades (Kennedy et al. 1986; Mullis et al. 1993). The underrepresentation of minority students among high academic achievers also begins at the elementary level and involves youngsters from low-, medium-, and high-SES families (Okada et al. 1972; Anderson 1990, 1991; Borman et al. 1998). Middle- and high-SES non-Asian minority students, not simply the extremely disadvantaged, labor under the (multifaceted) pressures of racial prejudice. The combined home/school human capital available to many non-Asian minority students may be less than for their white and Asian counterparts at each social class level (Miller 1995). Finally, some of the culture-specific strategies of academically successful groups are often initially implemented by the parents when their children are very young (Caplan et al. 1992; Chao 1998).

These factors lead me to the conclusion that sophisticated after-school, weekend, and summer programs need to be developed for very large numbers of minority students, from all social class backgrounds, beginning in the primary grades. Via such programs, many non-Asian minority youngsters could be exposed initially to group study and other peer-oriented learning approaches that are so valuable later in schooling. Participants also could be inducted into an intellectually very positive and demanding environment, which would support academic development in its own right and build valuable linkages with the children's schools. (For example, to staff the summer programs, teachers could be drawn from local public elementary schools.) And, in the case of after-school programs, help and support for the children's schoolwork would be provided. Although the primary grades are far from the college years, higher education may have a substantial role to play in the design and ongoing evaluation and modification of these supplementary programs, just as they have been playing a major role in the development and evaluation of many school reform strategies (Fashola and Slavin 1997).

Foundations, corporations, and wealthy individual donors could be approached to help pay for the design work as well as for the enrollment fees for many disadvantaged youngsters. But I believe that the programs should be developed on the assumption that middle-class and high-SES minority parents would typically pay their children's enrollment fees. This approach could ensure considerable core funding on a stable basis. Such a strategy would put an extra financial burden on middle-class minority parents, but it could provide their children with an enormously useful increment of educational opportunity.

Let me turn now to the need to target the academically best-prepared minority college students to ensure that they maximize their academic performance. Over the years, a great many of these students have generally been targeted in three other ways. First, a large proportion of them have been heavily recruited by selective colleges and universities. Second, a number of them have received generous financial aid packages, often with funds provided partly by corporate donors interested in hiring academically successful minority college graduates. And third, many have been encouraged to participate in (minority) support programs at their institutions, which were started primarily for the purpose of increasing minority retention and graduation rates. Among the most common of these programs are those run by schools of engineering — again reflecting in part the corporate interest in expanding the number of minority engineering and science graduates. (For reviews of many of these programs, see Gordon [1986] and Gandara [1998].)

About a decade ago, several program operators and others began to look more closely at the results that were being produced. They found that, in addition to the fact that academically underprepared African-American, Latino-American, and Native American students were generally earning low grades, many seemingly extremely well-prepared non-Asian minority students also had GPAs that were lower than those of similarly prepared whites and Asians (e.g., Phillips 1991). This meant not only that the average GPAs of non-Asian minority graduates were much lower than those of their white and Asian counterparts, but that few black, Latino, and American Indian students were graduating with honors.

Several promising strategies have been developed in response to these issues. Let me offer three examples. Via its Meyerhoff Scholars Program, the University of Maryland Baltimore County began recruiting top African-American students about a decade ago and providing them with an extensive amount of support for the purpose of dramatically increasing the proportion of black students who earn high grades in engineering and science at UMBC. Meyerhoff offers participants a summer bridge program prior to their freshman year, substantial group study opportunities, extensive financial aid, a variety of group support mechanisms during the school year, summer internships, and an overall milieu — carefully nurtured by UMBC's president — that pushes them toward high academic achievement (Mercer 1994; Hrabowski and Maton

1995). Encouragingly, African-American students in the Meyerhoff Program earn much higher grades than similarly prepared black students did in the past at UMBC. For example, in their freshman year, the Meyerhoff students have averaged a 3.4 GPA, while the similarly prepared black students have averaged about 2.8 (Hrabowski and Maton 1995).

At the University of Colorado at Boulder, the minority engineering program has for many years tended to recruit non-Asian minority students who are, on average, almost as well prepared for engineering as the white students, using traditional preparation measures such as SAT scores. Nonetheless, historically, the average GPA of these minority students was about a half-point lower than that of the white students. Through use of a learning community approach instituted by the program staff, this GPA gap was essentially eliminated over a period of years and a robust percentage of the participants began to graduate with above-average to high grades. For example, over half of the 35 non-Asian minority graduates in 1994–95 had GPAs over 3.0 and five had GPAs over 3.5. Unlike the Meyerhoff Program at UMBC, which was originally designed to serve black students, the minority engineering program at the University of Colorado has a large Hispanic student population (see Rubi 1995).

In Ohio, the Student Achievement in Research and Scholarship (STARS) Program targets high-GPA minority undergraduates in a wide range of academic disciplines at 17 institutions in the state to help prepare them for doctoral programs. Each student is provided with a faculty mentor, a paid research assistantship with their mentor, as well as with a variety of support services. STARS was established by the Ohio Board of Regents, and reflects the Board's awareness that it is very important to increase the number of high academic achieving minority students who earn doctorates and pursue academic careers (see Kroll 1994).

What conclusions can be drawn from these and other promising initiatives, such as the Challenge Program at Georgia Tech (Smothers 1994) and the 21st Century Program at the University of Michigan, which Claude Steele helped to start (Steele 1997)? First, in at least some settings, we have evidently learned how to eliminate the previously discussed SAT "overprediction" problem for a great many African-American and Latino students. Thus, if we make widespread use of this existing program "technology," it should be possible for academically well-prepared black and Latino students at a large number of colleges and universities to earn grades that are consistently about the same as those of similarly prepared white and Asian students at their institutions.

Second, we do not seem to have learned how, as yet, to get levels of academic performance for minority college students that are consistently a great deal higher than the levels that would be predicted by their high school grades, class rank, and SAT/ACT scores. This is true even for reasonably well-prepared minority students. For example, using existing strategies, minority students who are, say, 200 points off the combined SAT verbal and math average for engineering students at a particular selective institution, do not routinely approach the average GPA level for all engineering majors there.

Third, on the positive side, the best of the existing strategies do seem to close academic preparation gaps of modest size, for example, differences in average combined SAT scores of 50–60 points (Rubi 1995). This gives us reason to hope that even better designed and executed programs would allow somewhat larger gaps to be eliminated at the higher education level.

Fourth, high-quality programs tend to be those that effectively address major issues raised by the educational research base. For example, by making it clear that high academic achievement is both possible and expected for non-Asian minority students, these programs directly address the low academic expectations that often surround blacks, Latinos, and Native Americans, in large measure due to the problem of racial/ethnic prejudice, which was reviewed earlier. Similarly, the workshop/study group strategy that is widely used to improve minority students academic performance in calculus and several other courses is based on an approach that Uri Treisman developed after observing Asian students at Berkeley use group study techniques to maximize their performance in the freshman calculus course at that institution (Fullilove and Treisman 1990).

Fifth, successful programs tend to be those with a strong empirical orientation. High-quality information systems are established so that students' progress can be closely monitored and program modifications can be made when problems are encountered. (The Meyerhoff Scholars Program and the University of Colorado minority engineering program seem strong in the information system and program modification areas.)

And sixth, for strategies designed to raise minority students' academic performance to succeed, leadership must come not only from program operators, but from senior academic officials as well—from deans to presidents. This last point brings us to what I believe is a responsibility of rapidly growing importance for selective colleges and universities in the United States. Because they have preferential access to the nation's most academically successful college-bound seniors, selective institutions are expected to prepare these students for careers that will lead many into leadership positions in virtually all sectors of our society. Indeed, many of our selective institutions increasingly have genuinely multinational student bodies, which means that their leadership preparation responsibilities have taken on global dimensions.

It is essential, therefore, that our selective institutions make every effort to ensure that the high academic achievement dimension of leadership preparation extends to their black, Hispanic, and Native American students. This means that presidents and other senior officials should embrace high academic achievement for non-Asian minorities as a priority objective — one that leads them to make use of the best available strategies in this area. It also means that they should actively be seeking additional resources to implement these strategies and, where necessary, to develop more effective ones.

Presidents and senior officials typically will need to put much of their emphasis in this area on working to ensure that the well-prepared non-Asian minority students who attend their own institutions perform at a high level. But since many of these institutions are research universities, a great deal of effort also can — and should — be given to increasing the pool of top minority high school graduates, which means working as far back as the elementary school years, and possibly the preschool years as well.

I have mentioned funding. It is difficult to imagine that we can make rapid, sustained progress on the minority high-achievement front without a major commitment of philanthropic resources, especially since minority high achievement has not yet emerged as a pressing public policy issue (despite the elimination of affirmative action in admission decisions at public universities in some states in recent years). There is nothing surprising about the need to turn to private grant-making foundations, since they have long played an important role in promoting educational innovation in the United States, and have been the leading funders of most of the promising school reform strategies that have emerged in the current period of educational reform, which began in the early 1980s (Goodlad 1996). Private foundations and some corporate contributions units have also played a leading funding role in the development of the minority engineering and science program strategies discussed in this section (Gandara 1998).

Because this is a long-term problem, we are in great need of similarly long-term-oriented foundation grant programs — programs operated for 10–20 years or more. These programs should be designed to encourage development of better school reform, supplementary education, and higher education academic support strategies; to promote widespread use of the most effective approaches; and to monitor progress. And they should be designed to help minority organizations and parents provide leadership on the high-achievement front.

## Coda

Our nation has every incentive to work much, much harder in the future — through both public and private initiatives — to accelerate the rate of educational advancement of African-Americans, Latino-Americans, and Native Americans, as well as any other population segments that lag far behind the majority population educationally. Not only is this the right thing to do from the standpoint of offering each individual (and each group) genuine educational and social opportunity, I believe that it is likely to be essential, if we are to have a humane, reasonably cohesive society in the twenty-first century. Should we fail to increase greatly our society's efforts to address several minority groups' educational needs, we run the risk that our current racial/ethnic divisions will be deepened by continuing sharp human capital differences among groups, particularly at both the top and the bottom of the skills distribution.

In my view, these circumstances provide a powerful moral and practical rationale for retaining affirmative action in education, or, to use Edmund W. Gordon's term, to pursue *affirmative development* policies: policies that target minority students in various ways designed to significantly enhance their academic development. Yet, as noted earlier, public support evidently remains limited for policies focused primarily on needs of specific minority groups. Consistent with this reality, racial/ethnic affirmative action policies directed at admission decision processes or outreach programs of public universities in two of our most populous and diverse states, California and Texas, have been eliminated in recent years, owing to the passage of Proposition 209 in California and the *Hopwood v. Texas* decision by the Fifth Circuit Court of Appeals (Haro 1998).

Predictably, there has been a drop in non-Asian minority enrollment at a number of selective public college and university campuses in California and Texas as a result of these changes (Bronner 1998; Smith 1998). And opponents of affirmative action are continuing to press their case in the courts in several other states (Bronner 1997; Diaz 1997). Searching for alternatives to affirmative action, admission officers have understandably turned to social class criteria as one means of preserving enrollment of underrepresented minorities at selective institutions. But this approach has quickly run into the reality that few very disadvantaged black, Hispanic, and Native American students emerge from high school well prepared academically for selective colleges and universities (Selingo 1998). When affirmative action policies were in place, many non-Asian minority students admitted to these institutions had been from middle- to high-SES families, because they were more likely than their low-SES counterparts to be academically prepared for them (Healy 1998), although not as well prepared, on average, as most of the white and Asian students who were admitted. This is a major reason why social class is not a good surrogate for race/ethnicity in admission decisions. Moreover, even prior to the end of affirmative action in higher education in some states, little attention was being paid to needs of top minority students (Gandara 1998; Gordon 1986).

It is truly ironic that targeting top- and middle- to high-SES students, in addition to low-SES students, from non-Asian minority groups has become increasingly problematic for colleges and universities, even as evidence continues to accumulate that all of these student segments are encountering serious obstacles to academic success. The reality that many non-Asian minority students have important unmet needs, regardless of their social class circumstances or academic preparation levels, should be stimulating more extensive public and private actions concerned with accelerating the educational advancement of minorities. For some time to come, however, the greatest opportunities may be in expanding the scope and quality of efforts pursued by various private actors, owing to the likely continuing difficulty of establishing a stable national consensus for much greater public investments.

## REFERENCES

Acuna, R. 1988. *Occupied America: A History of Chicanos*, 3rd ed. New York: Harper & Row.

Anderson, B. T. 1990. *Reading Proficiency of Minority Students, 1971–1988: A Descriptive Analysis of Trend Data for Ages Nine and Thirteen by Background Factors* (unpublished paper, Educational Testing Service).

———. 1991. *Mathematics Proficiency of Minority Students, 1978–1990: A Descriptive Analysis of Trend Data for Ages Nine and Thirteen by Background Factors* (unpublished paper, Educational Testing Service).

Anderson, J. D. 1988. *The Education of Blacks in the South, 1860–1935*. Chapel Hill: University of North Carolina Press.

Baker, D. P., and D. L. Stevenson. 1986. "Mothers' Strategies for Children's School Achievement: Managing the Transition to High School." *Sociology of Education* 59: 156–67.

Bobo, L., and J. R. Kluegel. 1993. "Opposition to Race-Targeting: Self Interest, Stratification Ideology, or Racial Attitudes." *American Sociological Review* 58: 443–64.

Bodilly, S. 1996. *Lessons from New American Schools Development Corporation's Demonstration Phase*. Santa Monica, CA: Rand.

Borjas, G. J. 1993. "The Intergenerational Mobility of Immigrants." *Journal of Labor Economics* 11 (January): 113–35.

Borman, G. D., S. C. Stringfield, and R. Rachuba. 1998. *Advancing Minority High Achievement: National Trends and Promising Programs and Practices; A Report to the National Task Force on Minority High Achievement.* New York: College Board.

Boykin A. W. 1982. "Task Variability and the Performance of Black and White School Children: Vervistic Explorations." *Journal of Black Studies* 12: 469–85.

Bronner, E. 1997. "Group Suing U. of Michigan Over Diversity." *New York Times*, 14 October, A4.

———. 1998. "Fewer Minorities Entering U. of California." *New York Times*, 21 May, A28.

Bureau of the Census. 1995. *PPL-33, Tables in Support of P20–486, "The Foreign Born Population: 1994."* Washington, DC: U.S. Bureau of the Census.

Campbell, J. R., et al. 1996. *NAEP 1994 Reading Report Card for the Nation and the States: Findings from the National Assessment of Educational Progress and Trial State Assessments.* Washington, DC: U.S. Department of Education.

———. 1997. *NAEP 1996 Trends in Academic Progress: Achievement of U.S. Students in Science, 1969 to 1996; Mathematics, 1973 to 1996; Reading, 1971 to 1996; and Writing, 1984 to 1996.* Washington, DC: Educational Testing Service/U.S. Department of Education, U.S. Government Printing Office.

Caplan, C., M. H. Choy, and J. K. Whitmore. 1992. "Indochinese Refugee Families and Academic Success." *Scientific American* 266: 36–42.

Carnegie Forum on Education and the Economy. 1986. *A Nation Prepared: Teachers for the 21st Century.* New York: Carnegie Corporation.

Carnegie Foundation for the Advancement of Teaching. 1988. *An Imperiled Generation: Saving Urban Schools.* Princeton, NJ: Princeton University Press.

Chao, R. K. 1998. *Cultural Explanations for the Role of Parenting in the School Success of Asian Children*, paper for the National Invitational Conference on *Resilience Across Contexts: Family, Work, Culture, and Community*, Temple University Center for Research in Human Development and Education, Philadelphia, PA, 12–13 March.

Chen, C., and H. W. Stevenson. 1995. "Motivation and Mathematics Achievement: A Comparative Study of Asian-American, Caucasian-American, and East Asian High School Students." *Child Development* 66: 1216–34.

Coleman, J. S., et al. 1966. *Equality of Educational Opportunity.* Washington, DC: U.S. Government Printing Office.

College Entrance Examination Board. 1995a. *1995 College-Bound Seniors: Ethnic and Gender Profile of SAT and Achievement Test Takers for California.* New York: College Entrance Examination Board.

———. 1995b. *1995 College-Bound Seniors: Ethnic and Gender Profile of SAT and Achievement Test Takers for New York.* New York: College Entrance Examination Board.

———. 1995c. *1995 College-Bound Seniors: Ethnic and Gender Profile of SAT and Achievement Test Takers for Texas*. New York: College Entrance Examination Board.

————. 1995d. *1995 College-Bound Seniors: Ethnic and Gender Profile of SAT and Achievement Test Takers for the Nation*. New York: College Entrance Examination Board.

————. 1997. Unpublished data on 1995 senior SAT test takers prepared for the National Task Force on Minority High Achievement.

Committee for Economic Development. 1993. *Why Child Care Matters: Preparing Young Children for a More Productive America*. New York: Committee for Economic Development.

Cummings, W. K., and P. G. Altbach, eds. 1995. Special issue on "The Asian Educational Challenge." *Educational Policy* 9.

Day, J. C. 1996. *Population Projections of the United States by Age, Sex, Race, and Hispanic Origin: 1995–2050*. Washington, DC: U.S. Bureau of Census, Current Population Reports, P25–1130, U.S. Government Printing Office.

Denton, N. A., and D. S. Massey. 1989. "Residential Segregation of Blacks, Hispanics, and Asians by Socioeconomic Status and Generation." *Social Science Quarterly* 69: 797–817.

Diaz, I. M. 1997. "What's at Stake: The Court Decisions Affecting Higher Education and Diversity." *Black Issues in Higher Education*, 25 December, 19–21.

Dumenigo, A. R. 1997. *Cleveland Plain Dealer*, 1 March, 1–B and 6–B.

Dunn, A. 1995. "Cram Schools: Immigrants' Tools for Success." *New York Times*, 28 January, 1 and 24.

Dusek, J. B., and G. Joseph. 1986. "The Bases of Teacher Expectancies: A Meta-Analysis." *Journal of Educational Psychology* 75: 327–46.

Editors of *Education Week*. 1993. *From Risk to Renewal: Charting a Course for Reform*. Washington, DC: Editorial Projects in Education.

————. *Education Week*. 1997. *Quality Counts: A Report Card on the Condition of Public Education in the 50 States*. Supplement to *Education Week*, 22 January.

Elliott, R., et al. 1995. *Non-Asian Minority Students in the Science Pipeline at Highly Selective Institutions*, report submitted to the National Science Foundation, 1 July.

Entwisle, D. R., and K. L. Alexander. 1992. "Summer Setback: Race, Poverty, School Composition, and Mathematics Achievement in the First Two Years of School." *American Sociological Review* 57: 72–84.

Farver, J.A.M., Y. K. Kim, and Y. Lee. 1995. "Cultural Differences in Korean- and Anglo-American Preschoolers' Social Interaction and Play Behaviors." *Child Development* 66: 1088–99.

Fashola, O. S., and R. E. Slavin. 1997. "Promising Programs for Elementary and Middle Schools: Evidence of Effectiveness and Replicability." *Journal of Education for Students Placed At Risk* 2: 251–307.

Ferguson, R. F. 1995. "Shifting Challenges: Fifty Years of Economic Change Toward Black–White Earnings Equality." *Daedalus* 124: 37–76.

Fordham, S. 1990. "Racelessness as a Factor in Black Students' School Success." In *Facing Racism in Education*, N. M. Hidalgo, C.L. McDowell, and E. M.

Siddle, eds. Cambridge, MA: *Harvard Educational Review*, Reprint Series No. 21: 232–62.

Fordham, S., and J. U. Ogbu. 1986. "Black Students' School Success: Coping with the Burden of 'Acting White'." *Urban Review* 18: 176–206.

Fredrickson, G. M. 1988. *The Arrogance of Race: Historical Perspectives on Slavery, Racism, and Social Inequality*. Middletown, CT: Wesleyan University Press.

Fuchs, L. H. 1990. *The American Kaleidoscope: Race, Ethnicity, and the Civic Culture*. Hanover, NH: Wesleyan University Press/University Press of New England.

Fuligani, A. J., and H. W. Stevenson. 1995. "Time Use and Mathematics Achievement Among American, Chinese, and Japanese High School Students." *Child Development* 66: 831–42.

Fullilove, R. E., and P. R. Treisman. 1990. "Mathematics Achievement Among African American Undergraduates at the University of California, Berkeley: An Evaluation of the Mathematics Workshop Program." *Journal of Negro Education* 59: 463–78.

Gamoran, A. 1991. "Access to Excellence: Assignment to Honors English Classes in the Transition from Middle to High School." *Educational Evaluation and Policy Analysis* 14: 185–204.

Gandara, P. 1998. *A Review of Programs that Aim to Raise the Achievement of Underrepresented Minority Undergraduates: A Report to the National Task Force on Minority High Achievement of the College Board*. New York: College Board.

General Accounting Office. 1994. *Elementary School Children: Many Change Schools Frequently, Harming Their Education*. Washington, DC: United States General Accounting Office.

———. 1995. *Early Childhood Centers: Services to Prepare Children for School Often Limited*. Washington, DC: United States General Accounting Office.

Glazer, N. 1985. "Introduction." In *Clamor at the Gates: The New American Immigration*, N. Glazer, ed. San Francisco: Institute for Contemporary Studies, 3–13.

Goodlad, J. I. 1996. "Sustaining and Extending Educational Renewal." *Phi Delta Kappa*, November, 228–33.

Gordon, E. W. 1986. *A Descriptive Analysis of Programs and Trends in Engineering Education for Ethnic Minority Students: A Report to the Field*. New Haven, CT: Institution for Social and Policy Studies, Yale University.

Greenbaum, P. E., and S. D. Greenbaum. 1983. "Cultural Differences, Nonverbal Regulation, and Classroom Interaction: Sociolinguistic Interference in American Indian Education." *Peabody Journal of Education* 61: 16–33.

Hafner, A., S. Ingels, B. Schneider, and D. Stevenson. 1990. *A Profile of the American Eighth Grader: NELS:88 Student Descriptive Summary, National Educational Longitudinal Study of 1988*. Washington, DC: National Center for Education Statistics, U.S. Government Printing Office.

Haro, R. 1998. "At the Point of the Lance: Challenges to Diversity." *On Target*, Spring: 5–9.

Hauser, R. M., and D. L. Featherman. 1976. "Equality of Schooling: Trends and Prospects." *Sociology of Education* 49: 99–120.

Haynes, N. M., C. L. Emmons, and D. W. Woodruff. 1998. "School Development Program Effects: Linking Implementation to Outcomes." *Journal of Education for Students Placed At Risk* 3: 71–85.

Healy, P. 1998. "Berkeley Struggles to Stay Diverse in Post-Affirmative-Action Era." *Chronicle of Higher Education*, 29 May, A31–33.

Heath, S. B. 1982. "Questions at Home and School." In *Doing the Ethnography of Schooling*, G. Spindler, ed. New York: Holt, Rinehart & Winston.

Herrnstein, R. J., and C. Murray. 1994. *The Bell Curve: Intelligence and Class Structure in American Life*. New York: The Free Press.

Hess, R. D., and H. Azuma. 1990. "Cultural Support for Schooling: Contrasts Between Japan and the United States." *Educational Researcher* 9: 2–8.

Heynes, Barbara. 1987. "Schooling and Cognitive Development: Is There a Season for Learning?" *Child Development* 58: 1151–60.

Hill, C. R., and F. P. Stafford. 1980. "Parental Care of Children: Time Diary Estimates of Quantity, Predictability, and Variety." *Journal of Human Resources* 15: 219–39.

Holmes, S. A. 1995. "Surprising Rise in Immigration Stirs Up Debate." *New York Times*, 30 August, A1, A15.

Howard, J., and R. Hammond. 1985. "Rumors of Inferiority." *New Republic*, 9 September, 17–21.

Hrabowski, F. A., and K. I. Maton. 1995. "Enhancing the Success of African-American Students in the Sciences: Freshman Year Outcomes." *School Science and Mathematics* 95: 19–27.

Husen, T., and A. Tuijnman. 1991. "The Contribution of Formal Schooling to the Increase in Intellectual Capital." *Educational Researcher* 20: 17–25.

Irvine, J. J. 1990. *Black Students and School Failure: Policies, Practices, and Prescriptions*. Westport, CT: Greenwood.

Jaynes, G. D., and R. M. Williams. 1989. *A Common Destiny: Blacks and American Society*. Washington, DC: National Research Council, National Academy Press.

Kennedy, M. K., R. K. Young, and M. E. Orland et al. 1986. *Poverty, Achievement and the Distribution of Compensatory Education Services*. Washington, DC: Department of Education, U.S. Government Printing Office.

Kerbow, D. 1996. "Patterns of Urban Student Mobility and Local School Reform." *Journal of Education for Students Placed At Risk* 1: 147–69.

Kirsch, I. S., et al. 1993. *Adult Literacy in America: A First Look at the Results of the National Adult Literacy Survey*. Washington, DC: Educational Testing Service/U.S. Department of Education.

Klitgaard, R. 1985. *Choosing Elites*. New York: Basic Books.

Kluegel, J. R. 1990. "Trends in Whites' Explanations of the Black–White Gap in Socioeconomic Status, 1977–1989." *American Sociological Review* 55: 512–25.

Kroll, J. L. 1994. *Student Achievement in Research and Scholarship*, evaluation report conducted by Horizon Research, Inc. of Chapel Hill, NC, for the Ohio Board of Regents, May 1994.

Leibowitz, A. 1977. "Home Investments in Children." *Journal of Political Economy* 82: 219–239.

Levine, D. U., and E. E. Eubanks. 1990. "Achievement Disparities Between Minority and Nonminority Students in Suburban Schools." *Journal of Negro Education* 59: 186–94.

Lewis, A. C. 1993. *Changing the Odds: Middle School Reform in Progress, 1991–1993.* New York: Edna McConnell Clark Foundation.

Massey, D. S., and N. A. Denton. 1993. *American Apartheid: Segregation and the Making of the American Underclass.* Cambridge, MA: Harvard University Press.

Matute-Bianchi, M. E. 1986. "Ethnic Identities and Patterns of School Success and Failure Among Mexican-Descent and Japanese-American Students in a California High School: An Ethnographic Analysis." *American Journal of Education* 95: 233–55.

McHugh, B., and S. Spath. 1997. "Carter G. Woodson Elementary School: The Success of a Private School Curriculum in an Urban Public School." *Journal of Education for Students Placed At Risk* 2: 121–35.

Mercer, J. 1994. "Guiding Black Prodigies." *Chronicle of Higher Education*, 22 June, A22, A24.

Miller, L. S. 1995. *An American Imperative: Accelerating Minority Educational Advancement.* New Haven, CT: Yale University Press.

Miller, L. S., M. Fredisdorf, and D. C. Humphrey. 1992. *Student Mobility and School Reform.* New York: Council for Aid to Education.

Moore, E.G.J. 1987. "Ethnic Social Milieu and Black Children's Intelligence Test Achievement." *Journal of Negro Education* 56: 44–52.

Mullis, I.V.S., et al. 1993. *NAEP 1992 Mathematics Report Card for the Nation and the States.* Washington, DC: Educational Testing Service/U.S. Department of Education, U.S. Government Printing Office.

Muncey, D. E., and P. J. McQuillan. 1996. *Reform and Resistance in Classrooms: An Ethnographic View of the Coalition of Essential Schools.* New Haven, CT: Yale University Press.

Neidert, L. J., and R. Farley. 1985. "Assimilation in the United States: An Analysis of Ethnic and Generational Differences in Status and Achievement." *American Sociological Review* 50: 840–50.

Nettles, M. T., A. R. Thoeny, and E. R. Gosman. 1986. "Comparative and Predictive Analyses of Black and White Students' College Achievement and Experiences." *Journal of Higher Education* 57: 289–318.

Newman, L., and S. L. Buka. 1990. *Every Child a Learner: Reducing Risks of Learning Impairment During Pregnancy and Infancy.* Denver, CO: Education Commission of the States.

Oakes, J. 1985. *Keeping Track: How Schools Structure Inequality.* New Haven, CT: Yale University Press.

———. 1990. *Multiplying Inequalities: The Effects of Race, Social Class, and Tracking on Opportunities to Learn Mathematics and Science.* Santa Monica, CA: Rand Corporation.

Ogbu, J. U. 1988. "Diversity and Equity in Public Education: Community Forces and Minority School Adjustment and Performance." In *Policies for*

*America's Public Schools: Teachers, Equity, and Indicators*, R. Haskins and D. Macrae, eds. Norwood, NJ: Ablex.

———. 1990. "Overcoming Racial Barriers to Equal Access." In *Access to Knowledge: An Agenda for Our Nation's Schools*, J. I. Goodlad and P. Keating, eds. New York: College Entrance Examination Board, 65–84.

———. 1992. "Understanding Cultural Diversity and Learning." *Educational Researcher* 20: 5–14.

Okada, T., W. M. Cohen, and G. W. Mayeske. 1972. "Growth in Achievement for Different Racial, Regional, and Socio-economic Groupings of Students," paper, U.S. Office of Education, 1969, cited in F. Mosteller and D. P. Moynihan, "A Pathbreaking Report." In *On Equality of Educational Opportunity: Papers Deriving From the Harvard University Faculty Seminar on the Coleman Report*, F. Mosteller and D. P. Moynihan, eds. New York: Random House: 3–65.

O'Neill, J. 1990. "The Role of Human Capital in Earnings Differences Between Black and White Men." *Journal of Economic Perspectives* 4: 25–45.

Owings, J., et al. 1995. *Statistics in Brief: Making the Cut: Who Meets Highly Selective College Entrance Criteria*. Washington, DC: U.S. Department of Education.

Pennock-Roman, M. 1990. *Test Validity and Language Background: A Study of Hispanic-American Students at Six Universities*. New York: College Entrance Examination Board.

Phillips, T. R. 1991. *ABET/Exxon Minority Engineering Student Achievement Profile*. New York: Accreditation Board for Engineering and Technology.

Population Reference Bureau. 1992. *The Challenge of Change: What the 1990 Census Tells Us About Children*. Washington, DC: Center for the Study of Social Policy.

Puma, J. M. et al. 1997. *Prospects: Final Report on Student Outcomes*. Washington, DC: U.S. Department of Education.

Quality Education for Minorities Project. 1990. *Education That Works: An Action Plan for the Education of Minorities*. Cambridge, MA: MIT.

Ramirez, J. D., et al. 1990. *Executive Summary Final Report: Longitudinal Study of Immersion Strategy, Early-Exit and Late-Exit Transitional Bilingual Education Programs for Language-Minority Children*. San Mateo, CA: Aguirre International, submitted to the U.S. Department of Education.

Ramist, L., C. Lewis, and L. McCamley-Jenkins. 1994. Student Group *Differences in Predicting College Grades: Sex, Language, and Ethnic Groups*. New York: College Entrance Examination Board.

Raudenbush, S. W., and R. M. Kasim. 1998. "Cognitive Skill and Economic Inequality: Findings from the National Adult Literacy Study." *Harvard Educational Review* 68 (Spring): 33–79.

Rosenbaum, J. E., M. J. Kulieke, and L. S. Rubinowits. 1987. "Low-Income Black Children in White Suburban Schools: A Study of School and Student Responses." *Journal of Negro Education* 56 (Winter): 35–43.

Rubi, I. 1995. *The Minority Engineering Program, University of Colorado, Boulder: 1994–95 MEP Annual Report and 1995–96 MEP Program Plan*. Boulder, CO: Minority Engineering Program, University of Colorado.

Schneider, B., and Y. Lee. 1990. "A Model for Academic Success: The School and Home Environment of East Asian Students." *Anthropology and Education Quarterly* 21: 358–77.

Scribner, S., and M. Cole. 1973. "Cognitive Consequences of Formal and Informal Schooling." *Science* 182: 553–59.

Sears, D. O., et al. 1997. "Is It Really Racism? The Origins of White Americans' Opposition to Race-Targeted Policies." *Public Opinion Quarterly* 61 (Spring): 16–53.

Selingo, J. 1998. "Affirmative-Action Plan for the '90s? Wisconsin Tries for Diversity Without Numerical Goals." *Chronicle of Higher Education*, 8 May, A40–41.

Shade, B. J. 1989. "The Influence of Perceptual Development on Cognitive Style: Cross Ethnic Comparisons." *Early Child Development and Care* 51: 137–55.

Slavin, R. E., et al. 1996. "Success for All: Summary of Research." *Journal of Education for Students Placed At Risk* 1: 41–76.

Smith, J. T., and F. Welch. 1986. *Closing the Gap: Forty Years of Economic Progress for Blacks*. Santa Monica, CA: Rand Corporation.

Smith, S. 1998. "Minority Enrollment Creeps Upward at Texas Universities." *Black Issues in Higher Education*, 11 June, 10–11.

Smith, T. W. 1990. *Ethnic Images*, GSS Topical Report No. 19. Chicago: National Opinion Research Center, University of Chicago.

Smothers, R. 1994. "To Raise the Performance of Minorities, a College Increased Its Standards." *The New York Times*, 29 June, A21.

Solorzano, D. G., and R. W. Solorzano. 1995. "The Chicano Educational Experience: A Framework for Effective Schools in Chicano Communities." *Educational Policy* 9: 293–314.

Steele, C. M. 1997. "A Threat in the Air — How Stereotypes Shape Intellectual Identity and Performance." *American Psychologist*, 613–29.

Steele, C. M., and J. Aronson. 1995. "Stereotype Threat and the Intellectual Test Performance of African Americans." *Journal of Personality and Social Psychology* 69: 797–811.

Steinberg, L. 1996. *Beyond the Classroom*. New York: Simon & Schuster.

Steinberg, L., S. M. Dornbusch, and B. B. Brown. 1992. "Ethnic Differences in Adolescent Achievement: An Ecological Perspective." *American Psychologist* 47: 723–27.

Stevenson, D. L., and D. P. Baker. 1987. "The Family–School Relation and the Child's School Performance." *Child Development* 58: 1348–57.

Stevenson, H. W. 1998. "A Study of Three Cultures: Germany, Japan, and the United States — An Overview of the TIMSS Case Study Project." *Phi Delta Kappa*, March: 524–29.

Stevenson, H. W., and J. W. Stigler. 1992. *The Learning Gap: Why Our Schools Are Failing and What We Can Learn from Japanese and Chinese Education*. New York: Summit Books.

Stringfield, S., M. A. Millsap, and R. Herman. 1997. *Urban and Suburban/Rural Special Strategies for Educating Disadvantaged Children*. Washington, DC: U.S. Department of Education.

Tharp, R. G. 1989. "Psychocultural Variables and Constants: Effects of Teaching and Learning on Schools." *American Psychologist* 44: 349–59.

Tharp, R. G., and R. Gallimore. 1988. *Rousing Minds to Life: Teaching, Learning, and Schooling in Social Context.* Cambridge, UK: Cambridge University Press.

Tinsley, J. 1997. "Grim Numbers: Shaker Residents Unite for Task of Bridging the Gap Between Black and White Students." *Cleveland Plain Dealer*, 16 March, 1-A and 19-A.

Tomas Rivera Policy Institute and National Association of Latino Elected and Appointed Officials Education Fund. 1997. *Diversifying the Los Angeles Area Latino Mosaic: Salvadoran and Guatemalan Leaders' Assessment of Community Public Policy Needs.* Claremont, CA: Tomas Rivera Policy Institute.

Useem, E. L., et al. 1997. "Reforming Alone: Barriers to Organizational Learning in Urban School Change Initiatives." *Journal of Education for Students Placed At Risk* 2: 55–78.

U.S. Department of Education, National Center for Education Statistics. 1997. *Pursuing Excellence: A Study of Eighth-Grade Mathematics and Science Teaching, Learning, Curriculum, and Achievement in International Context,* NCES 97-198. Washington, DC: U.S. Government Printing Office.

Wacquant, L. C., and W. J. Wilson. 1989. "The Cost of Racial and Class Exclusion in the Inner City." *Annals of the American Association of Political and Social Science*, 501.

Wagner, R. 1997. "Intelligence, Training, and Employment," *American Psychologist* 52 (October): 1059–69.

Weinberg, M. A. 1977. *A Chance to Learn: The History of Race and Education in the United States.* New York: Cambridge University Press.

Welniak, E. J., and M. S. Littman. 1990. "Money Income and Poverty Status in the U.S. 1989." *Current Population Reports Series P-60, NO. 168.* Washington, DC: Bureau of the Census, U.S. Government Printing Office.

White, K. R. 1982. "Relation Between Socioeconomic Status and Academic Achievement." *Psychological Bulletin* 91: 461–81.

White, P. A., et al. 1996. "Upgrading the High School Math Curriculum: Math Course-Taking Patterns in Seven High Schools in California and New York." *Educational Evaluation and Policy Analysis* 18 (Winter): 285–307.

Willingham, W. W. 1985. *Success in College: The Role of Personal Qualities and Academic Ability.* New York: College Entrance Examination Board.

Wilson, W. J. 1987. *The Truly Disadvantaged: The Inner City, the Underclass, and Public Policy.* Chicago: University of Chicago Press.

# *Three*

## A THREAT IN THE AIR

### *HOW STEREOTYPES SHAPE*

### *INTELLECTUAL IDENTITY AND PERFORMANCE*

CLAUDE M. STEELE

ORE THAN HALF A CENTURY AGO, Gunnar Myrdal counterposed the experience of women and the experience of Negroes in an appendix to *An American Dilemma*. Myrdal suggested — but did not develop at length — a connection between what blacks and women experience as a result of how the dominant culture limited their opportunities for participation and achievement (Myrdal 1972, 1073). My own teaching and research have taught me that this observation continues to have a poignant relevance. What I term "stereotype threat" appears to persist in situations that in many respects are characterized by commitment to nondiscrimination and inclusion. The patterns I describe here are patterns I have researched at both the University of Michigan and Stanford.

In this chapter I develop evidence for a theory describing the ways in which the academic performance of high-achieving blacks and women is compromised by the stereotype threatening experience in circumstances of academic pressure. Our strongest students in our strongest and, as is frequently the case, some of our most progressive and selective institutions are affected by this threat. I have undertaken this work to understand better, and to suggest how we can address, this critical institutional and pedagogical dilemma.

From an observer's standpoint, the situations of a boy and a girl in a math classroom or of a black student and a white student in any classroom are essentially the same. The teacher is the same; the textbooks are the same; and in better classrooms, these students are treated the same. Is it possible, then, that they could still experience the classroom differently, so differently, in fact, as to significantly affect their performance and achievement there? This is the central question of this chapter, and in seeking an answer, it has both a practical and a theoretical focus. The practical focus is on the perhaps obvious need to better understand the processes that can hamper a group's school performance and on what can be done to improve that performance. The theoretical focus is on how societal stereotypes about groups can influence the intellectual functioning and identity development of individual groups members. To show the generality of these processes and their relevance to important outcomes, this theory is applied to two groups: African-Americans, who must contend with negative stereotypes about their abilities in many scholastic domains, and women, who must do so primarily in math and the physical sciences. In trying to understand the schooling outcomes of these two groups, the theory has a distinct perspective, that of viewing people, in Sartre's (1946/1965) words, as "first of all beings in a situation" such that if one wants to understand them, one "must inquire first into the situation surrounding [them]" (p. 60).

The theory begins with an assumption: that to sustain school success one must be identified with school achievement in the sense of its being a part of one's self-definition, a personal identity to which one is self-evaluatively accountable. This accountability—that good self-feelings depend in some part on good achievement—translates into sustained achievement motivation. For such an identification to form, this reasoning continues, one must perceive good prospects in the domain, that is, that one has the interests, skills, resources, and opportunities to prosper there, as well as that one belongs there, in the sense of being accepted and valued in the domain. If this relationship to schooling does not form or gets broken, achievements may suffer. Thus, in trying to understand what imperils achievements among women and African-Americans, this logic points to a basic question: What in the experience of these groups might frustrate their identification with all or certain aspects of school achievement?

One must surely turn first to social structure: limits on educational access that have been imposed on these groups by socioeconomic disadvantage, segregating social practices, and restrictive cultural orientations, limits of both historical and ongoing effect. By diminishing one's educational prospects, these limitations (e.g., inadequate resources, few role models, preparational disadvantages) should make it more difficult to identify with academic domains. To continue in math, for example, a woman might have to buck the low expectations of teachers, family, and social gender roles in which math is seen as unfeminine, as well as anticipate spending her entire professional life in a male-dominated world. These realities, imposed on her by societal structure, could so reduce her sense of good prospects in math as to make identifying with it difficult.

But this chapter focuses on a further barrier, one that has its effect on the already identified, those members of these groups who, having survived structural obstacles, have achieved identification with the domain (of the present groups, school-identified African-Americans and math-identified women). It is the social–psychological threat that arises when one is in a situation or doing something for which a negative stereotype about one's group applies. This predicament threatens one with being negatively stereotyped, with being judged or treated stereotypically, or with the prospect of conforming to the stereotype. Called *stereotype threat*, it is a situational threat — a threat in the air — that, in general form, can affect the members of any group about whom a negative stereotype exists (e.g., skateboarders, older adults, white men, gang members). Where bad stereotypes about these groups apply, members of these groups can fear being reduced to that stereotype. And for those who identify with the domain to which the stereotype is relevant, this predicament can be self-threatening.

Negative stereotypes about women and African-Americans bear on important academic abilities. Thus, for members of these groups who are identified with domains in which these stereotypes apply, the threat of these stereotypes can be sharply felt and, in several ways, hampers their achievement.

First, if the threat is experienced in the midst of a domain performance — classroom presentation or test taking, for example — the emotional reaction it causes could directly interfere with performance. My colleagues and I (Spencer et al. 1997; Steele and Aronson 1995) have tested this possibility with women taking standardized math tests and African-Americans taking standardized verbal tests. Second, when this threat becomes chronic in a situation, as for the woman who spends considerable time in a competitive, male-oriented math environment, it can pressure *disidentification*, a reconceptualization of the self and of one's values so as to remove the domain as a self-identity, as a basis of self-evaluation. Disidentification offers the retreat of not caring about the domain in relation to the self. But as it protects in this way, it can undermine sustained motivation in the domain, an adaptation that can be costly when the domain is as important as schooling.

Stereotype threat is especially frustrating because, at each level of schooling, it affects the vanguard of these groups, those with the skills and self-confidence to have identified with the domain. Ironically, their susceptibility to this threat derives not from internal doubts about their ability (e.g., their internalization of the stereotype) but from their identification with the domain and the resulting concern they have about being stereotyped in it. (This argument has the hopeful implication that to improve the domain performance of these students, one should focus on the feasible task of lifting this situational threat rather than on altering their internal psychology.) Yet, as schooling progresses and the obstacles of structure and stereotype threat take their cumulative toll, more of this vanguard will likely be pressured into the ranks of the unidentified. These students, by not caring about the domain vis-à-vis the self, are likely to underperform in it regardless of whether they are stereotype threatened there. Thus, although the identified among these groups are likely to underperform only under stereotype threat, the unidentified (casualties of sociocultural disadvantage or prior internalization of stereotype threat) are likely to underperform and not persist in the domain even when stereotype threat has been removed.

In these ways, then, the present analysis sees social structure and stereotypes as shaping the academic identities and performance outcomes of large segments of society. But first, for the two groups under consideration, what are these outcomes?

As is much discussed, these outcomes are in a crisis state for African-Americans. Although black students begin school with standardized test scores that are not too far behind those of their white counterparts, almost immediately a gap begins to appear (e.g., Alexander and Entwistle 1988; Burton and Jones 1982; Coleman et al. 1966) that, by the sixth grade in most school districts, is two full grade levels (Gerard 1983). There have been encouraging increases in the number of African-Americans completing high school or its equivalence in recent years: 77% for black students versus 83% for white students (American Council on Education 1995–1996). And there have been modest advances in the number of African-American high school graduates enrolling in college, although these have not been as substantial as in other groups (American Council on Education 1995–1996). Perhaps most discouraging has been the high dropout rate for African-American college students. The dropout rate for those who do not finish college within six years is 62%, compared with a national dropout rate of 41% (American Council on Education 1995–1996). And there is evidence of lower grade performance among those who do graduate of, on average, two-thirds of a letter grade lower than those of other graduating students (Nettles 1988). On predominantly white campuses, black students are also underrepresented in math and the natural sciences. Although historically black colleges and universities now enroll only 17% of the nation's black college students, they produce 42% of all black bachelor of science (BS) degrees in natural science (Culotta & Gibbons 1992). At the graduate level, although black women have recently shown modest gains in PhDs received, the number awarded to black men has declined over the past decade more than for any other subgroup in society (American Council on Education 1995–1996).

Women clearly thrive in many areas of schooling. But in math, engineering, and the physical sciences, they often endure lesser outcomes than men. In a meta-analysis involving over 3 million participants, Hyde et al. (1990), for example, found that through elementary and middle school, there are virtually no differences between boys and girls in performance on standardized math tests but that a trend toward men doing better steadily increases from high school (standard deviation [SD] = .29) through college (SD = .41) and into adulthood (SD = .59). And, as their college careers begin, women leave these fields at a rate two and a half times that of men (Hewitt & Seymour 1991). Although white women constitute 43% of the U.S. population, they earn only 22% of the BS degrees and 13% of the PhDs and occupy only 10% of the jobs in physical science, math, and engineering, where they earn only 75% of the salary paid to men (Hewitt & Seymour 1991).

These inequities have compelled explanations ranging from the sociocultural to the genetic. In the case of African-Americans, for example, past and ongoing socioeconomic disadvantage, cultural orientations (e.g., Ogbu 1986), and genetic differences (e.g., Herrnstein & Murray 1994; Jensen 1969) have all been proposed as factors that, through singular and accumulated effect, could undermine their performance. In the case of women's performance in math and the physical sciences, there are parallel arguments: structural and cultural gender role constraints that shunt women away from these areas; culturally rooted expectations (e.g., Eccles 1987; Eccles-Parsons et al. 1983); and, again, genetic limitations (Benbow & Stanley 1980, 1983). But several findings show that these analyses are not fully sufficient.

For one thing, minority student achievement gaps persist even in the middle and upper socioeconomic classes. Using data from the Coleman report (Coleman et al. 1966) and a more recent College Board study of Scholastic Assessment Test (SAT) scores, Miller (1995, 1996) found that the gaps in academic performance (grades as well as standardized test scores) between whites and non-Asian minorities (e.g., African-Americans, Hispanics, and Native Americans) in the upper and middle classes (as measured by parental education and occupation) were as large as or larger than in the lower classes. Group differences in socioeconomic status (SES), then, cannot fully explain group differences in academic performance.

Another point is that these differences are not even fully explained by group differences in skills. This is shown in the well-known *overprediction* or *underperformance* phenomenon of the test bias literature. Overprediction occurs when, at each level of performance on a test of preparation for some level of schooling (e.g., the SAT), students from one group wind up achieving less—getting lower college grades, for example—than other students with the same beginning scores. In this sense, the test scores of the low-performing group overpredict how well they will actually achieve, or, stated another way, the low-performing group underperforms in relation to the test's prediction. But the point here is that because the students at each test-score level have comparable initial skills, the lower eventual performance of one group must be due to something other than skill deficits they brought with them.

In the case of African-Americans, overprediction across the academic spectrum has been so reliably observed as to be almost a lawful phenomenon in American society (e.g., Jensen 1980; Vars and Bowen 1997). Perhaps the most extensive single demonstration of it comes from a recent Educational Testing Service study (Ramist et al. 1994) that examined the predictiveness of the SAT on 38 representative college and university campuses. As is typically the case, the study found that the predictive validity to the SAT—its correlation with subsequent grades—was as good for African-American, Hispanic, and Native American students as for white and Asian students. But for the three non-Asian minority groups, there was sizable overprediction (underperformance) in virtually all academic areas. That is, at each level of preparation as measured by the SAT, something further depressed the grades of these groups once they arrived on campus.

The same study found evidence of SAT overprediction for female students (i.e., women performing less well than men at comparable SAT levels) in technical and physical science courses such as engineering, economics, and computer science but not in nontechnical areas such as English. It is interesting though that women in this study were not overpredicted in math per se, a seeming exception to this pattern. The overprediction of women's college math performance has generally been unreliable, with some studies showing it (e.g., Benbow & Arjmand 1990; Levin & Wyckoff 1988; Lovely 1987; Ware et al. 1985) and others not (e.g., Adelman 1991; DeBoer 1984; Ware & Dill 1986). However, a recent study (Strenta et al. 1993) involving over 5000 students at four prestigious northeastern colleges identified a pattern of effects that suggests why these different results occur: Underperformance reliably occurred among women who were talented in math and science and who, perhaps for that reason, took courses in these areas that were intended for majors, whereas it did not occur among women with less math and science preparation who took courses in these areas intended for nonmajors. Thus, women may be reliably overpredicted in math and the physical sciences, just as black students are more generally, but only when the curriculum is more advanced and only among women who are more identified with the domain. Among this vanguard, though, something other than skill deficits depresses their performance. What are these further processes?

## SOCIAL AND STEREOTYPE STRUCTURE AS OBSTACLES
## TO ACHIEVEMENT IDENTIFICATION

The proposed answer is that at least one of these processes is a set of social psychological phenomena that obstructs these groups' identification with domains of schooling.[1] I turn first to school identification.

### Academic Identification

As noted, this analysis assumes that sustained school achievement depends on identifying with school, that is, forming a relationship between oneself and the domains of schooling such that one's self-regard significantly depends on achievement in those domains. Extrinsic rewards, such as better career outcomes, personal security, parental exhortation, and so on, can also motivate school achievement. But it is presumed that sustaining motivation through the ebb and flow of these other rewards requires school identification. How, then, is this identification formed?

Not a great deal is known about the process. But several models (e.g., Schlenker and Weigold 1989; C.M. Steele 1988; Tesser 1988) share an implicit reasoning, the first assumption of which is that people need positive self-regard, a self-perception of "adaptive and moral adequacy" (C.M. Steele 1988, p. 289). Then, the argument goes, identification with a given domain of life depends, in large part, on the self-evaluative prospects it offers. James (1890/1950) described the development of the self as a process of picking from the many, often incompatible, possible selves, those "on which to stake one's salvation" (p. 310). This choice and the assessment of prospects that goes into it are, of course, multifaceted: Are the rewards of the domain attractive or important? Is an adequate opportunity structure available? Do I have the requisite skills, talents, and interests? Have others like me succeeded in the domain? Will I be seen as belonging in the domain? Will I be prejudiced against in the domain? Can I envision wanting what this domain has to offer? and so on. Some of these assessments undergird a sense of efficacy in the domain (e.g., Bandura 1977, 1986). Others have to do with the rewards, importance, and attractiveness of the domain itself. And still others have to do with the feasibility and receptiveness of the domain. The point here is that students tacitly assess their prospects in school and its subdomains, and, roughly speaking, their identifications follow these assessments: increasing when they are favorable and decreasing when they are unfavorable. As for the two groups under consideration, then, this analysis suggests that something systematically downgrades their assessments of, and thus their identification with, critical domains of schooling.

## Threats to Academic Identification

### STRUCTURAL AND CULTURAL THREATS

Both groups have endured and continue to endure sociocultural influences that could have such effects. Among the most replicable facts in the schooling literature is that SES is strongly related to school success and cognitive performance (e.g., Coleman et al. 1966; Miller 1996). And because African-Americans have long been disproportionately represented in lower socioeconomic classes, this factor surely contributes to their achievement patterns in school, both through the material limitations associated with lower SES (poor schools, lack of resources for school persistence, etc.) and through the ability of these limitations, by downgrading school-related prospects, to undermine identification with school. And beyond socioeconomic structure, there are cultural patterns within these groups or in the relation between these groups and the larger society that may also frustrate their identification with school or some part of it, for exmaple, Ogbu's (1986) notion of a lower-class black culture that is "oppositional" to school achievement or traditional feminine gender roles that eschew math-related fields (e.g., Eccles-Parsons et al. 1983; Linn 1994).

### STEREOTYPE THREAT

Beyond these threats, waiting for those in these groups who have identified with school is yet another threat to their identification, more subtle perhaps but nonetheless profound: that of stereotype threat. I define it as follows: the event of a negative stereotype about a group to which one belongs becoming self-relevant, usually as a plausible interpretation for something one is doing, for an experience one is having, or for a situation one is in, that has relevance to one's self-definition. It happens when one is in the *field* of the stereotype, what Cross (1991, p. 195) called a "spotlight anxiety," such that one can be judged or treated in terms of a racial stereotype. Many analyses have referred to this predicament and the pressure it causes (e.g., Allport 1954; Carter 1991; Cose 1993; Goffman 1963; Howard & Hammond 1985; Jones et al. 1984; Sartre 1946/1965; C.M. Steele 1975; C.M. Steele & Aronson 1995; S. Steele 1990). The present definition stresses that for a negative stereotype to be threatening, it must be self-relevant. Then, the situational contingency it establishes — the possibility of conforming to the stereotype or of being treated and judged in terms of it — becomes self-threatening. It means that one could be limited or diminished in a domain that is self-definitional. For students from groups in which abilities are negatively stereotyped in all or some school domains and yet who remain identified with those domains, this threat may be keenly felt, felt enough, I argue, to become a further barrier to their identification with the domain.

There is, however, a more standard explanation of how negative stereotypes affect their targets. Beginning with Freud (as cited in Brill 1938) in psychology and Cooley (1956) and Mead (1934) in sociology, treatises on the experience of oppression have depicted a fairly standard sequence of events: Through long exposure to negative stereotypes about their group, members of prejudiced-against groups often internalize the stereotypes, and the resulting sense of inadequacy becomes part of their personality (e.g., Allport 1954; Bettelheim 1943; Clark 1965; Grier & Coobs 1968; Erikson 1956; Fanon 1952/1967; Kardiner & Ovesey 1951; Lewin 1941).

In recent years, the tone of this argument has constructively lightened, replacing the notion of a broad self-hatred with the idea of an inferiority anxiety or low expectations and suggesting how situational factors contribute to this experience. S. Steele's (1990) essays on *racial vulnerability* (i.e., a vulnerability of both blacks and whites that stems, in part, from the situational pressures of reputations about their groups) offered an example. This work depicts the workings of this anxiety among African-Americans in an interconnected set of ideas: *integration shock* that, like Goffman (1963), points to settings that integrate blacks and whites as particularly anxiety arousing; *objective correlatives* or race-related situational cues that can trigger this anxiety; and the inherent sense of risk, stemming from an internalized *inferiority anxiety* and from a *myth of inferiority* pervading integrated settings, of being judged inferior or of confirming one's own feared inferiority. Howard and Hammond (1985) earlier made this argument specifically in relation to the school achievement of black students. They argued that once "rumors of inferiority" (stereotypes; p. 18) about black students' abilities pervade the environment — through, for example, national debates over the genetic basis of racial differences in IQ — they can intimidate black students; become internalized by them; and, in turn, lead to a low sense of self-efficacy, demotivation, and underperformance in school. Analogous arguments have been applied to women interested in math-related areas (cf. Eccles-Parsons et al. 1983).

These models recognize the situational influence of negative stereotypes (e.g., Allport 1954; Howard & Hammond 1985; S. Steele 1990) but most often describe it as a process in which the stereotype, or more precisely the possibility of being stereotyped, triggers an internalized inferiority doubt or low expectancy. And because this anxiety is born of a socialization presumed to influence all members of the stereotyped group, virtually all members of the group are presumed to have this anxiety, to one degree or another.

Stereotype threat, in contrast, refers to the strictly situational threat of negative stereotypes, the threat that does not depend on cueing an internalized anxiety or expectancy. It is cued by the mere recognition that a negative group stereotype could apply to oneself in a given situation. How threatening this recognition becomes depends on the person's identification with the stereotype-relevant domain. For the domain identified, the situational relevance of the stereotype is threatening because it threatens diminishment in a domain that is self-definitional. For the less domain identified, this recognition is less threatening or not threatening at all, because it threatens something that is less self-definitional.

Stereotype threat, then, as a situational pressure "in the air," so to speak, affects only a subportion of the stereotyped group and, in the area of schooling, probably affects confident students more than unconfident ones. Recall that to be identified with schooling in general, or math in particular, one must have confidence in one's domain-related abilities, enough to perceive good prospects in the domain. This means that stereotype threat should have its greatest effect on the better, more confident students in stereotyped groups, those who have not internalized the group stereotype to the point of doubting their own ability and have thus remained identified with the domain — those who are in the academic vanguard of their group.[2]

Several general features of stereotype threat follow:

1. Stereotype threat is a general threat not tied to the psychology of particular stigmatized groups. It affects the members of any group about whom there exists some generally known negative stereotype (e.g., a grandfather who fears that any faltering of memory will confirm or expose him to stereotypes about the aged). Stereotype threat can be thought of as a subtype of the threat posed by negative reputations in general.

2. That which turns stereotype threat on and off, the controlling mechanism, so to speak, is a particular concurrence: Whether a negative stereotype about one's group becomes relevant to interpreting oneself or one's behavior in an identified-with setting. When such a setting integrates stereotyped and nonstereotyped people, it may make the stereotype, as a dimension of difference, more salient and thus more strongly felt (e.g., Frable et al. 1990; Goffman 1963; Kleck & Strenta 1980; Sartre 1946/1965; S. Steele 1990). But such integration is neither necessary nor sufficient for this threat to occur. It can occur even when the person is alone, as for a woman taking an important math test alone in a cubicle but under the threat of confirming a stereotyped

limitation of ability. And, in integrated settings, it need not occur. Reducing the interpretive relevance of a stereotype in the setting, say in a classroom or on a standardized test, may reduce this threat and its detrimental effects even when the setting is integrated.[3]

3. This mechanism also explains the variabilities of stereotype threat: the fact that the type and degree of this threat vary from group to group and, for any group, across settings. For example, the type and degree of stereotype threat experienced by white men, black people, and people who are overweight differ considerably, bearing on sensitivity and fairness in the first group, on school performance in the second, and on self-control in the third. Moreover, for any of these groups, this threat will vary across settings (e.g., Goffman 1963; S. Steele 1990). For example, women may reduce their stereotype threat substantially by moving across the hall from math to English class. The explanation of this model is straightforward. Different groups experience different forms and degrees of stereotype threat because the stereotypes about them differ in content, in scope, and in the situations to which they apply.

4. To experience stereotype threat, one need not believe the stereotype nor even be worried that it is true of oneself. The well-known African-American social psychologist James M. Jones (1997) wrote, "When I go to the ATM machine and a woman is making a transaction, I think about whether she will fear I may rob her. Since I have no such intention, how do I put her at ease? Maybe I can't . . . and maybe she has no such expectation. But it goes through my mind" (p. 262). Jones felt stereotype threat in this situation even though he did not believe that the stereotype characterized him. Of course, this made it no less a life-shaping force. One's daily life can be filled with recurrent situations in which this threat pressures adaptive responses.

5. The effort to overcome stereotype threat by disproving the stereotype — for example, by outperforming it in the case of academic work — can be daunting. Because these stereotypes are widely disseminated throughout society, a personal exemption from them earned in one setting does not generalize to a new setting where either one's reputation is not known or where it has to be renegotiated against a new challenge. Thus, even when the stereotype can be disproved, the need to do so can seem Sisyphean, everlastingly recurrent. And in some critical situations, it may not be disprovable. The stereotypes considered in this work allege group-based limitations of ability that are often reinforced by the structural reality of increasingly small group representations at more advanced levels of the schooling domain. Thus, for group members working at these advanced levels, no amount of success up to that point can disprove the stereotype's relevance to their next, more advanced performance. For the advanced female math student who has been brilliant up to that point, any frustration she has at the frontier of her skills could confirm the gender-based limitation alleged in the stereotype, making this frontier, because she is so invested in it, a more threatening place than it is for the non-

stereotyped. Thus, the work of dispelling stereotype threat through performance probably increases with the difficulty of work in the domain, and whatever exemption is gained has to be re-won at the next new proving ground.

## EMPIRICAL SUPPORT FOR A THEORY OF STEREOTYPE THREAT AND DISIDENTIFICATION

In testing these ideas, the research of my colleagues and me has had two foci: The first is on intellectual performance in the domain in which negative group stereotypes apply. Here, the analysis has two testable implications. One is that for domain-identified students, stereotype threat may interfere with their domain-related intellectual performance. Analysts have long argued that behaving in a situation in which one is at risk of confirming a negative stereotype about one's group, or of being seen or treated stereotypically, causes emotional distress and pressure (e.g., Cross 1991; Fanon 1952/1967; Goffman 1963; Howard & Hammond 1985; Sartre 1946/1965; C.M. Steele & Aronson 1995; S. Steele 1990). The argument here is that for those who identify with the domain enough to experience this threat, the pressure it causes may undermine their domain performance. Disruptive pressures such as evaluation apprehension, test anxiety, choking, and token status have long been shown to disrupt performance through a variety of mediating mechanisms: interfering anxiety, reticence to respond, distracting thoughts, self-consciousness, and so on (Baumeister & Showers 1984; Green 1991; Lord & Saenz 1985; Sarason 1980; Wine 1971). The assumption of this model is that stereotype threat is another such interfering pressure. The other testable implication is that reducing this threat in the performance setting, by reducing its interfering pressure, should improve the performance of otherwise stereotype-threatened students.

The second research focus is the model's implication that stereotype threat, and the anticipation of having to contend with it unceasingly in school or some domain of schooling, should deter members of these groups from identifying with these domains, and, for group members already identified, it should pressure their disidentification.[4]

### Stereotype Threat and Intellectual Performance

Steven Spencer, Diane Quinn, and I (Spencer et al. 1997) first tested the effect of stereotype threat on intellectual performance by testing its effect on the standardized math test performances of women who were strong in math.

THE STEREOTYPE THREAT OF WOMEN PERFORMING MATH

At base, of course, the stereotype threat that women experience in math-performance settings derives from a negative stereotype about their math ability that is disseminated throughout society. But whether this threat impaired their performance, we reasoned, would depend on two things. First, the performance would have to be construed so that any faltering would imply the limitation of ability alleged in the stereotype. This means that the performance would have to be difficult enough so that faltering at it would imply having reached an ability limit but not so difficult as to be nondiagnostic of ability. And second, as has been much emphasized, the women in question would have to be identified with math, so that faltering and its stereotype-confirming implication would threaten something they care about, their belongingness and acceptance in a domain they identify with. Of course, men too (at least those of equal skill and identification with math) could be threatened in this situation; faltering would reflect on their ability too. But their faltering would not carry the extra threat of confirming a stereotyped limitation in math ability or of causing them to be seen that way. Thus, the threat that women experience, through the interfering pressure it causes, should worsen their performance in comparison to equally qualified men. Interestingly, though, these otherwise confident women should perform as well as equally qualified men when this situational threat is lessened.

To explore these questions, Spencer, Quinn, and I (Spencer et al. 1997) designed a basic research paradigm: We recruited female and male students, mostly college sophomores, who were both good at math and strongly identified with it in the sense of seeing themselves as strong math students and seeing math as important to their self-definition. We then gave them a very difficult math test one at a time. The items were taken from the advanced math Graduate Record Examination (GRE) and we assumed would frustrate the skills of these students without totally exceeding them. As expected, and presumably reflecting the impairing effects of stereotype threat, women significantly underperformed in relation to equally qualified men on this difficult math test. But more important, in another condition of this experiment, in which the test was an advanced literature test rather than a math test, and in which participants had been selected and matched for their strong literature skills and identification, women performed just as well as equally qualified men. This happened, we reasoned, because women are not stereotype threatened in this area.

A second experiment replicated women's underperformance on the difficult math test and showed that it did not happen when the test was easier, that is when the items, taken from the regular quantitative section of the GRE, were more within the skills of these strong math students. The lack of performance frustration on this easier test, presumably, reduced women's stereotype threat by making the stereotype less relevant as an interpretation of their performance.

STEREOTYPE THREAT VERSUS GENES

So went our interpretation. But an alternative was possible: The biological limits of women's math ability do not emerge until the material tested is difficult. It is this very pattern of evidence that Benbow and Stanley (1980, 1983) used to suggest a genetic limitation in women's math ability. Thus, the first two experiments reproduced the gender effects on math performance reported in the literature: that women underperform primarily in math and mainly when the material is difficult. But they fall short of establishing our interpretation.

To do this, we would need to give women and men a difficult math test (one capable of producing women's underperformance) but then experimentally vary stereotype threat, that is, vary how much women were at risk of confirming the stereotype while taking the test. A third experiment did this by varying how the test (the same difficult one used in the earlier experiments) was represented. Participants were told either that the test generally showed gender differences, implying that the stereotype of women's limitations in math was relevant to interpreting their own frustration, or that it showed no gender differences, implying that the gender stereotype was not relevant to their performance and thus could not be confirmed by it on this particular test. The no-gender-differences representation did not challenge the validity of the stereotype; it simply eliminated the risk that the stereotype could be fulfilled on this test. In the gender-differences condition, we expected women (still stereotype threatened) to underperform in relation to equally qualified men, but in the no-gender-differences condition, we expected women (with stereotype threat reduced) to perform equal to such men. The genetic interpretation, of course, predicts that women will underperform on this difficult test regardless of how it is represented.

In dramatic support of our reasoning, women performed worse than men when they were told that the test produced gender differences, which replicated women's underperformance observed in the earlier experiments, but they performed equal to men when the test was represented as insensitive to gender differences, even though, of course, the same difficult "ability" test was used in both conditions (see Figure 1). Genetic limitation did not cap the performance of women in these experiments. A fourth experiment showed that reducing stereotype threat

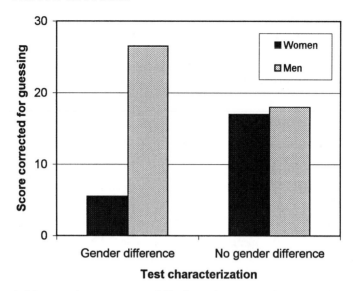

Figure 1. Mean performance on a difficult math test as a function of gender and test characterization.

(through the no-gender-differences treatment) raised women's performance to that of equally qualified men, even when participants' specific performance expectancies were set low, that is, when participants were led to expect poor test performance. Also, a fifth experiment (that again replicated the treatment effects of the third experiment) found that participants' post-treatment anxiety, not their expectancies or efficacy, predicted their performance. Thus, the disruptive effect of stereotype threat was mediated more by the self-evaluative anxiety it caused than by its lowering of performance expectations or self-efficacy.

INTERNAL OR SITUATIONAL THREAT

These findings make an important theoretical and practical point: The gender-differences conditions (including those in which the possibility of gender differences was left to inference rather than stated directly) did not impair women's performance by triggering doubts they had about their math ability. For one thing, these women had no special doubts of this sort; they were selected for being very good at math and for reporting high confidence in their ability. Nor was this doubt a factor in their test performance. Recall that the math test was represented as an ability test in all conditions of these experiments. This means that in the no-gender-differences conditions, women were still at risk of showing their own math ability to be weak — the same risk that men had in these conditions. Under this risk (when their own math ability was on the line), they performed just as well as men. Whatever performance-impairing anxiety they had, it was no greater than that of equally qualified men. Thus, the gender-differences conditions (the normal condition under which people take these tests) could not have impaired their performance by triggering some greater internalized anxiety that women have about their own math ability — an anxiety acquired, for example, through prior socialization. Rather, this condition had its effect through situational pressure. It set up an interpretive frame such that any performance frustration signaled the possible gender-based ability limitation alleged in the stereotype. For these women, this signal challenged their belongingness in a domain they cared about and, as a possibly newly met limit to their ability, could not be disproved by their prior achievements, thus its interfering threat.

## THE STEREOTYPE THREAT OF AFRICAN-AMERICANS ON STANDARDIZED TESTS

Joshua Aronson and I (C.M. Steele & Aronson 1995) examined these processes among African-American students. In these studies, black and white Stanford University students took a test composed of the most difficult items on the verbal GRE. Because the participants were students admitted to a highly selective university, we assumed that they were identified with the verbal skills represented on standardized tests. The first study varied whether the stereotype about black persons' intellectual ability was relevant to their performance by varying whether the test was presented as *ability-diagnostic*, that is, as a test of intellectual ability, or as *ability-nondiagnostic*, that is, as a laboratory problem-solving task unrelated to ability and thus to the stereotype about ability. Analysis of covariance was used to remove the influence of participants' initial skills, measured by their verbal SAT scores, on their test performance. This done, the results showed strong evidence of stereotype threat: Black participants greatly underperformed white participants in the diagnostic condition but equaled them in the nondiagnostic condition (see Figure 2). A second experiment produced the same pattern of results with an even more slight manipulation of stereotype threat: whether or not participants recorded their race on a demographic questionnaire just before taking the test (described as nondiagnostic in all conditions). Salience of the racial stereotype alone was enough to depress the performance of identified black students (see Figure 3).

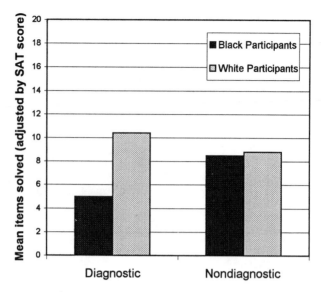

Figure 2. Mean performance on a difficult verbal test as a function of race and test characterization.

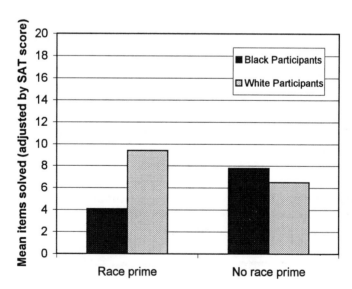

Figure 3. Mean performance on a difficult verbal test as a function of whether race was primed.

THE COGNITIVE MEDIATION OF STEREOTYPE THREAT

Stereotype threat, then, can impair the standardized test performance of domain-identified students. This effect generalizes to several ability-stereotyped groups, and its mediation seems to involve anxiety more than expectancies. But do these manipulations cause a specific state of stereotype threat, that is, a sensed threat specifically about being stereotyped or fitting the stereotype? To address this question, Aronson and I (C.M. Steele & Aronson 1995) tested two things: whether manipulating stereotype threat actually activates the racial stereotype in the thinking and information processing of stereotype-threatened test takers and whether it produces in them a specific motivation to avoid being seen stereotypically. Again, black and white participants were run in either an ability-diagnostic or ability-nondiagnostic condition, except that just after the condition instructions and completion of the sample test items (so that participants could see how difficult the items were) and just before participants expected to take the test, they completed measures of stereotype activation and avoidance. The stereotype-activation measure asked them to complete 80 word fragments, 10 of which we knew from pretesting could be completed with, among other words, words symbolic of African-American stereotypes (e.g., _ _ce [race], la_ _ _[lazy], or _ _or [poor] and 5 of which could be completed with, among other words, words signifying self doubts (e.g., lo_ _ _ _[loser], du_ _[dumb], or sha_ _ _[shame]). The measure of participants' motivation to avoid being seen stereotypically simply asked them how much they preferred various types of music, activities, sports, and personality traits, some of which a pretest sample had rated as stereotypic of African-Americans.[5]

If expecting to take a difficult ability-diagnostic test is enough to activate the racial stereotype in the thinking of black participants and to motivate them to avoid being stereotyped, then these participants, more than those in the other conditions, should show more stereotype and self-doubt word completions and fewer preferences for things that are African-American. This is precisely what happened. Black participants in the diagnostic condition completed more word fragments with stereotype- and self-doubt-related words and had fewer preferences for things related to African-American experience (e.g., jazz, basketball, hip-hop) than black participants in the nondiagnostic conditions or white participants in either condition, all of whom were essentially the same (see Figure 4). Also, as a last item before participants expected to begin the test, they were given the option of recording their race, a measure we thought might further tap into an apprehension about being viewed stereotypically. Interestingly, then, all of the black partici-

**(a) Stereotype activation measure**

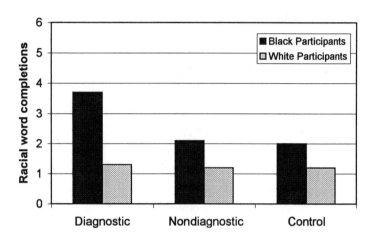

**(b) Self-doubt activation measure**

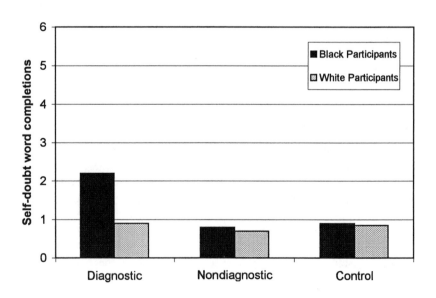

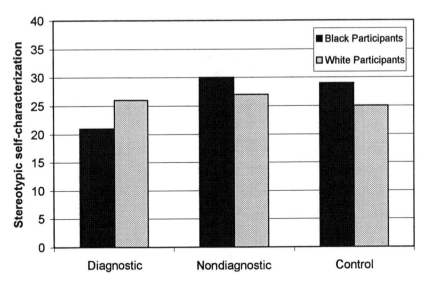

Figure 4. Indicators of stereotype threat: (a) stereotype activation measure, (b) self-doubt activation measure, and (c) stereotype avoidance measure.

pants in the nondiagnostic condition and all of the white participants in both conditions listed their race, whereas only 25% of the black participants in the diagnostic condition did so.

SELF-REJECTION OR SELF-PRESENTATION?

A troubling implication of the earlier mentioned internalization models (e.g., Allport 1954; Bettelheim 1943; Clark 1965; Grier & Coobs 1968; Erikson 1956; Fanon 1952/1967; Kardiner & Ovesey 1951) is that negative stereotypes about one's group eventually become internalized and cause rejection of one's own group, even of oneself — *self-hating* preferences. The famous finding of Clark and Clark (1939) that black children preferred white dolls over black dolls has been interpreted this way. The preferences of black participants in the diagnostic conditions fit this pattern; with negative stereotypes about their group cognitively activated, they valued things that were African-American less than any other group. But the full set of results suggests a different interpretation. In those conditions in which black participants did not have to worry about tripping a stereotypic perception of themselves, they valued things that were African-American more strongly than did other participants. Thus, rather than reflecting self- or own-group rejection, their devaluation of things that were African-American in the diagnostic condition was apparently a strategic self-presentation aimed at cracking the stereotypic lens through which they could be seen. So it could be, then, in the general case, that rather than reflecting real self-concepts, behavior that appears group rejecting or self-rejecting may reflect situation-bound, self-presentational strategies.

STEREOTYPE THREAT AND DOMAIN IDENTIFICATION

Not being identified with a domain, our (C.M. Steele & Aronson 1995) theory reasons, means that one's experience of stereotype threat in the domain is less self-threatening. Although we have yet to complete a satisfactory test of this prediction, partially completed experiments and pretests show that stereotype threat has very little, if any, effect on participants not identified with the domain of relevance. Most typically, these participants give up and underperform on the difficult test regardless of whether they are under stereotype threat. Although not yet constituting a complete test of this implication of the theory, these data do emphasize that the above results generalize only to domain-identified students.

STEREOTYPE THREAT AND THE INTERPRETATION OF GROUP DIFFERENCES IN STANDARDIZED TEST PERFORMANCE

Inherent to the science of quantifying human intelligence is the unsavory possibility of ranking societal groups as to their aggregated intelligence. It is from this corner of psychology that the greatest controversy has arisen, a controversy that has lasted throughout this century and that is less about the fact of these group differences than about their interpretation (cf. Herrnstein & Murray 1994; Kamin 1974). To the set of possible causes for these group differences, our findings (C.M. Steele & Aronson 1995) add a new one: the differential impact of stereotype threat on groups in the testing situation itself. Thus, stereotype threat may be a possible source of bias in standardized tests, a bias that arises not from item content but from group differences in the threat that societal stereotypes attach to test performance. Of course, not every member of an ability-stereotyped group is going to be affected by stereotype threat every time he or she takes a test. As our research has shown, the experience of success as one takes the test can dispel the relevance of the stereotype. Nonetheless, among the most identified test takers in the stereotype-threatened group — those in its academic vanguard who have the greatest confidence and skills — this threat can substantially depress performance on more difficult parts of the exam. And this depression could contribute significantly to the group's underperformance in comparison with nonstereotype-threatened groups.[6]

## Reaction of Disidentification

Stereotype threat is assumed to have an abiding effect on school achievement — an effect beyond its impairment of immediate performance — by preventing or breaking a person's identification with school, in particular, those domains of schooling in which the stereotype applies. This reasoning has several implications for which empirical evidence can be brought to bear: the resilience of self-esteem to stigmatization; the relationship between stigmatized status and school achievement; and, among ability-stigmatized people, the relationship between their school performance and self-esteem.

### SELF-ESTEEM'S RESILIENCE TO STIGMATIZATION

In a recent review, Crocker and Major (1989) were able to make a strong case for the lack of something that common sense suggests should exist: a negative effect of stigmatization on self-esteem. Following the logic of the internalization models described above and viewing stigmatization as, among other things, an assault to self-esteem, one might expect that people who are stigmatized would have lower self-esteem than people who are not. Yet, as Crocker and Major reported, when the self-esteem of stigmatized groups (e.g., blacks, Chicanos, the facially disfigured, obese people) is actually measured, one finds that their self-esteem is as high as that of the nonstigmatized.

Crocker and Major (1989) offered the intriguing argument that stigma itself offers esteem-protective strategies. For example, the stigmatized can blame their failures on the prejudice of out-group members, they can limit their self-evaluative social comparisons to the in-group of other stigmatized people, and they can devalue the domains in which they feel devalued. Other models have also described esteem-saving adaptations to stigma. For example, models that assume internalization of stereotype-related anxieties often posit compensatory personality traits (e.g., grandiosity) that protect self-esteem but leave one poorly adapted to the mainstream (e.g., Allport 1954; Clark 1965; Grier & Coobs 1968; Kardiner & Ovesey 1951; S. Steele 1990). In the present reasoning, stigmatization stems from stereotype threat in specific domains. Thus, it adds to the list of stigma adaptations the possibility of simple domain disidentification, the rescuing of self-esteem by rendering as self-evaluatively irrelevant the domain in which the stereotype applies.

Herein may lie a significant source of the self-esteem resilience shown in stigmatized groups. This idea also implies that once domain disidentification is achieved, the pressure for adaptations of attribution and personality may be reduced.

## A UNIVERSAL CONNECTION BETWEEN STIGMATIZATION AND POOR SCHOOL ACHIEVEMENT

If disidentification with school, and the resulting underachievement, can be a reaction to ability-stigmatizing stereotypes in society, then it might be expected that ability stigmatization would be associated with poor school performance wherever it occurs in the world. Finding such a relationship would not definitely prove the present theory; the direction of causality could be quarreled with, as could the mediation of such a relationship. Still, it would be suggestive, and, in that respect, Ogbu (1986) reported an interesting fact: Among the caste-like minorities in industrial and nonindustrial nations throughout the world (e.g., the Maoris of New Zealand, the Baraku of Japan, the Harijans of India, the Oriental Jews of Israel, and the West Indians of Great Britain), there exists the same 15-point IQ gap between them and the nonstigmatized members of their society as exists between black and white Americans. These groups also suffer poorer school performance, higher dropout rates, and related behavior problems. Moreover, these gaps appear even when the stigmatized and nonstigmatized are of the same race, as in the case of the Baraku and other Japanese. What these groups share that is capable of explaining their deficits is a caste-like status that, through stereotypes in their societies, stigmatizes their intellectual abilities — sowing the seeds, I suggest, of their school disidentification.

## THE DISASSOCIATION OF SELF-ESTEEM AND SCHOOL ACHIEVEMENT

If the poor school achievement of ability-stigmatized groups is mediated by disidentification, then it might be expected that among the ability stigmatized, there would be a disassociation between school outcomes and overall self-esteem. Several kinds of evidence suggest this process among African-Americans. First, there is the persistent finding that although black students underperform in relation to white students on school outcomes from grades to standardized tests (e.g., Demo & Parker 1987; Simmons et al. 1978; C.M. Steele 1992), their global self-esteem is as high or higher than that of white students (e.g., Porter & Washington 1979; Rosenberg 1979; Wylie 1979). For both of these facts to be true, some portion of black students must have acquired an imperviousness to poor school performance.

Several further studies suggest that this imperviousness is rooted in disidentification. In a study of desegregated schools in Champaign, Illinois, Hare and Costenell (1985) measured students' school achievement; overall self-esteem; and self-esteem in the specific domains of home life, school, and peer-group relations. Like others, they found that although black students performed less well than white students, they still had comparable levels of overall self-esteem. Their domain-specific measures suggested why: Although black students were lower than white students in school and home-life self-esteem, blacks slightly exceeded whites in peer-group self-esteem. Here, then, perhaps, was the source of their overall self-regard: disidentification with domains in which their evaluative prospects were poor (in this case, school and home life) and identification with domains in which their prospects were better (i.e., their peers).

A recent study suggests that this may be a not uncommon phenomenon. Analyzing data available from the National Educational Longitudinal Survey (National Center for Educational Statistics 1992; a nationally representative longitudinal survey begun in 1988), Osborne (1994) found that from the 8th through the 10th grades, black students had lower achievement and somewhat higher self-esteem than white students, which replicated the general pattern of findings described above. But more than this, he found evidence of increasing black students' disidentification over this period: The correlation between their school achievement and self-esteem for this period decreased significantly more for black than for white students. Also, using a scale measure of school disidentification, Major et al. (in press) found that black students were more disidentified than white students in several college samples and that for disidentified students of both races, negative feedback about an intellectual task had less effect on their self-esteem than it did for identified students. Major et al. further showed that when racial stereotypes were primed, neither negative nor positive feedback affected black students' self-esteem, whereas the self-esteem of white students followed the direction of the feedback. Ability stigmatization of the sort experienced by African-Americans, then, can be associated with a protective "disconnect" between performance and self-regard, a disconnect of the sort that is consistent with disidentification theory.

Can stereotype threat directly cause this disconnect? To test this question, Kirsten Stoutemeyer and I varied the strength of stereotype threat that female test takers (Stanford students) were under by varying whether societal differences between women and men in math performance were attributed to small but stable differences in innate ability (suggesting an inherent, gender-based limit in math ability) or to social causes such as sex-role prescriptions and discrimination (suggesting no inherent, gender-based limit in math ability). We then measured their identification with math and math-related careers, either before or after they took a difficult math test. Regardless of when identification was measured, women under stronger stereotype threat disidentified with math and math-related careers more than women under weaker stereotype threat. Although domain identification has several determinants, these findings suggest that stereotype threat is an important one of them.

## "Wise" Schooling: Practice and Policy

As a different diagnosis, the present analysis comes to a different prescription: The schooling of stereotype-threatened groups may be improved through situational changes (analogous to those manipulated in our experiments) that reduce the stereotype threat these students might otherwise be under. As noted, psychological diagnoses have more typically ascribed the problems of these students to internal processes ranging from genes to internalized stereotypes. On the face of it, at least, internal states are more difficult to modify than situational factors. Thus, the hope of the present analysis, encouraged by our research, is that these problems might be more tractable through the situational design of schooling, in particular, design that secures these students in the belief that they will not be held under the suspicion of negative stereotypes about their group. Schooling that does this, I have called *wise*, a term borrowed from Irving Goffman (1963), who borrowed it from gay men and lesbians of the 1950s. They used it to designate heterosexuals who understood their full humanity despite the stigma attached to their sexual orientation: family and friends, usually, who knew the person beneath the stigma. So it must be, I argue, for the effective schooling of stereotype-threatened groups.

Although "wisdom" may be necessary for the effective schooling of such students, it may not always be sufficient. The chief distinction made in this analysis (between those of these groups who are identified with the relevant school domain and those who are not) raises a caution. As noted, stereotype threat is not keenly felt by those who identify little with the stereotype-threatening domain. Thus, although reducing this threat in the domain may be necessary to encourage their identification, it may not be sufficient to build an identification that is not there. For this to occur, more far-reaching strategies that develop the building blocks of domain identification may be required: better skills, greater domain self-efficacy, feelings of social and cultural comfort in the domain, a lack of social pressure to disidentify, and so on.

But for the identified of these groups, who are quite numerous on college campuses, the news may be better than is typically appreciated. For these students, feasible changes in the conditions of schooling that make threatening stereotypes less applicable to their behavior (i.e., wisdom) may be enough. They are already identified with the relevant domain, they have skills and confidence in the domain, and they have survived other barriers to identification. Their remaining problem is stereotype threat. Reducing that problem, then, may be enough to bring their performance on par with that of nonstereotyped persons in the domain.

This distinction raises an important and often overlooked issue in the design of schooling for stereotype-threatened students, that of *triage*, the issue of rendering onto the right students the right intervention. Mistakes can easily be made. For example, applying a strategy to school-identified students (on the basis of their membership in a stereotype-threatened group) that assumes weak identification, poor skills, and little confidence could backfire. It could increase stereotype threat and underperformance by signaling that their abilities are held under suspicion because of their group membership. But the opposite mistake could be made by applying a strategy that assumes strong identification, skills, and confidence to those who are actually unidentified with the relevant domain. Merely reducing stereotype threat may not accomplish much when the more primary need of these students is to gain the interests, resources, skills, confidences, and values that are needed to identify with the domain.

Some wise strategies, then, may work for both identified and unidentified students from these groups, but others may have to be appropriately targeted to be effective. I offer some examples of both types:

### For Both Domain-Identified and Domain-Unidentified Students

1. *Optimistic teacher–student relationships.* The prevailing stereotypes make it plausible for ability-stigmatized students to worry that people in their schooling environment will doubt their abilities. Thus, one wise strategy, seemingly suitable for all students, is to discredit this assumption through the authority of potential-affirming adult relationships. The Comer (1988) Schools Project has used this strategy with great success at the elementary school level, and Johnides et al. (1992) have used it in designing a mentoring program for incoming minority and other students at the University of Michigan. In analogous laboratory experiments, Geoffrey Cohen, Lee Ross, and I (Cohen et al. 1997) found that critical feedback to African-American students was strongly motivating when it was coupled with optimism about their potential.

2. *Challenge over remediation.* Giving challenging work to students conveys a respect for their potential and thus shows them that they are not

regarded through the lens of an ability-demeaning stereotype. Uri Treisman (1985) used this strategy explicitly in designing his successful group-study workshops in math for college-aged women and minorities. Taking students where they are skill-wise, all students can be given challenging work at a challenging, not overwhelming, pace, especially in the context of supportive adult–student relationships. In contrast, remedial work reinforces in these students the possibility that they are being viewed stereotypically. And this, by increasing stereotype threat in the domain, can undermine their performance.

3. *Stressing the expandability of intelligence.* The threat of negative-ability stereotypes is that one could confirm or be seen as having a fixed limitation inherent to one's group. To the extent that schooling can stress what Carol Dweck (1986) called the *incremental* nature of human intelligence — its expandability in response to experience and training — it should help to deflect this meanest implication of the stereotype. Aronson (1996) recently found, for example, that having African-American college students repeatedly advocate the expandability of intelligence to their elementary school tutees significantly improved their own grades.

## For Domain-Identified Students

1. *Affirming domain belongingness.* Negative-ability stereotypes raise the threat that one does not belong in the domain. They cast doubt on the extent of one's abilities, on how well one will be accepted, on one's social compatibility with the domain, and so on. Thus, for students whose primary barrier to school identification is stereotype threat, direct affirmation of their belongingness in the domain may be effective. But it is important to base this affirmation on the students' intellectual potential. Affirming social belonging alone, for those under the threat of an ability stereotype, could be taken as begging the question.

2. *Valuing multiple perspectives.* This refers to strategies that explicitly value a variety of approaches to both academic substance and the larger academic culture in which that substance is considered. Making such a value public tells stereotype-threatened students that this is an environment in which the stereotype is less likely to be used.

3. *Role models.* People from the stereotype-threatened group who have been successful in the domain carry the message that stereotype threat is not an insurmountable barrier there.

## For Domain-Unidentified Students

1. *Nonjudgmental responsiveness.* Research by Lepper et al. (1993) has identified a distinct strategy that expert tutors use with especially poor students: little direct praise, Socratic direction of students' work, and minimal attention to right and wrong answers. For students weakly identified with the domain, who are threatened by a poor reputation, and who probably hold internalized doubts about their ability, this Socratic strategy has the wisdom of securing a safe teacher–student relationship in which there is little cost of failure and the gradual building of domain efficacy from small gains.

2. *Building self-efficacy.* Based on Bandura's (1977, 1986) theory of self-efficacy, this strategy attempts to build the student's sense of competence and self-efficacy in the schooling domain. Howard and Hammond (1985) have developed a powerful implementation of this strategy for African-American and other minority students, especially in inner-city public schools.

## Existence Proof: A Wise Schooling Intervention

Providing a definitive test of wise schooling theory will require, of course, an extensive research program. But as a first step, something might be learned from what Uri Treisman (1985) called an existence proof, in this case, a demonstration that an intervention derived from the theory could stop or reverse a tenacious negative trajectory in the school performance of stereotype-threatened students. Such an intervention would of necessity confound things: different wise practices as well as other practices and structures, peculiar to that setting, that could also affect academic outcomes. It could not stand as a test of the psychological theory per se. But if a particular architecture of wise strategies succeeded, it would encourage their applicability to the real-world schooling of these students.

With this rationale, my colleagues and I (Steven Spencer, Richard Nisbett, Mary Hummel, David Schoem, Kent Harber, and Ken Carter) implemented a freshman-year program at the University of Michigan aimed at the underachievement and low retention rates of African-American students. Each year, the program included approximately 250 freshmen in the ethnic proportions of the larger campus but with an oversampling of approximately 20% black students and 20% nonblack minority students (i.e., Asian, Hispanic, and Native American students as a single group). Program students were randomly selected from the students admitted to Michigan and then recruited by phone to participate. All program participants lived together in the wing of a large, 1200-student dormitory throughout their freshman year.

In this context, we implemented several wise strategies. The program was presented as a transition program aimed at helping students maximize the advantages of university life. We also recruited students honorifically; they were told that, as Michigan admittees, they had survived a very competitive selection process and that our program was designed to help them maximize their strong potential. These practices represented the program as nonremedial and represented the university as having acknowledged their intellectual potential and as having high expectations for them—all things that signal the irrelevance of negative group stereotypes. Once the students were in the program, these expectations were reinforced by their being offered a "challenge" workshop, modeled on those developed by Treisman (1985) for calculus, in either freshman calculus, chemistry, physics, or writing. These were taken on a voluntary basis in the dormitory. Students also participated in small weekly discussion groups, centered on brief readings, that allowed discussion of adjustment-relevant social and even personal issues. This activity has the wisdom of letting students know that they, or other members of their group, are not the only ones with concerns about adjusting to university life—an insight that can deflect the relevance of negative group stereotypes. These formal program components lasted for the first 10 weeks of the school year, and, as voluntary activities, approximately half of the students regularly participated in either one or both of them.

The first-semester grades averaged over the first two years of this ongoing project give a reliable picture of the program's initial impact. To show the size of the program's effect on students at different levels of preparation, Figure 5 graphs first-semester grades, using regression lines, for the different student groups as a function of standardized test scores on entry into the university (they are presented as standard deviation units in this figure to provide a common scale for students who took either the SAT or American College Test exam). The first thing to notice is the two essentially parallel lines for white and black students outside of any program at Michigan. They replicate the standard over-prediction–underperformance of black students alluded to earlier and it is against this pattern that the effects of the program can be evaluated. Looking first at the line for white students in our program, there is a modest tendency for these students to do better than the white control students (i.e., those outside the program), but given our accumulation of $n$ throughout these first two years, this difference is not significant.

It is the results for black students in our program (but who were not also in the campus minority program) that are most promising. Their line is considerably above that for black control students (i.e., black students outside any program) and, even with the modest sample size ($n = 27$), is significantly higher than this control line in the top one-third of the standardized test distribution, $t = 2.72$, $p < .05$. It is important that this group of black students showed almost no underperformance; in the top two-thirds of the test distribution, they had essentially the same grades as white students. We also know from follow-up data that their higher grade performance continued at least through their sophomore year and that as long as four years later, only one of them had dropped out.

Theoretically just as important is the bottom line in Figure 5, depicting the results for black students in a large minority remediation program. Despite getting considerable attention, they performed worse than the other groups at nearly every level of preparation. The differ-

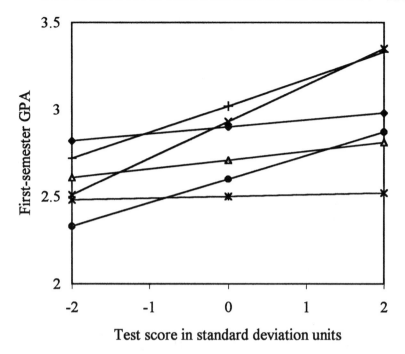

Figure 5. First-semester grade point average (GPA) as a function of program and race controlling for high school GPA.

—◆— White participants in contemporary control group (*n* = 6.515)
—+— White participants in 21st century program (*n* = 288)
—△— Black participants in contemporary control and not in remedial program (*n* = 313)
—×— Black participants in 21st century and not in remedial program (*n* = 27)
—✳— Black participants in contemporary control and in remedial program (*n* = 459)
—●— Black participants in 21st century and in remedial programs

ence between black students in the minority program and black students not in any program becomes significant at 1.76 standard deviations below the mean for test performance and is significant from that point on, *ps* < .05. Also, by the beginning of their junior year, 25% of these students had failed to register, and among those who entered with test scores in the top one-third of the test distribution, this figure was 40%. Some selection factor possibly contributed to this. Despite our having controlled for test scores and high school grade point averages in these analyses, some portion of these students may have been assigned to this program because they evidenced other risk factors. Still, these results suggest that the good intentions of the minority-remediation framework for schooling African-American students can backfire by, in our terms, institutionalizing the racial stereotype by which they are already threatened.

Although these findings are preliminary and we do not know that they were mediated as our theory claims, they are a step toward an existence proof; they show that wise practices can reduce black students' underachievement in a real-school context, and, just as important, that unwise practices seem to worsen it.

## CONCLUSION

In social psychology, we know that as observers looking at a person or group, we tend to stress internal, dispositional causes of their behavior, whereas when we take the perspective of the actors, now facing the circumstances they face, we stress more situational causes (e.g., E.E. Jones and Nisbett 1972; Ross 1977). If there is a system to the present research, it is that of taking the actor's perspective in trying to understand the intellectual performance of African-American and female students. It is this perspective that brings to light the broadly encompassing condition of having these groups' identification with domains of schooling threatened by societal stereotypes. This is a threat that in the short run can depress their intellectual performance and over the long run can undermine the identity itself, a predicament of serious consequence. But it is a predicament — something in the interaction between a group's social identity and its social psychological context, rather than something essential to the group itself. Predicaments can be treated and intervened on, and it is in this respect that I hope the perspective taken in this analysis and the early evidence offer encouragement.

## NOTES

The research reported in this chapter was supported by National Institutes of Health Grant MH51977, Russell Sage Foundation Grant 879.304, and Spencer Foundation and James S. McDonnell Foundation postdoctoral fellowships. Completion of the research was aided by the Center for Advanced Study in the Behavioral Sciences.

1. Other factors may also contribute. For example, there are persistent reports of women and minorities being treated differently in the classroom and in other aspects of schooling (e.g., Hewitt and Seymour 1991). This treatment includes both the "chilly-climate" sins of omission — the failure to call on them in class or to recognize and encourage their talents, and so on — and, in the case of low-income minorities, sins of commission — disproportionate expulsion from

school, assignment to special education classes, and administration of corporal punishment (National Coalition of Advocates for Students Report 1988).

2. The point is not that negative stereotypes are never internalized as low self-expectancies and self-doubts. It is that in such internalization, disidentification is the more primary adaptation. That is, once the stereotype-relevant domain (e.g., math) is dropped as a self-definition, the negative stereotype (e.g., that women are limited in math) can be accepted as more self-descriptive (i.e., internalized) without it much affecting one's self-regard (as for the woman who, not caring about math, says she is lousy at it). But this internalization is probably resisted (e.g., Crocker and Major 1989) until disidentification makes it less self-threatening. Once this has happened, the person is likely to avoid the domain because of both disinterest and low confidence regardless of whether stereotype threat is present.

3. As a process of social devaluation, stereotype threat is both a subform of stigmatization and something more general. It is that form of stigmatization that is mediated by collectively held, devaluing group stereotypes. This means that it does not include stigmatization that derives from nonstereotyped features such as a facial disfigurement or, for example, what Goffman (1963) called abominations of the body. Stereotype threat is a situational predicament. And, in this sense, it is also more general than stigmatization. It is a threat that can befall anyone about whom a negative reputation or group stereotype exists.

4. Moreover, a protective avoidance of identification can become a group norm. In reaction to a shared sense of threat in school, for example, it can become a shared reaction that is transmitted to group members as the normative relation to school. Both research (e.g., Ogbu 1986; Solomon 1992) and the media have documented this reaction in minority students from inner-city high schools to Harvard University's campus. Thus, disidentification can be sustained by normative pressure from the in-group as well as by stereotype threat in the setting.

5. Participants did not actually take the test in this experiment, as completing these measures would likely have activated the stereotype in all conditions.

6. Those who are less domain-identified in the stereotype-threatened group may also underperform on standardized tests. Because they care less about the domain it represents, they may be undermotivated or they may withdraw effort in the face of frustration. And for all of the reasons I have discussed, the greater portion of the stereotype-threatened group may be academically unidentified. This fact, too, then, may contribute to the group's overall weaker performance on these tests in comparison with nonstereotype-threatened groups.

## REFERENCES

Adelman, C. 1991. "Women at Thirty-Something: Paradoxes of Attainment." Washington, DC: U.S. Department of Education, Office of Research and Development.

Alexander, K. L., and D. R. Entwistle. 1988. "Achievement in the First Two

Years of School: Patterns and Processes." *Monographs of the Society for Research in Child Development* 53(2).

Allport, G. 1954. *The Nature of Prejudice.* New York: Doubleday.

American Council on Education. 1995–96. "Minorities in Higher Education." Washington, DC: Office of Minority Concerns.

Aronson, J. 1996. *Advocating the Malleability of Intelligence as an Intervention to Increase College Grade Performance.* Unpublished manuscript, University of Texas.

Bandura, A. 1977. "Self-efficacy: Toward a Unifying Theory of Behavior Change." *Psychological Review* 84: 191–215.

———. 1986. *Social Foundations of Action: A Social-Cognitive Theory.* Englewood Cliffs, NJ: Prentice Hall.

Baumeister, R. F., and C. J. Showers. 1984. "A Review of Paradoxical Performance Effects: Choking Under Pressure in Sports and Mental Tests. *European Journal of Social Psychology* 16: 361–83.

Benbow, C. P., and O. Arjmand. 1990. "Predictions of High Academic Achievement in Mathematics and Science by Mathematically Talented Students: A Longitudinal Study." *Journal of Educational Psychology* 82: 430–41.

Benbow, C. P., and J. C. Stanley. 1980. "Sex Differences in Mathematical Ability: Fact or Artifact? *Science* 210: 1262–4.

———. 1983. "Sex Differences in Mathematical Reasoning Ability: More Facts." *Science* 222: 1029–31.

Bettelheim, B. 1943. "Individual and Mass Behavior in Extreme Situations." *Journal of Abnormal and Social Psychology* 38: 417–52.

Brill, A. A., ed. 1938. *The Basic Writings of Sigmund Freud.* New York: Random House.

Burton, N. W., and L. V. Jones. 1982. "Recent Trends in Achievement Levels of Black and White Youth." *Educational Researcher* 11: 10–7.

Carter, S. 1991. *Reflections of an Affirmative Action Baby.* New York: Basic Books.

Clark, K. B. 1965. *Dark Ghetto: Dilemmas of Social Power.* New York: Harper & Row.

Clark, K. B., and M. K. Clark. 1939. "The Development of Consciousness of Self and the Emergence of Racial Identification of Negro School Children." *Journal of Social Psychology* 10: 591–9.

Cohen, G., C. M. Steele, and L. Ross. 1997. *Giving Feedback across the Racial Divide: Overcoming the Effects of Stereotypes.* Unpublished manuscript, Stanford University.

Coleman, J. S., E. Q. Campbell, C. J. Hobson, J. McPartland, A. M. Mood, F. D. Weinfield, and R. L. York. 1966. "Equality of Educational Opportunity." Washington, DC: U.S. Government Printing Office.

Comer, J. 1988. "Educating Poor Minority Children." *Scientific American* 259 (November): 42.

Cooley, C. H. 1956. *Human Nature and the Social Order.* New York: Free Press.

Cose, E. 1993. *The Rage of a Privileged Class.* New York: Harper Collins.

Crocker, J., and B. Major. 1989. "Social Stigma and Self-esteem: The Self-protective Properties of Stigma." *Psychological Review* 96: 608–30.

Cross, W. E., Jr. 1991. *Shades of Black: Diversity in African-American Identity.* Philadelphia: Temple University Press.

Culotta, E., and A. Gibbons, eds. 1992. "Minorities in Science [Special section]." *Science* 258 (13 November): 1176–232.

DeBoer, G. 1984. "A Study of Gender Effects in Science and Mathematics Course-Taking Behavior Among Students Who Graduated from College in the Late 1970s." *Journal of Research in Science Teaching* 21: 95–103.

Demo, D. H., and K. D. Parker. 1987. "Academic Achievement and Self-esteem Among Black and White College Students." *Journal of Social Psychology* 4: 345–55.

Dweck, C. 1986. "Motivational Processes Affecting Learning." *American Psychologist* 41: 1040–8.

Eccles, J. S. 1987. "Gender Roles and Women's Achievement-Related Decisions." *Psychology of Women Quarterly* 11: 135–72.

Eccles-Parsons, J. S., T. F. Adler, R. Futterman, S. B. Goff, C. M. Kaczala, J. L. Meece, and C. Midgley. 1983. "Expectations, Values, and Academic Behaviors." In *Achievement and Achievement Motivation*, J. T. Spence, ed. New York: Freeman, 75–146.

Erikson, E. 1956. "The Problem of Ego-Identity." *Journal of the American Analytical Association* 4: 56–121.

Fanon, F. 1967. *Black Skins, White Masks.* New York: Grove Press. (Original work published 1952)

Frable, D., T. Blackstone, and C. Sherbaum. 1990. "Marginal and Mindful: Deviants in Social Interaction." *Journal of Personality and Social Behavior* 59: 140–9.

Gerard, H. 1983. "School Desegregation: The Social Science Role." *American Psychologist* 38: 869–78.

Goffman, E. 1963. *Stigma: Notes on the Management of Spoiled Identity.* New York: Touchstone.

Green, R. G. 1991. "Social Motivation." *Annual Review of Psychology* 42: 377–99.

Grier, W. H., and P. M. Coobs. 1968. *Black Rage.* New York: Basic Books.

Hare, B. R., and L. A. Costenell. 1985. "No Place to Run, No Place to Hide: Comparative Status and Future Prospects of Black Boys." In *Beginnings: The Social and Affective Development of Black Children*, M. B. Spencer, G. K. Brookins, and W. Allen, eds. Hillsdale, NJ: Erlbaum, 201–14.

Herrnstein, R. A., and C. Murray. 1994. *The Bell Curve.* New York: Grove Press.

Hewitt, N. M., and E. Seymour. 1991. *Factors Contributing to High Attrition Rates Among Science and Engineering Undergraduate Majors.* Unpublished report to the Alfred P. Sloan Foundation.

Howard, J., and R. Hammond. 1985. "Rumors of Inferiority." *New Republic* 72 (9 September): 18–23.

Hyde, J. S., E. Fennema, and S. J. Lamon. 1990. "Gender Differences in Mathematics Performance: A Meta-analysis." *Psychological Bulletin* 107: 139–55.

James, W. 1950. *The Principles of Psychology*, Vol. 1. New York: Dover. (Original work published 1890)

Jensen, A. R. 1969. "How Much Can We Boost IQ and Scholastic Achievement?" *Harvard Educational Review* 30: 1–123.

———. 1980. *Bias in Mental Testing*. New York: Free Press.

Johnides, J., W. von Hippel, J. D. Lerner, and B. Nagda. 1992. *Evaluation of Minority Retention Programs: The Undergraduate Research Opportunities Program at the University of Michigan*. Paper presented at the 100th Annual Convention of the American Psychological Association, Washington, DC.

Jones, E. E., and R. E. Nisbett. 1972. "The Actor and the Observer: Divergent Perceptions of the Causes of Behavior." In *Attribution: Percieving the Causes of Behavior*, E. E. Jones, D. E. Kanouse, H. H. Kelley, R. E. Nisbett, S. Valins, and B. Weiner, eds. Morristown, NJ: General Learning Press, 79–94.

Jones, E. E., A. Farina, A. H. Hastorf, H. Markus, O. T. Miller, and R. A. Scott. 1984. *Social Stigma: The Psychology of Marked Relationships*. New York: Freeman.

Jones, J. M. 1997. *Prejudice and Racism*, 2d ed. New York: McGraw-Hill.

Kamin, L. 1974. *The Science and Politics of I.Q.* Hillsdale, NJ: Erlbaum.

Kardiner, A. and L. Ovesey. 1951. *The Mark of Oppression: Explorations in the Personality of the American Negro*. New York: Norton.

Kleck, R. E., and A. Strenta. 1980. "Perceptions of the Impact of Negatively Valued Physical Characteristics on Social Interactions." *Journal of Personality and Social Psychology* 39: 861–73.

Lepper, M. R., M. Woolverton, D. L. Mumme, and J.-L. Gurtner. 1993. "Motivational Techniques of Expert Human Tutors: Lessons for the Design of Computer-Based Tutors." In *Computers as Cognitive Tools*, S. P. Lajoie and S. J. Derry, eds. Hillsdale, NJ: Erlbaum, 75–104.

Levin, J., and J. Wyckoff. 1988. "Effective Advising: Identifying Students Most Likely to Persist and Succeed in Engineering." *Engineering Education* 78: 178–82.

Lewin, K. 1941. *Resolving Social Conflict*. New York: Harper & Row.

Linn, M. C. 1994. "The Tyranny of the Mean: Gender and Expectations." *Notices of the American Mathematical Society* 41: 766–9.

Lord, C. G., and D. S. Saenz. 1985. "Memory Deficits and Memory Surfeits: Differential Cognitive Consequences of Tokenism for Tokens and Observers." *Journal of Personality and Social Psychology* 49: 918–26.

Lovely, R. 1987. *Selection of Undergraduate Majors by High Ability Students: Sex Difference and Attrition of Science Majors*. Paper presented at the annual meeting of the Association for the Study of Higher Education, San Diego, CA.

Major, B., S. Spencer, T. Schmader, C. Wolfe, and J. Crocker. In press. "Coping with Negative Stereotypes About Intellectual Performance: The Role of Psychological Disengagement." *Personality and Social Psychology Bulletin*.

Mead, G. H. 1934. *Mind, Self, and Society*. Chicago: University of Chicago Press.

Miller, L. S. 1995. *An American Imperative: Accelerating Minority Educational Advancement*. New Haven, CT: Yale University Press.

———. 1996. *Promoting High Academic Achievement Among Non-Asian Minorities*. Paper presented at the Princeton University Conference on Higher Education, Princeton, NJ.

Myrdal, Gunnar. 1972. *An American Dilemma: The Negro Problem and Modern Democracy*. New York: Pantheon Books.

National Center for Educational Statistics. 1992. *National Educational Longitudinal Study of 1988: First Follow-up. Student Component Data File User's Manual*. Washington, DC: U.S. Department of Education, Office of Educational Research and Improvement.

National Coalition of Advocates for Students Report. 1988. *The Ann Arbor News*, 12 December, A1, A4.

Nettles, M. T. 1988. *Toward Undergraduate Student Equality in American Higher Education*. New York: Greenwood.

Ogbu, J. 1986. "The Consequences of the American Caste System." In *The School Achievement of Minority Children: New Perspectives*, U. Niesser, ed. Hillsdale, NJ: Erlbaum, 19–56.

Osborne, J. 1994. "Academics, Self-esteem, and Race: A Look at the Underlying Assumption of the Disidentification Hypothesis." *Personality and Social Psychology Bulletin* 21: 449–55.

Porter, J. R., and R. E. Washington. 1979. "Black Identity and Self-esteem: A Review of the Studies of Black Self-concept, 1968–1978." *Annual Review of Sociology* 5: 53–74.

Ramist, L., C. Lewis, and L. McCamley-Jenkins. 1994. *Student/Group Differences in Predicting College Grades: Sex, Language, and Ethnic Groups* (College Board Report No. 93-1, ETS No. 94.27). New York: College Entrance Examination Board.

Rosenberg, M. 1979. *Conceiving Self*. New York: Basic Books.

Ross, L. 1977. "The Intuitive Psychologist and His Shortcomings: Distortions in the Attribution Process." In *Advances in Experimental Social Psychology*, Vol. 10, L. Berkowitz, ed. New York: Academic Press, 337–84.

Sarason, I. G. 1980. "Introduction to the Study of Test Anxiety." In *Test Anxiety: Theory, Research, and Applications*, I. G. Sarason, ed. Hillsdale, NJ: Erlbaum, 57–78.

Sartre, J. P. 1965. *Anti-Semite and Jew*. New York: Schocken Books. (Original work published 1946)

Schlenker, B. R., and M. F. Weigold. 1989. "Goals and the Self-identification Process: Constructing Desired Identities." In *Goals Concepts in Personality and Social Psychology*, L. A. Pervin, ed. Hillsdale, NJ: Erlbaum, 243–90.

Simmons, R. G., L. Brown, D. M. Bush, and D. A. Blyth. 1978. "Self-esteem and Achievement of Black and White Adolescents." *Social Problems* 26: 86–96.

Solomon, R. P. 1992. *Forging a Separatist Culture*. Albany: State University of New York Press.

Spencer, S., C. M. Steele, and D. Quinn. In press. "Under Suspicion of Inability: Stereotype Threat and Women's Math Performance." *Journal of Experimental Social Pyschology*.

Steele, C. M. 1975. "Name-Calling and Compliance." *Journal of Personality and Social Psychology* 31: 361–69.

———. 1988. "The Psychology of Self-affirmation: Sustaining the Integrity of the Self." In *Advances in Experimental Social Psychology*, Vol. 21, L. Berkowitz, ed. New York: Academic Press, 261–302.

Steele, C. M. 1992. "Race and the Schooling of Black Americans." *The Atlantic Monthly* April: 68–78.

Steele, C. M., and J. Aronson. 1995. "Stereotype Threat and the Intellectual Test Performance of African Americans." *Journal of Personality and Social Psychology* 69: 797–811.

Steele, S. 1990. *The Content of Our Character*. New York: St. Martin's Press.

Strenta, A. C., R. Elliott, R. Adair, J. Scott, and M. Matier. 1993. *Choosing and Leaving Science in Highly Selective Institutions*. Unpublished report to the Alfred P. Sloan Foundation.

Tesser, A. 1988. "Toward a Self-evaluation Maintenance Model of Social Behavior." In *Advances in Experimental Social Psychology*, Vol. 21, L. Berkowitz, ed. New York: Academic Press, 181–227.

Treisman, U. 1985. *A Study of Mathematics Performance of Black Students at the University of California, Berkeley*. Unpublished report.

Vars, F. E., and W. G. Bowen. 1997. *SAT Scores, Race, and Academic Performance: New Evidence from Academically Successful Colleges*. Unpublished manuscript.

Ware, N. C., and D. Dill. 1986. *Persistence in Science Among Mathematically Able Male and Female College Students with Pre-college Plans for a Scientific Major*, March. Paper presented at the annual meeting of the American Educational Research Association, San Francisco.

Ware, N. C., N. A. Steckler, and J. Leserman. 1985. "Undergraduate Women: Who Chooses a Science Major?" *Journal of Higher Education* 56: 73–84.

Wine, J. 1971. "Test Anxiety and Direction of Attention." *Psychological Bulletin* 76: 92–104.

Wylie, R. 1979. *The Self-concept*, Vol. 2. Lincoln: University of Nebraska Press.

# Four

## A PRACTITIONER'S VIEW FROM TEXAS

*COMMENTS ON THE ESSAYS BY L. SCOTT MILLER*

*AND CLAUDE M. STEELE*

Philip Uri Treisman

I T IS MY INTENT to respond to the papers of Scott Miller and Claude Steele as a practitioner who has been deeply engaged by the questions they examined. The complementarity of their efforts and explicit focus on differing patterns of academic achievement force us to reckon with what is, perhaps, the most agonizingly unresolved dilemma of affirmative action on college campuses. Both Miller and Steele challenge dominant presuppositions of the conventional wisdom about affirmative action and diversity, and raise important questions about the ways in which the motif of "remediation" has informed institutional practices about inclusion of under represented minorities.

The intriguing patterns of stereotype vulnerability and the provocative suggestion that "affirmative action" can still be done "right" remind us of the work remaining to make good on the promise of a diverse educational community in which all students are empowered to achieve their highest potential. Nothing set forth in Scott Miller's essay about the still too small numbers of high achieving blacks can be a surprise to anyone who has observed the processes and patterns of educational institutions seeking to diversify their student populations over the last 20 years. At the University of Texas, the Emerging Scholars program — based on a prototype initially developed at the University of California, Berkeley — has begun to have important success in raising academic achievement levels for blacks and Latino students. It is a program based on the idea that higher levels of achievement will follow from a program that sets high standards and provides a context in which such standards can be met. Like the twenty-first-century program that Claude Steele described — a program that encouraged underrepresented minority students to maximize their development as students — Emerging Scholars is based on a belief that academic success can be achieved if the stigmatizing notion of remediation is supplanted by ambition to excel. Through the provision of a series of honors calculus courses that required more student commitment and by creation of a multiethnic community of students who worked *together* on academic problems and formed a group who did other things together as well, we began to observe noticeable improvements in academic performance for all students and we eliminated the pattern of underperformance by black students.

In Emerging Scholars we seek to apply what we have learned about the group process of supportive mutual learning that we had observed in interactions among Asian-Americans (and to a lesser extent in white student groups) to the experiences of blacks and Hispanics. We did this by forming communities (classes) of students who were ambitious, who were prepared to do more work than was assigned in "regular" calculus, and who would commit to participation in the other parts of the program that stressed building multiethnic communities based on shared intellectual interests.

Emerging Scholars works differently from many programs similar to it in that its sponsorship and its objectives are centered on academic issues and it encourages a high degree of faculty involvement. Most affirmative action programs in colleges and universities have been introduced during socially and politically volatile periods. This fact, as well as the special conditions associated with admissions, led administrators to take principal responsibility for their efforts during the 1960s and 1970s. Because admission standards were relaxed, these programs tend to be based on the need for remediation; they assume implicitly that the students are not quite good enough. During roughly the same period, the rising importance of research pressured faculty away from undergraduate education and into more intense commitment to disciplinary specialization. The professionalization of student services occurring during this same period consolidated the pattern in which diversity/pluralism efforts were predominantly sponsored by administrators.

Let me tell you about some of the results of this program we have seen at Austin, where in 1990, six years ago, there were six Hispanic math majors and one black math major. In the fall of 1994, there were 151 black and Hispanic math majors at Austin. Many of the winners of the undergraduate math competition — the Bennett exam — over the last four years have been black and Hispanic. The first winner, who was also the first female winner, came from a poor family from the Rio Grande valley in Donna, Texas. These results represent a radical transformation about who succeeds academically. We have essentially "reconstructed" the undergraduate math program at the University.

I like to be personal about these issues. I want to tell you about another impressive person. Frankie White is a black graduate student completing her studies in math at Austin. She did her undergraduate work at Berkeley in one of those multiethnic class sections I described. We have a beautiful videotape of the following encounter in which she "stars."

> It is the first day of class. There are 10 blacks and 3 Asians, some whites, a few Hispanics in a 24-student section. The instructor sets a problem on the blackboard. A Chinese-American student looks at it and responds "3 over pi squared." You can feel the tension in the room. The stereotype drama is being played out. You can *feel* the ethnic tension. The teacher praises the precocious Chinese-American. Then, the teacher poses the second question. One of the other Chinese-American students, all sitting together the first day, falls into the trap, is caught by the trick and gives a wrong answer. Frankie White looks over and says, "You fell into his trap." The Chinese-American students look at the black students, the blacks look at the Chinese-Americans and Frankie White has the courage to say, "You don't think we can do this stuff." (It's on tape, beautiful tape!) The Chinese-American students say, "You know, we know you're good, you always sit together and you do good work. How do you do it?" The black students and the white students who work together say, "We stay up all night and we work 'til we drop" and the Chinese-American students say, "That's what *we* do!"

The tragedy is, there are virtually no environments in higher education where African-American students and Chinese-American students comfortably interact around shared intellectual interests, common professional goals, and shared passions. The encounter described in this videotape is very unusual.

What are the results of these kinds of programs? The latest ones at Wisconsin, Kentucky, and Michigan State produced very similar results to those demonstrated by the Michigan data. They eliminate the underperformance of underrepresented minority students. At Austin now, 83% of black and Hispanic students get A's or B's in second-semester calculus, 35% graduate in the sciences with 3.5 GPAs (grade point averages) or better, 19 have gone on to doctoral programs—a significant portion of the national pool outside of historically black colleges, which, of course, is a major producer—58% are graduating with 3.0 or better in the sciences. We believe we can compensate for about 120 points of SAT (Scholastic Assessment Test) scores through these kinds of efforts.

In particular, the predicament confronting African-American students remains a source of deep concern. Many of the students I have studied—first, at Berkeley and now at Austin—came from middle class backgrounds and attended integrated high schools. By the time they settled into college habits of peer group association, two different patterns were evident: Either they had only black friends or they had no black friends. Paradoxically, at the college level, what seemed to happen had the effect of unraveling the commitment to integrated association that many of these students had begun to experience in high school and to which both of these universities had made strong commitments. Within the racially isolated black group, as Claude Steele has observed in other contexts, it became apparent that disidentification with academic achievement was taking place (Steele 1992). This disidentification was reflected both in attitudes about academic work and in lower than anticipated levels of academic performance.

I believe strongly that the success of Emerging Scholars is based in significant measure on the ways in which it unites a small, diverse student community around shared academic tasks and aspirations, building further on that commitment a dedication to service and to extracurricular engagement. In this kind of program intervention, there is an additional bonus: The theme of remediation as a dominant institutional posture toward black students, a pressure that can also encourage disidentification, is replaced by a commitment to high academic standards and service that cuts across racial boundaries. Emerging Scholars is, I think, an example of how affirmative action can be done "right."

How does this happen? It happens in an environment in which diversity can become a resource for enhancing what I like to call *civitas*, a Latin word for citizenship. Students who share academic commitments and goals are encouraged to identify other kinds of commitments to share. For example, now that Emerging Scholars has emerged as a program of the math department at Austin, our students are developing the habit of doing community service as a group. To be sure, many students were in the habit of doing volunteer work as individuals on their own. Now they do it as an extension of their involvement in Emerging Scholars. We have more than a hundred of these students working in local elementary schools tutoring math and helping teachers teach and younger students learn. The fact that our students came together initially around math means that the community service activity has created a second, inclusive social bond overlapping with their base academic group. Students are learning to live in different worlds simultaneously while learning the skills they need to navigate the boundaries among those worlds. We see its benefits in the richness of departmental life. Students report liking the energy and excitement and the unexpectedness of what happens in the classroom. A shared commitment to *civitas* has revitalized the teaching and learning experience. Normally, academic programs do not foster these kinds of experiences. We now have a larger number of math majors of all races than we did six years ago.

.   .   .   .   .

I want to make an observation on Miller's comment about the importance of high school intervention. In recent months I have visited the 10 elementary schools in Texas where blacks and Hispanics perform a standard deviation better than all students. I go in as a substitute teacher for a day. It is the only way to learn about schools. I have also visited the 15 high schools that have the largest number of female black and Hispanic students passing the AP (Advanced Placement) calculus exam. We have a significant number of schools that have learned how to improve performance dramatically. The single most impressive fact is that higher education is involved in none of them. When you watch these schools you see what I would describe as strong principals and entrepreneurial "scavengers" as teachers. Universities are not resources to these schools. If you look at policy issues that support good schools—that means common uniformly high standards for all children—higher education is not a major player in demanding, in formulating meaningful high standards for all children. The business community is a more active participant in requiring high standards for students than higher education. This is deeply disturbing. If we do not get involved in these efforts to improve performance at the precollege level we will continue to serve the population we now serve, which will be a smaller and smaller population of America, and we will play a counterproductive role in this society.

Finally, I must, as a professor at the University of Texas, comment about the meaning and the significance of the *Hopwood* case, a challenge that in my judgment will reverberate for some time to come throughout public and private higher education. Efforts like Emerging Scholars and the Twenty-first Century Program provide a rare and needed opportunity to promote research about the benefits of diversity as an educational strategy. This kind of research has not been done, even though for the nearly 20 years following the Bakke decision, it has been common for colleges and universities to make claims about these benefits as rationales for inclusive admissions policies.

It will be very important to consider the following kinds of questions as we prepare for a post-Hopwood period in higher education.

- First, what is the evidence for asserting that diversity is a "compelling interest" in higher education? Does diversity contribute to the traditional mission of education, i.e., cognitive growth and preparation for leadership and citizenship?

- Second, the desegregation literature suggests that diversity has modest effects for majority students. Yet many analysts are privately asserting that more recent research will provide strong arguments that these benefits have been overstated. Of course, it is hardly a fair test of diversity to look for its benefits in environments that were designed to limit diversity. It is, therefore, extremely important to characterize environments in which diversity does have broad and positive effects. What are these environments and what are the dynamics that create their success?

- Third, it has been pointed out by a number of scholars, including Claude Steele and Scott Miller, that standardized measures of performance like the SAT overpredict the actual performance of underrepresented minority students. I regard this phenomenon as an index of institutional inhospitality. It will be interesting to analyze these outcomes as a function of institutional type. Virtually no private institutions have adopted programs like Emerging Scholars, for example. Yet elite private institutions have been among the most aggressive in recruiting high-ability underrepresented minority students.

We face a period of important transition and difficult questions. The *Hopwood* case is about the instability of the consensus that supports what many of us in higher education regard as a fundamental article of belief: that there is a profound relationship between an inclusive sense of fairness and excellence. Our challenge now is to develop the evidence for this belief and to muster the intelligence necessary to defend it as a common interest of a diverse national community.

## REFERENCES

Steele, C. M. 1992. "Race and the Schooling of Black Americans." *The Atlantic Monthly* April: 67–78.

# Five

## ASSESSMENT AND STUDENT DIVERSITY

### COMMENTS ON THE ESSAYS BY L. SCOTT MILLER

### AND CLAUDE M. STEELE

RICHARD J. LIGHT

MY CONCERNS revolve around the importance of empirical experience and the role of accurate data that help us understand what we want to accomplish and what we have learned about diversity and higher education. Both the Miller and the Steele essays substantially advance our understanding about the experience of diversity in high education, but do this in different ways.

Scott Miller's paper gives several examples of the magnitude of our challenges. I would call it a macro approach. He lays out, clearly, three big ideas. First, he presents concrete evidence about the dramatic increase in the diversity among students at colleges now. I have two daughters, both of whom graduated from college in the past three years. When I was an undergraduate more than 30 years ago, there were, as I remember, a grand total of two black students and perhaps a handful of Asian-American and Latino students out of my graduating class of about 2000. My daughters, in contrast, although they both attended a different college from me, had as their classmates a nonwhite enrollment of 38%. Their experience just couldn't have been more different from mine. We talked a lot about the differences. It was easy to agree that now is better.

In his second big theme, Professor Miller reminds us with compelling evidence that in the macro sense, thinking nationally, troublingly large gaps remain among the average performance of different ethnic groups. I expect that many people are not surprised at all to hear that differences exist among ethnic group means on SAT (Scholastic Assessment Test) scores, GPAs (grade point averages), or other measures of performance. Yet the *starkness* of these differences, especially when they are averaged across tens of thousands of individuals within each ethnic group, demands that we think hard about remedies, about what can be done to narrow some of these gaps.

The third big theme is the one I think has received the least work among scholars and among policy makers. Yet it is the most challenging of all. It is what a statistician would call the challenge of "selection at the right tail." For a place like Princeton, or any other of the several dozen truly selective colleges, the disparity among ethnic groups as to what fraction of each group is extraordinarily productive — meaning those with extraordinarily high SAT scores, or high school GPAs — this is a deeply troubling finding. Yet it is clearly true. If a first step toward working to solve a problem is identifying its dimensions in a clear and compelling way, Professor Miller has succeeded. Big time.

Claude Steele's presentation, on the other hand, is quite different. In a highly creative, concrete, empirical investigation, he is working to help us understand why some black students, with admissions credentials basically similar to those of whites, simply don't fare as well. As a statistician, I could nitpick, arguing that the samples are not that big, or that all the data are from one institution. But I do not want to say those things because this work is among the best I have seen. It is one of very few serious efforts to understand why some students substantially underperform what we might expect from them.

I am especially struck by two features of Professor Steele's work. First, by applying his ideas about social context and the importance of students' perceptions to both blacks as an ethnic group and also to women, he enriches his findings enormously. Again, if I may lapse into a magic moment of statistical jargon, working with both women and blacks adds the strength of making his findings about stereotyping more robust. As a result, they are more compelling, and more exciting, than if they were limited to one subset of a single ethnic group.

The second feature I find exciting is that it is one of very few examples of an actual intervention that was tried in a selective college. And it seems to hold promise for positive change. I notice that while the details are different, this work is done in the same spirit as Uri Treisman's major contribution about 10 years ago. Rather than just handwringing about black students' performance in math or science, he actually worked to implement a concrete intervention. And Uri's intervention made a difference. Other colleges, including my own, are trying various versions of encouraging students to study productively outside of class in groups, which Uri finds offers several benefits.

I hope Claude Steele's work will, similarly, begin to help faculty members, advisors, and indeed even student leaders. It can help them both to understand, and then to grapple with the importance of self-stereotyping among different subgroups of students. It illustrates a two-step process. Step one is to begin to understand why certain students aren't succeeding as well as we hope. And, thanks to Professor Steele, we now have a concrete idea about a possible step two — to think of constructive ways to knock down stereotyping, self-stereotyping in particular, as a way to enhance each student's performance.

These two superb pieces of work illustrate the constructive purposes to which well-conceived empirical work can be put. But I can't help thinking that what makes both of these presentations so special is precisely the concrete, substantial, and very careful presentation of evidence to back up just about every argument each of these authors makes.

Their work provokes a more extended reflection about the kinds of evidence we have about the role of diversity in our colleges and universities, particularly in our selection institutions, where so many pressures must be mediated. The topic is remarkably underresearched. Exploring it in a sustained way would help all of us.

In his recent president's report to the Harvard Board of Overseers, Neil Rudenstine addressed the importance of having a diverse student body both for learning and for the well being of our society. He makes a powerful case for the advantages of colleges working hard to ensure genuine diversity. President Rudenstine takes a distinctly scholarly, historical perspective. It is not polemical. He quotes from the work of John Stuart Mill, St. Augustine, De Tocqueville, Adam Smith, and other distinguished philosophers. He cites former Harvard presidents. Their writings buttress the case for the sometimes difficult, sometimes even painful, but hopefully constructive interplay of different ideas put forth by different people from different backgrounds, who care deeply about these ideas and who are willing and able to argue their positions in a civil manner.

He and I have talked about his essay. It challenges us to explore two unanswered questions, and I do not believe many of my colleagues around the country are really digging in on either one. They remain fertile ground. The first question is, given the increasing diversity among students on nearly all campuses, how can we, as faculty members, deans, advisors, or administrators in general, capitalize on this diversity to enhance college life, in the most positive sense, rather than just "letting what happens, happen"?

As part of a long-term project at my institution, I direct something called the Harvard Assessment Seminars. Indeed, its initial funding came from a generous start-up grant from the Mellon Foundation. It has different aspects. Part of the work involves my sitting one-to-one with our undergraduates and interviewing them. I do this in depth, often for more than two hours per chat. I have now interviewed 900 students over eight years. A message that comes through loud and clear is that a large fraction of Harvard undergraduates choose the place precisely because of its great diversity. They expect to meet fellow students who are different, who are smart, from whom they can learn, and some of whom will ultimately become their friends, perhaps lifelong friends.

So someone might ask the direct question, "How is it going?" And that is exactly the first challenge I would like to mention. I believe on most campuses, the honest answer is "We don't quite know." Of course, we all have our impressions, our hunches, our particular anecdotes. But how can we assess or evaluate in any systematic way whether and how students from all ethnic groups are actually benefiting from our dramatically increased diversity? For example, Harvard undergraduates have remarkably little use for the usual summary statistics in admissions brochures that simply report, "9% of our student body are members of ethnic group X, while 14% are from ethnic group Y, and so on." They are focused, like a laser beam, on what is the actual interplay, the interaction that the new diversity really brings out among students.

So I would like to pose the challenge: How might we get clearer measures of how it's going? And how might we gather information that would help us, and even more importantly help our students, to capitalize productively and positively on growing student diversity? It seems to me this broad question is best divided into parts. One part focuses on the impact of diversity outside of the classroom. That is, after all, where all students spend the overwhelming proportion of their time — interacting with one another. That is especially true of residential campuses, such as Princeton or Harvard. The second part focuses on what impact, if any, diversity among students is having on learning inside the classroom.

So that is what we will undertake in the Harvard Assessment activities as our next project. We will explore both questions. First, how well is diversity working outside of the classroom? Is it accomplishing most of the good purposes my president wrote about, most of the time? And what can our university do, what can any university do, structurally and institutionally, to maximize the good that can come from the new diversity? Second, what can individual faculty do, faculty like me who teach day-in and day-out, to take advantage of the new diversity in the educational process inside our classrooms?

We are not starting this exploration entirely devoid of evidence. Let me share one concrete example of evidence about inside-the-classroom impact, and one concrete example of outside-the-classroom impact. I hope this first example from inside the classroom will illustrate how assessment evidence has changed the way some of my colleagues and I organize our classes day-in and day-out.

The example comes from an assessment project done by Anne Clark, a student I supervised who was a graduating senior. She found from in-depth student interviews that many students identify the format of creating conflict within small classes and assigning subgroups within a class to argue different sides of an issue as an exceptionally good strategy for engaging learning in the social sciences. Then, in the spirit of focusing on diversity, make sure each group, if possible, includes students from diverse backgrounds. To illustrate, I taught a class last year called Controversies in American Education. The class had 24 students. For one assignment, I created a "debate for the following week" on ability grouping in American public schools. My question for the students was: What does the empirical evidence show?

To describe the format concretely, there were six Asian-American students in this class. I divided the 24 students overall into three working groups of eight. One group of eight was assigned to present published evidence in favor of ability grouping and to argue for it. The second group was assigned to find and present published evidence against ability grouping and to argue against it.

The third group was assigned to make a compelling argument based on empirical evidence, not on hunches, that ability grouping helps the highest skill children and hurts the lowest skill children, and therefore actually widens the gaps. Now here is the key point. I divided the six Asian-American students randomly, but assigned two to each of the three groups. The next week, in class, we had a vigorous, three-way debate.   At the end of the semester, I got feedback from all 24 students about each of the semester's classes. They singled out this particular class as especially effective. They emphasized its productive structure, or format, for maximizing their engagement and learning.

First—What did arranging this format cost me, as the professor, in terms of time or cost or effort? About three minutes. I had to set up the groups, which I created, and then to give the assignments.

Second—What did the students do? They met as small groups, outside of class, several times during that week to prepare their arguments. They tracked down research findings. They divided some of the labor. They argued among themselves, in the best sense, about what the evidence showed and how they could most effectively present it.

Third—What did this incredibly simple, low-tech idea, accomplish in terms of capitalizing on students' diversity?
- Each student, of any ethnic group, is working as a team member with other diverse colleagues.
- Each student is working with other students of his own ethnic group, around a substantive, educational, debatable topic, not in a pep rally format, but with a focus on evidence.

- Different members with the same ethnicity are in all three groups, arguing constructively for different perspectives.

What is the outcome? Students report, and I take their reports at face value, that this simple technique was particularly useful for capitalizing on, using, and strengthening the diversity among themselves, in what ultimately became a comfortable and enjoyable format for academic engagement and interaction. They also report that not always, but often, these academic projects spill over nicely into ongoing social interactions.

An example like this illustrates just one simple way that in-class instruction can be organized to capitalize on diversity. No doubt there are many other ways. And there are likely to be ideas that haven't occurred to me. But the big message is that surely the topic is worth pursuing.

Now, let's switch over to the "outside of class" question. The dilemma I pose is how do we really know if educating students in our remarkably different student body from 30 years ago is actually having all, or even some, of the positive effects that St. Augustine, John Stuart Mill, Adam Smith, and other people of good will had hoped for and expected?

To put it crassly, what concrete assessment evidence might we gather that would help us to answer this? I pose this question as a challenge. I am also posing it to my Assessment Seminars colleagues. Let me give just one example, again in the spirit of concreteness, that I invite the readers to interpret for themselves. Perhaps there are better ones, but this will serve as an illustration.

I posed this question about outside of class impact of diversity to the Assessment Seminars undergraduate student interviewers. I invited them to make suggestions. One suggestion immediately was unanimously accepted by our group as constructive, easy to implement, and a good starting point.

Here is what happened. I invited each member of the group to imagine being a *U.S. News and World Report* reporter writing an article about students from different backgrounds living together well, or not so well, at any college. What could they do to measure concretely how is it going? Several liked that question. They proposed elaborate student interviews. They proposed observational studies. Then one young man came up with what I consider a winning idea. Since I'm a statistician, it won my heart. He just said, "Well, each of us gets to choose our own roommates after freshman year. Most students live in groups of four. Suppose we could just find out what fraction of seniors choose freely, on their own, to live with one or more roommates from a different ethnic group at some time as an undergraduate. That would give a great first cut of concrete evidence about the quality of ethnic group relations and friendships on campus."

Well, this young man hit the jackpot. I had actually done a study about two years ago where I asked graduating seniors that exact question. I found that 76% of seniors had chosen to live, at some time, with at least one roommate from a different ethnic group. A second, follow-up survey found 78%. Whatever the precise fraction, to the second decimal place, that ballpark figure in the high seventies is a far higher proportion than I would have guessed. And it at least begins to tell us something about ethnic group relations on our campus. It is one bit of concrete data.

## CONCLUSION

I have a short conclusion to these remarks. Assessment at Harvard has led to some pretty solid substantive findings. It has changed how faculty teach and how students learn. And now it is leading us to confront some new challenges. Assessment certainly focuses our attention. I think maybe the big point here is that all of these examples, both those where our evidence and answers are already good and also those that are only starting up, share a few common underlying principles. One is the principle that a little bit of data can go a long way. For example, instead of simply asserting things about diversity on campus, as is so common on my campus and many others that I visit, I believe our effort to harness assessment techniques to search for ways to enhance it creates and reinforces a good-spirited culture of evidence-based exploration.

A second underlying principle is to focus on what students say and to take it seriously. What better way to honor students than to ask them about their experiences and then actually listen and make some changes in the way we organize courses and outside-of-class opportunities in response to what we learn from students? Students, in turn, are almost uniformly thrilled to have this opportunity to shape their institution, and they take it very seriously. Instead of accepting everything in their environment and just saying, "That's the way it is," any assessment process that invites students' responses in depth and takes those responses seriously generates an increasing focus among students to reflect on their own engagement with learning and to improve their own effectiveness as students.

Finally, to close, the reader will notice that several of my examples take assessment, which is a form of research, and show how teaching has changed because of that research. This is a time when so many of our colleagues, on so many campuses, are grappling with tensions be-tween teaching and research. It is a time when external constituencies, as well as our own students, are concerned about achieving a good balance. One of the most fulfilling aspects of doing this work is that we can actually harness assessment, a form of research, in the service of improving teaching and learning. Probably there are some elaborate words to capture this idea, like synergy, or feedback loops, or mutual reinforcement, or some other such snappy expression. To me, doing this work is simply a good thing. It is good for our campuses, good for our own effectiveness, and ultimately, most importantly, good for our students.

*PART III*

## Six

## EQUITY AND EXCELLENCE—STRANGE BEDFELLOWS?

### A CASE STUDY OF SOUTH AFRICAN HIGHER EDUCATION

MAMPHELA RAMPHELE

THE LINK between equity and excellence often evokes attacks from two diametrically opposed camps in the South African context. Those fearing an erosion of "standards" as a consequence of what they perceive as politically correct approaches to redress past inequalities in higher education charge that "You are prepared to sacrifice excellence on the alter of equity. If you want to develop [the University of Cape Town] as a center of excellence, then race and sex are irrelevant. At this stage in the development of South Africa, excellence and equity may be terms in contradiction."[1]

Those who have been excluded from higher educational opportunities in the past, and are anxious not to be shortchanged in the current transforming South Africa, contend that: "Focusing on excellence is a strategy for protecting existing privilege and elitism in higher education, which serves to perpetuate the exclusion of previously disadvantaged groups. Redress must be the focus now; excellence will come over time."[2]

The purpose of this paper is to explore whether there is a way of reconciling these opposing views in redesigning higher education policy in South Africa. The very future of the system depends on the extent to which this question is adequately addressed. The first part of the paper focuses on the political context of the debate, the second on the tensions between the nature of higher education and the pressure for redress, and the third part proposes a framework that identifies some of the tensions between equity and excellence and sketches a way forward for the South African higher education system in which equity and excellence would not only coexist but be seen as complementary.

TABLE 1

|  | South African Population | Bachelor's Degree | Master's Degree | Doctorate |
|---|---|---|---|---|
| White | 78% | 89% | 90% | 91% |
| Indian | 7% | 3% | 3% | 1% |
| Colored | 4% | 5% | 4% | 4% |
| African | 12% | 4% | 3% | 4% |
| Total | 100% | 100% | 100% | 100% |

Note: Figures are rounded up to the nearest percent; thus, the first two columns actually total 101%.

## THE POLITICAL CONTEXT

The most devastating aspect of the legacy of apartheid is the criminal neglect of human resource development particularly for Africans who constitute the majority of the South African population (approx. 75%). There are vast visible inequalities which stare one in the face in everyday life. Higher education reflects these inequalities most starkly.

A 1992 study by the Development Bank of South Africa showed that over a third of the total African population had no formal educational qualifications, and fewer than 1% (0.6%) had tertiary educational qualifications. In contrast, 25% of the total white population had tertiary educational qualifications and only 8% had no formal qualifications. In other words, of the total number of people in South Africa who had no formal education, 90% were African, 5% colored, 4% white, and 1% were Asian.

A review of formal educational qualifications in South Africa by racial classification undertaken by Bunting is shown in Tables 1–3 (Budlender and Sutherland 1995; Development Bank 1991). The figures in Table 1 translate into the profile of academic staff in institutions of higher learning in Table 2.

TABLE 2

|  | Instruction/ Research Staff | Administrative Staff | Service Staff | Total Staff |
|---|---|---|---|---|
| African | 7% | 12% | 71% | 30% |
| White | 87% | 71% | 4% | 54% |
| Colored | 3% | 11% | 22% | 12% |
| Indian | 3% | 7% | 3% | 4% |
| Total | 9971 | 11,413 | 10,479 | 31,863 |

TABLE 3

|  | F | M | T | % |
|---|---|---|---|---|
| Permanent academic staff | | | | |
| African | 8 | 20 | 28 | 4% |
| Colored | 5 | 8 | 13 | 3% |
| Indian | 2 | 6 | 8 | 2% |
| White | 137 | 477 | 614 | 92% |
| Unknown | 1 | 0 | 1 | — |
| Total | 153 | 511 | 664 | 100% |
| Temporary academic staff | 123 | 141 | 264 | |
| Grand total | 276 | 652 | 928 | |
| Permanent administrative, service, and support staff | | | | |
| African | 52 | 65 | 117 | 6% |
| Colored | 421 | 604 | 1025 | 53% |
| Indian | 12 | 13 | 25 | 2% |
| White | 549 | 210 | 759 | 39% |
| Unknown | 1 | 0 | 1 | — |
| Total | 1035 | 892 | 1927 | 100% |
| Temporary academic staff | 108 | 45 | 153 | |
| Grand total | 1143 | 937 | 2080 | |

Gender inequalities are less stark when viewed in global terms, but when desegregated by racial classification the position of African women is shocking. In 1992, 30% of academic staff at universities were women. This ranged from a low 22% at the universities of the Free State, Cape Town, and Stellenbosch, to a high 42% at UNISA.[3] Table 3 shows the position of University of Cape Town (UCT) academic staff profile in 1995.

The late 1980s and 1990s have brought about a surge in black student numbers into the higher education system. For example, at UCT the proportion of black students rose from about 15% of the total student body in 1984 to about 43% in 1995. This rise has created its own political crisis, given the less successful changes in staff profiles, which reflect that in 1994, 94% of teaching and research staff were white, the majority of whom were males (96% of all professors in 1995 were white males).[4]

The mismatch between significant black student access to higher education and a continuing dominance of teaching, research, and administrative positions by whites, particularly white males, is potentially explosive. There is a crisis of expectations in higher education in South Africa, which could plunge the system into chaos and ruin as has happened in many other postcolonial African countries (Saunders 1992).

The challenge is to manage the crisis in a creative way to enable South Africa to emerge as a winning nation, and thereby become an engine of growth for a continent in desperate need of success stories.

## TENSIONS BETWEEN THE NATURE OF THE BEAST AND POLITICAL IMPERATIVES

Higher education, particularly university education, is by its very nature elitist. Only a minority of citizens of even the most highly developed countries gain access to university education or have an interest in gaining such access. Open access to the university system cannot be a desirable social goal. There are alternative means of gaining skills that may add more value to the life of a given nation than university education.

In the South African context, where there was traditionally near universal access to university education for any white person who desired it, it is difficult to make a rational case for limiting access when opportunities for blacks are beginning to open up. The attachment to the status conferred by a university degree rather than an evaluation of the skills it confers has seen many university graduates gaining positions of power out of proportion to the value they may be adding to societal good.

An important added distortion to the university system is the impact of the post-1948 National Party's affirmative action program for Afrikaners, which further devalued the academic currency. Doctorates became easy to attain in Afrikaner institutions, which had no system of external examination nor a strong peer review system to ensure independent quality control within the university sector.

Many black students are expecting that what was made possible by the Nationalist Party for Afrikaners should be available to them under a government in which the African National Congress (ANC) commands a clear majority. Anything short of that is seen as a failure by the government to make good election promises made. Pressures for redress along the old Afrikaner route ignore a crucial difference between redressing inequity for a minority versus doing the same for a majority. Nationalist Party type affirmative action for Afrikaners ruined both the education system and the economy. It is mind boggling to contemplate what the impact of similar action on a massive scale would entail for South Africa's future. Is there a way out of this dilemma?

David Court's comments on the dismal state of most postcolonial universities are important to bear in mind. The pressure to embrace the concept of "developmental universities" put many universities under strain as they tried to be everything for everybody in the context of countries facing enormous developmental challenges. Court correctly concluded that universities must keep a focus on their missions as special types of institutions: "[T]he comparative advantage of African universities is not in leading community action or providing social services, but in fulfilling the university's traditional role of training professional and scientific manpower (sic), conducting research and providing an arena for the exchange of ideas" (Court 1980).

The nature of the university is best captured by Guy Neave, the editor of the *Quarterly Journal of the International Association of Universities:* "[U]niversities are essentially institutions which function in the long term. . . . they work to a time-scale that is largely independent of the rhythm imposed on politics by the ballot box or to delivery datelines to which industry claims to work. It is a time scale determined by the pace of individual disciplines, by rhythms of projects in hand and by the nature of the knowledge universities are entrusted with purveying and elaborating" (Neave 1995).

Living up to the ideal of what universities are all about is difficult in the South African situation where the "rhythm imposed on politics by the ballot box" has traditionally shaped universities and in many cases interfered with their focus on the long term. Dealing with that legacy is likely to impose its own constraints on the long-term vision. The legacy of the past generates tensions between the ideal and the reality.

## TENSIONS BETWEEN EQUITY AND EXCELLENCE

Equity is used in this paper to refer to equality tempered by contextual factors that allow for the fair though not necessarily uniform treatment of all people, ensuring that they have equal opportunities to develop their full potential. An equitable approach to social policy is based on the premise that talent is randomly distributed in society, and its development depends on access to opportunities that was constrained for those sectors of society who are currently underrepresented in the higher levels of human resource profiles. Thus, in the South African case, the underrepresentation of black people in academia can be directly attributed to the denial of opportunities for them to realize their full potential. The same can be said for women. An equity policy framework in higher education would thus have to take race and gender as important contextual factors in approaching student and staff development. Failure to do so may lead to further inequities. Equal treatment of unequals in social policy terms may produce greater inequity.

But there are various levels at which equity in the university system applies. There are equity considerations at the individual level. How one treats an individual person in relation to another has to be subjected to an equity lens. For example, equitable treatment of an individual black student will depend on the student's academic ability, social class position, gender, and so on. Whereas categories of black students may on the whole be treated equitably, ignoring the class differences between them or the constraints of gender on some could lead to inequity. Equity in the South African sense also applies to both inter- and intrainstitutional levels. The differentiation between institutions is a real one given the history of higher education. Major inequities exist between those institutions historically set aside for black people and others. The burden of disadvantage in terms of requisite human resource development capacity and infrastructure has fallen on historically black institutions. Achieving equity within the higher education system is a major challenge.

Excellence is used here to refer to striving for performance at a level that exceeds the ordinary. It also implies a constant focus on performance at higher levels than those attained to date. Excellence in academia entails originality of mind, creativity, and a track record that can stand the test of time in world-class terms and not being satisfied with being the best in a given limited contest. It has also been referred to as striving to "do ordinary things extraordinarily well" (Wallace Mgoqi[5]).

The legacy of apartheid has created tensions between equity and excellence in a number of important ways. First, criteria for measuring excellence in performance have become a matter of dispute, given that the skills and the power to set socioeconomic standards are currently monopolized by the white minority. There is a body of opinion that questions the validity of the standards by which performance is judged. For example, one could question the excellence of professional training that prepares young people for work in a multilingual society that does not insist on or create opportunities for them to develop language competence beyond their own mother tongue. This applies particularly to white South Africans who are likely to be competent at the very best only in the two traditional official languages, Afrikaans and English.

Second, the lack of access to opportunity has made the striving for excellence difficult. However hard one may try to excel in higher education, the shaky foundation inherited from poor home socioeconomic conditions, inadequate schooling, and the lack of preparation for critical scholarship make excellence an unattainable goal for the majority of black people. A focus on excellence is thus seen as one that automatically excludes the disadvantaged. For example, however hard an African student from a disadvantaged educational background at UCT works, the chances of gaining a first class or honors pass are slim.

Third, racism and prejudice continue to influence perceptions in South Africa. There is a tendency by many whites to assume that the very presence of blacks in higher education is testimony that standards of performance have fallen. Such racist notions use standards as a metaphor for exclusivity. The racist view holds that only white people, particularly white males, have the capacity to attain acceptable levels of performance and to excel. For example, critics of policies for increased access to university education for black students charge that the acceptance of African students who are judged to have the potential to succeed despite lower matriculation scores than those generally accepted from other students from better educational backgrounds automatically means a lowering of standards. They pay scant attention to the importance of distinguishing between entry and exit standards. The latter are more important as measures of performance of the university system. Interestingly, some of the strongest critics of broadening access to university education are themselves beneficiaries of the post-World War II access policies that allowed returning veterans to enter university without matriculation certificates. The underlying assumption seems to be that the white male status was enough to guarantee high standards.

Apartheid has in a sense delegitimated the very notion of excellence in the minds of a significant number of those who were excluded from opportunities to succeed. How is the higher education system to deal with this legacy?

## A Framework for Tackling Tensions Between Equity and Excellence

The University of Cape Town for over a decade has been pursuing a transformation process to change both the student and staff profiles from the legacy of a predominance of white males. The transformation process was further sharpened in 1991 around a framework that has three foci:

- Increasing access
- Promoting personal development and high performance
- Changing the institutional culture into a more inclusive one

Increasing access has two components: student and staff. There has been greater success in significantly changing the student profile than has been the case for staff. The reasons for the difference in success rates is outlined later in the text.

## Student Access

The success of the change in student profiles results from the following policy interventions: the admission policy, financial aid, and student housing. UCT admission policy has two thrusts:

- The identification and attraction of the best students irrespective of color, gender, or educational background as measured by their previous educational performance at school or another tertiary educational institution. Our records show that we consistently attract a large share of students from all over the country with A and B aggregates in their matriculation examinations.
- The identification of the potential to succeed among those applicants who have not had the educational experience to provide them with an opportunity to demonstrate their abilities. This has led to the development of the Alternative Admissions Research Project (AARP). AARP has developed tools to test applicants' ability in mathematics and English, which have been shown to correlate fairly well with the potential to succeed at UCT. The tools are being continually refined, and have been adapted for use by other universities.

Financial aid is intended to ensure that students with the potential to succeed are not excluded from opportunities because of poverty. UCT has an annual financial aid budget of about $8.6 million, of which $2 million is allocated from the general operating budget. Allocations of a combination of loans and grants are made by the Financial Aid committee, which has both staff and students, using a stringent means test. Additional resources are made available to needy students in the form of part-time jobs.

UCT also has merit entrance scholarships to attract high-performing students. Given the shortage of skills in the science and technology area, more emphasis is placed on this sector in awarding merit scholarships.

Student housing is an important part of UCT access policies to ensure that students live in an environment that promotes academic endeavor. In 1984 only 19% of the student body was in residence, 94% of whom were white, compared to 30% in 1994 of whom 65% are African. The investment in the student housing budget is considerable.

The Academic Development Program (ADP) is aimed at ensuring that students who have gained access to UCT succeed and excel. The ADP has a number of foci:

- Creating a supportive environment for students to learn how to learn. This is crucial, given the tendency within the entire education system to promote rote learning rather than critical enquiry. This problem is particularly marked among those coming from schools that were set aside for Africans by the apartheid system, which continue to underperform. A lot of work is done to help UCT academics learn to teach more effectively in a more interactive way.

- Curriculum reform and restructuring to ensure that differently prepared students enter courses at the right level, where necessary foundation courses are created to help underprepared students gain the necessary competencies before moving on. In some cases courses are extended by six months to a year to allow time for the consolidation of a more solid foundation.
- Providing support for the mastering of specific skills in the form of the Writing Centre and the Professional Communications Unit is crucial to the pursuit of excellence. Students are encouraged to drop in and get help, and even high performers are assisted in becoming more proficient.

## Staff Access

Staff access has shown little success in spite of the adoption of the Equal Opportunity Employment Policy in 1991 by both Senate and Council. The policy makes provision for affirmative action to be taken in the recruitment of staff to ensure that black people and women are targeted. The staff remains largely white and male. Reasons for failure are numerous:

- The pool of available people with the requisite skills is very limited — another legacy of apartheid. In 1990, 91% of South Africans with doctorates and 90% with master's degrees were whites, compared to 4 and 3% Africans with similar qualifications.
- Academic salaries militate against the attraction and retention of the few available black people. Their scarcity tends to push up their market price. The opening of opportunities in government and the private sector has created a competitive environment in which academic institutions are the losers. Academic salaries lag 12% behind those in the private and public sector.
- The long career path to the top in academia puts a limit to the pace of change in the staff profiles. Academics are like oak trees in that they take a long time to mature.

## STAFF DEVELOPMENT

The Equal Opportunity Employment Policy hinges on two important thrusts:

1. The University of Cape Town will adhere without exception to a policy of searching thoroughly for good applicants in respect of all its vacancies and of appointing, in every case in the context of a particular post, only the person who can be expected to make the greatest contribution to the work and reputation of the University.

2. The University will carry out affirmative action in the specific sense of doing everything in its power to help prepare black persons and women to become equal competitors for every post on its establishment.

Given the problems outlined above, a number of initiatives have been taken to address them:

- The appointment of an Equal Opportunity Officer, and the specific assignment of executive responsibility for the advancement of black persons and women at UCT to a Deputy Vice Chancellor.
- The creation of master's, doctoral, and postdoctoral fellowships to increase the number of black postgraduate students who have the potential to embark on an academic career.
- The introduction of vacation employment projects in academic departments, specifically to develop the academic and research skills of black students.
- The creation of one-year internships to prepare young graduates for the world of work so that they can have the kind of exposure that enables them to develop the skills for negotiating recruitment, selection, placement, and social relations that are part of the employment scene.
- The creation of three-year contract developmental posts to give very good black and/or women candidates opportunities for advancing their academic careers. Such candidates are part of the "growing our own timber" program, which is aimed at enlarging the pool of good academics. Beneficiaries come to the program via two routes. First, those candidates who were unsuccessful candidates for particular posts but were judged by the selection committees to have good potential as future academics. Second, each department is encouraged to identify high flyers from their own senior post graduate students and to nurture and encourage them to apply for the annually allotted posts to each Faculty where they compete with their peers for limited developmental three-year posts.

The success of the above measures will depend on the commitment of heads of departments and deans to support younger academics, as well as the determination of the persons concerned to succeed. Institutional support provides the environment for success, but cannot guarantee success. Each individual remains personally responsible for successful performance.

Similar steps are being taken in the administrative arena to increase the pace of change in the staff profiles. The internship program is specifically geared to "growing our own administrative timber." It should be easier to make progress in this area, but initial assessments are not encouraging. The commitment from senior staff to supporting interns, on one hand, and determination of juniors to succeed is not yet at the level it should be.

## CHANGING THE INSTITUTIONAL CULTURE

Part of the nature of the beast is that university education is embedded in an institutional cultural framework that is the result of complex processes that are shaped by the participants within a given institution and reflects power relations within a given institution. The extent to which one shapes the cultural milieu of any institution into which one enters is shaped to a large extent by the power position one holds within it. It is often asserted that university education is intended for self-starters who are able to cope with being thrown in at the deep end and being able to swim. Those who sink are assumed not to have what it takes to make it. The ability to swim is often determined by subtle factors.

First, the identification with, or alienation from, the culture of any institution should be taken into account. The swim or sink approach often obscures the existence of "lifeboats" that some new entrants come with, given their family and other networks that prepare them for their entry. Second, the "swimming pool" is often designed with certain body types in mind, thus predisposing others to failure unless they can crack the code that leads to success. For example, women who have to divide their time between academia and domestic responsibilities have a more difficult and slower path to the top than their male counterparts whose domestic needs are more often than not taken care of by the women in their lives. Similarly, black graduate students tend to come from an older age cohort, bringing with them family responsibilities that weigh them down.

Third, the standards by which one judges success or failure to swim is sometimes colored by the cultural lens one is using to examine performance. There is often little dispute in assessing performance in technical disciplines such as mathematics and science, whereas in the humanities and social sciences a measure of subjectivity can and does intrude. Second-language English speakers are in some cases unfairly assessed because of their nontraditional accents or writing styles which color the substance of their academic knowledge. It takes a conscious effort on the part of academics to go beyond the coloring and assess the substance. The discomfort some may feel with people who do not look like them or whose artistic expression is out of the mainstream can also be a factor in rating performance.

The creation of a supportive environment to promote excellence includes paying careful attention to the cultural climate within a given institution. The legacy of racism and sexism has had an impact on the relationships between black and white people, as well as on those between women and men. Racism and sexism have a profound impact on the pecking order of intrainstitutional relations. Ignoring the impact of institutional culture in setting the tone for social and academic relations has serious consequences for excellence. One cannot expect new entrants at a given institution to simply fit into an existing culture without doing harm to their sense of self.

Institutional culture has overt and covert manifestations. Overt ones relate to language in all its manifestations, such as tone, accent, metaphors, and so on; symbols of success; and rituals and ceremonies, including what is to be celebrated and what form such celebrations should take. The naming of important edifices and the identification of heroes create the symbolic framework of a given institution. Graduation ceremonies are at the heart of the enactment of the drama and symbolism of academic social relations and the celebration of excellence at the end of the academic year.

Covert manifestations are more difficult to pin down. "The way things happen here" is often an intangible set of norms and conventions that have become part of the fabric of social relationships and that are so deeply ingrained that they often defy detailed description. What is important is not a preoccupation with hidden assumptions, but a sensitivity to the possibility of not being able to hear or be heard, understand and be understood, perceive and be perceived in ways that one would ordinarily take for granted.

For example, a pilot study conducted by the Equal Opportunity Project of the UCT on the learning environment students experience in selected classes suggests that black and white students often differ in their perceptions and interpretations of the same classroom situation. A lecturer who is inattentive or unenthusiastic in teaching is often seen as such by white students, whereas some black students may perceive the lecturer's attitude as being motivated by racism and/or personally directed against them. So, too, the response of women students to lecturers may be mediated by their perceptions of sexism in the person concerned, which may or may not have been intended.

UCT has taken active steps to address institutional cultural issues:

- Adoption of policies against sexual and racial harassment, with mechanisms to deal with infringements

- Adoption of general antidiscrimination measures to ensure that all persons are protected from intolerant behavior and have recourse wherever they feel wronged.
- The establishment of a Naming, Ritual and Ceremonies Committee to examine any complaints or suggestions about changes to the symbols, rituals, and ceremonies of the University. Our graduation ceremonies have undergone changes that have made them more spontaneous and joyous occasions, while still retaining the sense of pomp and ceremony that are the core of these moments in the academic calendar.

## The Unanswered Questions

UCT's model of transformation attempts to balance the imperatives of equity and excellence, but there are many unanswered questions. The National Commission on Higher Education is currently drawing up a report that is intended to lay the foundation for restructuring higher education nationally. Some of the problems that UCT faces at the micro level have a national dimension, others are peculiar to a university focusing on research, and still others are essentially national problems with local institutional manifestations. Finally, some of the problems have resonance beyond national borders, offering both opportunities and threats to international scholarship.

### MICROLEVEL PROBLEMS

A research university has great difficulties adjusting to opening opportunities in an educational environment that does not promote excellence. UCT has responded to the legacy of apartheid education by using its research skills to experiment with models of identifying potential, selection, and academic development. There are major areas of success in that 90% of students from underprivileged backgrounds meet the readmissions criteria, 65% proceed to next level of study (compared to 85% of first time entering white students), and the majority of these students graduate. UCT has contributed a third of the black engineering graduates in the country over the last five years or so. It also makes other major contributions to the science and technology areas essential to South Africa's success as an international player in both the teaching and research through the training of master's and doctoral students.

Problems at this level are numerous, but only a few will be highlighted. First, there is the difficulty of motivating researchers who are hard-pressed for time to devote extra time for teaching and mentoring both undergraduate and postgraduates who are underprepared. Although excellence in teaching is recognized and honored, productivity in research remains a more visible and reliable measure of excellence.

Second, how does one enforce behavioral change in terms of curriculum changes without infringing on the "academic freedom" of individual academics? After all, the right to define what to teach and who to teach are fundamental tenants of academic freedom. Those who are now being asked to change their teaching styles could argue with some success that their job contracts were entered into with an entirely different understanding of the job content, and that they have a right to negotiate the redefinition of their job descriptions.

Third, how does one ensure compliance with the spirit of the Equal Opportunity Employment Policy in the administrative area where networks have traditionally largely governed who gets employed at UCT? Sabotaging new entrants without being caught is fairly easy in any given institution. One simply needs to play the game by the rules and let the new person falter from want of that extra helping hand of support.

Fourth, how does one manage change in institutional culture in an institution where there are forces pulling in different directions? The traditionalists are fearful of change and the unknown into which it is likely to throw them, whereas new entrants are impatient and push for a faster pace of change. The combination of fear, anger, and resentment more often than not reinforces existing prejudices and further bedevils relationships.

Fifth, tenure as part of the tradition that has shaped employment contracts in academic institutions makes change in the staff profiles very difficult. A study of the age profile of academics in South Africa indicated a predominance of the 25–55 age group. This type of national staff profile leaves little room for changing the composition of the staff, which is currently predominantly white and male. In the UCT case we have opted for a policy option that takes the long-term view and optimizes the presence of mature white male senior academics as the strong branches around which one grows the younger cadre. The problem of nonproductive tenured staff remains a difficult one to deal with. Ideally, one should be pruning the academic tree and getting rid of deadwood and making room for young shoots. But deadwood has a tendency to hang on.

But how palatable is a gradualist policy at the national level where the pace of change is much more likely to be influenced by the rhythm of the politics of the ballot box? It remains to be seen whether politicians would impose a more rapid change process, and if so how such a process would be designed to balance equity with excellence.

Sixth, the adoption of policies against undesirable forms of behavioral patterns does not in itself stop such behaviors. The enforcement of policies such as antiharassment in terms of both sexism and racism is complex, bordering as it does on the infringement of the rights of adults to enter into relationships of their choice in the manner they see fit. High-profile cases in the United States of individuals suing institutions for violating their basic rights attest to the difficulties that policy makers face.

Skillful top management and a clear vision of an equitable prosperous future are key to success. Successful academic leadership rests on the principle of management by conversation. Hierarchical relationships hide the power that resides in ordinary academics, particularly professors and deans who can make or break a university leader who rides roughshod over them. But there is also the need to manage the pressure for change from the ranks of students and workers. They need to be assured that their aspirations are being taken into account, and that the management system allows them meaningful participation. It is not easy to keep the balance.

## National Challenges

Promoting equity and excellence in the higher education system nationally is likely to prove difficult given the tensions alluded to. First, how is the government going to succeed in resisting the pressure for open access to higher education? Some provincial governments that did not inherit universities from the apartheid era are demanding that they should be given the opportunity to establish such institutions. South Africa has 21 universities—far too many for its level of development and out of proportion to the needs within the system. Apartheid distorted higher education with the result that there are three university students for each technikon one instead of the other way round as is the case in successfully industrialized countries such as Germany. But most of the members of the new elite who are making these demands have no other yardstick to judge reality by. The practices of the previous regime, which have largely been misguided, are often cited by the new elites as policy options.

Is the government going to have the courage to close down some of the universities that cannot demonstrate a capacity for excellence in either teaching or research and convert them into technikons, which would produce the sorely needed technologically skilled personnel to contribute to economic growth? Or is there going to be a capacity-building program to support quality teaching and learning in those universities that are struggling with the legacy of the past?

The Technical Committee on Staff Access and Development has recommended that such a Human Resource Development Unit be set up in the National Ministry of Education to help support struggling institutions to clarify their missions to develop the capacity to add value to the higher education system in line with their missions. But what if there is no potential for success in a given institution? The devastating impact of apartheid has bred demotivated staff who in some cases have survived through cheating the system, which they saw as illegitimate. The corruption that results from that adaptive behavioral pattern has become a way of life for some. How does one deal with such people?

Second, balancing the needs of an elitist university education with those of a poorly resourced school system is difficult. South Africa spends 23% of its gross domestic product on education, of which 25% goes to higher education. It is unlikely that the slice of the cake will be increased. But who is to compensate universities for the role they have to play to deal with the legacy of the past such as the costs incurred in establishing and running bridging programs? In 1994 alone the ADP at UCT had an operating budget of $1.6 million, most of which the University had to fund from sponsorships sought in an aggressive fundraising drive. For the foreseeable future these programs will continue to underpin the quest for excellence and should, in the view of many of us, be funded by government as part of special grants until the school system begins to graduate better-prepared students who can interface with the university system at an appropriate level.

Third, there is also a dilemma in balancing the needs of individuals versus those of a larger cohort of individuals. To what extent can society support individuals who fail to perform, given the opportunity costs relating to those not yet afforded a chance to demonstrate their ability to succeed? The pressure from vocal students often drowns the voices of reason in this regard. Higher education is by its very nature a scarce resource that cannot be regarded as a right. The failure to take advantage of the given opportunity has serious consequences for all concerned. Individuals who have little chance of success can be kept within the system only at the expense of others waiting in the queue.

Fourth, how does the government intervene in higher education to promote equity without violating academic freedom? A carefully negotiated financial leverage policy that rewards universities that pursue equity and excellence while penalizing those who deliberately continue the legacy of the past could promote change toward more desirable policies. Greater emphasis on the carrot than the stick is more likely to lead to greater success. Significant resources would need to be invested in helping institutions to build capacity to meet national goals. But there is a real danger of the government violating institutional autonomy and academic freedom in pursuit of short-term political objectives. What safe-guards can society put in place in this regard?

There are no easy answers. Tough decisions will have to be made. The politically correct route out of the many dilemmas outlined above would be an inappropriate and expensive policy choice. University education has to retain its long-term focus, otherwise it would run the risk of mortgaging the future. Equity and excellence are inseparable in the higher educational environment of changing South Africa. The challenge is to manage the inevitable tensions between the two.

## NOTES

1. Quotations from a letter from a UCT alumnus following the announcement of my appointment as the new Vice Chancellor.

2. Views of some black students in private and public discussions.

3. Most of the statistics in this paper have their origin in a report by Budlender and Sutherland (1995) commissioned by Technical Committee 3 of the National Commission of Higher Education, which focused on Staff Access and Development.

4. Source of data is the UCT booklet entitled *The Transformation of the University of Cape Town 1984–1994: A Decade of Change* and an update of statistics produced at the beginning of 1996.

5. Wallace Mgoqi is an attorney-at-law currently heading the Land Restitution Commission.

## REFERENCES

Budlender, D., and C. Sutherland. 1995. "A Report on Staff Access and Development for the Technical Committee of the National Commission of Higher Education."

Court, D. 1980. "The Developmental Ideal in Higher Education: The Experience of Kenya and Tanzania Higher Education."

Development Bank. 1991. Cited in I. Bunting. 1994. *A Legacy of Inequality of Higher Education in South Africa.* Cape Town: UCT Press.

Neave, G. 1995. *Quarterly Journal of the International Association of Universities* 8(4).

Saunders, S. J. 1992. "Access to and Quality in Higher Education: A Comparative Study." Unpublished, Cape Town.

# Seven

## FACING THE DILEMMAS OF DIFFERENCE

*COMMENTS ON THE ESSAY BY MAMPHELA RAMPHELE*

RANDALL KENNEDY

HOW SHOULD AUTHORITIES address the consequences of racial oppression in societies engaged in transforming themselves from pigmentocracies into multiracial democracies? More specifically, how should authorities deal with the fact that racial exploitation often diminishes the skills of those who have been oppressed, making many of them less capable in important respects than those who have benefited from racial privilege? These are the broad questions upon which Mamphela Ramphele sheds light in her discussion of reforms in postapartheid South Africa. I shall address an aspect of these questions in the context of the affirmative action debate in the United States, drawing for inspiration upon the Vice Chancellor's paper. In particular, I shall concern myself with problems posed by openly and fully acknowledging the damage that has been inflicted upon American blacks by slavery, segregation, and current invidious racial discriminations. This damage includes restricted access to education and the attendant far-reaching losses stemming from such deprivations — losses that are reflected, for instance, by test scores and other indicia of skill and knowledge that often reveal large gaps between whites and blacks.

On the other hand, to acknowledge this damage and the difference it makes to present levels of skill and knowledge risks (1) legitimating myths of racial inferiority and (2) conceding the actuality of disabilities that some people will seize upon as a justification for policies that would continue to perpetuate racial inequalities. On the other hand, to disregard the damage and the difference it makes risks (1) obscuring deficiencies that are in need of remedy and (2) misallocating human resources; any society will suffer if it goes far toward ignoring distinctions between higher as opposed to lower levels of knowledge and skill. Martha Minow has given this dilemma a name — she calls it the dilemma of difference — and shown that variants of it shadow debates over treatment of gender, language, physical and mental disability, and other markers deemed to be socially significant. To satisfactorily address the dilemma of difference in the context of black–white conflict in the United States requires, among other things, an unflinching appreciation of the many ways in which both those who have been privileged and those who have been victimized will often try to escape reckoning with the full costs of racial oppression.

Those who have been beneficiaries of racial oppression often ignore or minimize its consequences. They act as if the formal cessation of invidious racial discrimination immediately creates a society in which all members are now on the same footing, a society in which it is unnecessary (not to mention unfair) to offer special policies to aid the victims of the former pigmentocracy. A striking but neglected illustration of this tendency was the presidential veto of the first federal civil rights law in the United States, the legislation that ultimately became the Civil Rights Act of 1866. This act proposed to extend citizenship immediately to all persons born in the United States and to prohibit states from treating any individuals differently than whites in terms of the rules governing contracts or the acquisition of property. President Andrew Johnson vetoed the legislation on grounds that will sound hauntingly familiar to anyone that has paid attention to struggles over civil rights in the United States during the past 50 years. Writing only three months after the constitutional abolition of slavery, President Johnson objected to the civil rights act as "special legislation" that would give "discriminating protection" to blacks insofar as it would "establish for the security of the colored race safeguards which go infinitely beyond any that the (federal government) has ever provided for the white race." In a certain limited sense, President Johnson was correct: The federal government had never before limited the power of states to discriminate against their white citizens and residents. Of course, whites had never been subjected to racial slavery and other forms of racial exploitation and so, for them, the need for such legislation had never arisen. This rather basic fact, however, did not stop President Johnson from asserting, ridiculously, that the Civil Rights Act represented legislation that "operate[d] in favor of the colored and against the white race."

President Johnson also asserted, moreover, that the civil rights bill was "fraught with evil" because it would wrongly intrude upon a situation in which, in the aftermath of slavery and absent any governmental intervention, blacks and whites would now have "equal power" in settling the terms of their interactions in employment and other markets. Johnson's perspective minimized egregiously the baleful consequences of slavery (illiteracy, inexperience in business, politics, and other spheres of activity, lack of access to capital, etc.) and the tendency of such consequences to perpetuate inequalities long into the future.

Unfortunately, the minimization expressed by President Johnson's (fortunately overridden) veto has not been idiosyncratic. It has emerged time and again when policy makers, academics, journalists, and other influential persons have underestimated the tenaciousness with which racial oppression retards the pace of change even in environments in which reform has attracted powerful support. Often ill-motivated impatience animates this minimization. This was so with President Johnson and the other enemies of America's First Reconstruction. Sometimes, though, minimization stems from fears felt by friends of change who are afraid that offering special solicitude for oppressed groups will stigmatize them. The great runaway slave and abolitionist Frederick Douglass initially objected to the special channeling of federal aid to the former slaves on precisely these grounds.

In the twentieth century, we have seen a replication of these patterns. Ideological descendants of Andrew Johnson have downplayed the damage wrought by segregation in order to minimize the compensatory bill. Ideological descendants of Frederick Douglass have downplayed the damage wrought by segregation to minimize potentially stigmatizing assertions of Negro incapacity.

Just as both enemies and friends of racial egalitarianism have minimized the extent to which racial oppression actually diminishes the abilities of its victims, so, too, have enemies and friends emphasized, and indeed exaggerated, the damage inflicted by past racial wrongs. Friends have done so to build support for compensatory or remedial affirmative action programs. By contrast, enemies of racial egalitarianism have done so to drive home the point that, whatever the cause, many blacks are in fact inferior to whites in terms of skills, training, and knowledge. President Johnson's veto message is again instructive. One of the grounds on which he objected to granting immediate citizenship to American-born blacks was that, in his view, slavery had deprived them of the background needed for good, responsible citizenship.

What is one to make of these strategic deployments of interpretations of the extent to which oppressed people have been damaged by wrongs inflicted upon them? One important lesson is that a given interpretation can be deployed for diametrically opposed purposes and on behalf of diametrically opposed policies. This lesson is important because two many people believe that facts (real or perceived) dictate policy. This is not so. Facts do not dictate a society's response to them. *Values* dictate the response. Values dictate that a group's victimization will elicit respectful solicitude, contemptuous pity, irrelevant indifference, or some other response.

In *Contempt & Pity: Social Policy and the Image of the Damaged Black Psyche, 1880–1996* (Chapel Hill: Universtiy of North Carolina Press, 1997), Darryl Michael Scott chronicles changing perceptions of the Negro, particularly the way that academics and policy makers have attempted to manipulate portrayals of the group's debilities, portrayals that Scott terms "damage imagery." He shows convincingly that damage imagery has been put to propagandistic use by racial aristocrats as well as racial egalitarians. "Often playing on white contempt towards blacks," Scott observes, "racial conservatives have sought to use findings of black pathology to justify exclusionary policies and to explain the dire conditions under which many black people live." By contrast, Scott notes, racial liberals, "often seeking to manipulate white pity . . . have used damage imagery primarily to justify policies of inclusion and rehabilitation."

Scott argues that, given current prevailing attitudes, it is a mistake to think that invoking damage imagery will succeed is eliciting a greater degree of solicitude for and investment in racial minorities. Now, he maintains, invoking damage imagery is more likely to trigger fear, contempt, and exclusion than pity, sympathy, and inclusion.

There is, unfortunately, considerable validity to Scott's sobering assessment. Recognizing this, some racial egalitarians deny or even suppress information that may reflect poorly on the racial reputation of African-Americans. This reaction is by no means new. Early in the twentieth century, W.E.B. Du Bois urged novelists, movie makers, social scientists, and other purveyors of images to forgo portraying blacks in ways that would confirm the negative stereotypes that largely defined them in the public mind. Du Bois put special pressure on black intellectuals and artists to present "best foot forward" imagery that would propagandize on behalf of the Negro masses. It should be noted, too, that blacks are not the only racial or ethnic group that has shown an acute attentiveness to its collective reputation. Many Jewish-Americans, Italian-Americans, and Asian-Americans have also engaged in robust efforts to discourage their group's defamation. Blacks, however, have suffered from a uniquely effective and long-lasting campaign of stigmatization that has added a special urgency to countervailing efforts.

It is right, of course, to oppose group vilification. It is wrong, however, to allow one's anxiety about a group's reputation to become the basis for an overheated defensiveness that prompts the ignoring or even suppressing of significant social facts. Some people of my orientation— the party of racial egalitarianism—have succumbed to that syndrome. The symptoms include certain strategies of argumentation deployed in debates over affirmative action. I will focus on two: a strategy of suppression and a strategy of denial.

The strategy of suppression has surfaced on several highly publicized occasions during the past few years when proponents of affirmative action have taken punitive action against virtually anyone revealing sizable differences between the credentials of students admitted to universities under conventional standards of admission and the credentials of students admitted pursuant to affirmative action programs. There are a variety of problems with this reaction. One is that it is profoundly counterproductive politically. American political culture is remarkably tolerant of various perceived sins and failings. It is notably intolerant, however, of cover-ups. Among the perceptions that have eroded popular support for affirmative action is the sense, felt by many, that its proponents are hiding or suppressing pertinent information, that they are failing to level with the public, that they are purposefully obscuring the aims, means, justifications, and costs of the programs they support.

The strategy of denial has emerged when proponents of affirmative action here argued that, actually, there exists no real issue of racial "preference" involved in assessing programs under which, for racial reasons, black applicants are selected over white applicants with superior conventional credentials. The argument takes two forms. One is that there is no real preference because the "extra" points awarded to black candidates only serves to fairly level the playing field. The argument runs that these putatively extra points merely counteract invidious racial discriminations that black candidates confront throughout their dealings in American society, including their dealings with racially biased tests and other dubious aspects of established schemes of recruitment, selection, and promotion. A second form of this argument is that the points awarded to black candidates pursuant to affirmative action are not really "extra" but an acknowledgment of the heretofore unrecognized benefit that racial minorities bring to institutions, including colleges and universities. This benefit, this heretofore unrecognized merit, is now often referred to as "diversity."

There is some force to both of these arguments. Given the headwinds that most blacks confront there is a rough basis of crediting a black American's accomplishment — say, a score of 90 on a standardized test — more than the identical accomplishment of a white American. Moreover, without embracing the fatuous notion that race alone determines opinion or sensibility, one can argue convincingly that the quality of educational and other institutions is adversely effected by the absence of certain highly noticeable groups in American society, particularly blacks.

The problem with these arguments is not that they are without basis. It is that they cannot bear the weight that they are asked to bear. Alone they do not provide a credible explanation or justification for the bulk of what constitutes affirmative action in practice. Affirmative action as actually practiced is primarily animated by considerations of compensatory and distributive justice: (1) The idea that special solicitude for blacks is appropriate because of the special wrongs to which they have been subjected and (2) the idea that America's multiracial democracy requires in substantial measure the presence of all major subgroups in the influential institutions of the society. Supporters of these ideas find them sufficiently weighty to justify assessing black applicants according to less exacting — hence less exclusionary — criteria than white applicants. What cannot honestly or reasonably be denied is that a necessary corollary to the application of less exacting standards is less qualified admittees. This does not mean unqualified admittees. It does mean that affirmative action necessarily entails a certain amount of real preference.

I noted above that some supporters of affirmative action contend that criteria that reflect racially disparate levels of ability or knowledge indicate deficiencies in lower-ranking applicants. This charge is undoubtedly valid in some instances. But in the context of American higher education this charge is more likely to be part of the strategy of denial, a way of avoiding the problem posed by *real* gaps as opposed to biased testing. I say this, in part, because of the exclusive focus on demographic outcomes shown by many who voice the charge under discussion. If this charge were truly aimed at the accuracy of testing, then the racial outcome of the test would not be determinative in assessing its propriety. An outcome that adversely affects disproportionately large numbers of blacks in the competition for positions should raise eyebrows and prompt questioning. But if, after investigation, the conclusion is reached that the selection scheme at issue accurately measures skills and knowledge properly expected by an institution, it should then be acknowledged that the problem resides not with the criteria but with the performance of lower-ranking applicants. One gets the impression that with many critics of established schemes of selection, the real concern is not the mode of evaluation but solely the racial demographics of outcomes.

I concede again that enemies of racial egalitarianism will use signs of relative weakness in the performance of black candidates *against* the cause of needed reform. As we have seen, though, facts can be spun to support a wide, indeed conflicting, array of policies. Those intent upon imposing or perpetuating unfair conditions will attempt to do so no matter what facts are available. With that point in mind, I urge the party of egalitarianism to be unafraid of any real facts, including those that indicate the relative weakness of black students seeking places in higher education. It is important to know about weaknesses to remedy them. It is important, moreover, to defend the idea of meritocracy, even if one decides for good reason to deviate in limited circumstances from its norms. The importance of doing so stems from the need of any modern, competitive society to differentiate performances that are bad, good, or excellent. When a society loses the willingness or ability to make such distinctions, when the notion prevails that merit is simply a myth, pathetic decline is certain to follow.

The party of racial egalitarianism in the United States would do well to embrace the ethos that infuses Vice Chancellor Ramphele's paper. She is appropriately harsh in her analysis of apartheid, noting that it produced a "criminal neglect" of human resources, which is also true, of course, of American slavery and segregation. She is attentive to the numerous, subtle ways in which a regime of racial privilege can perpetuate its baleful effects after its formal abolition. She demonstrates sensitivity to and impatience with the impediments that confront those who have long been victimized by racial oppression.

Vice Chancellor Ramphele, however, is also appropriately unsentimental in her stance toward the condition and aspirations of blacks recently emancipated from pigmentocracy. She recognizes that racial oppression imposes real disabilities upon its victims, that there is no good reason to be ashamed of these disabilities, and that, to the contrary, there is every good reason to identify and remedy them. She recognizes that her fellow blacks understandably desire to occupy *now* the most prestigious and selective positions in higher education. Yet she insists on preventing immediate, parochial ambitions from spoiling the long-range prospects for South African higher education, embracing rightly the belief that universities are managed best when they are managed with the long-term interest of society foremost in mind, even if this means slowing down somewhat the pace of reform. Cautioning that the fall of apartheid has occasioned "a crisis of expectations . . . which could plunge the system [of higher education] into chaos and ruin," she insists upon managing this crisis "in a creative way to enable South Africa to emerge as a winning nation." Part of the creative management she offers, ironically, is a strong endorsement of meritocratic ideals. Noting that undisciplined affirmative action for Afrikaaners under apartheid "ruined both the education system and the economy," she eschews replicating such a system for the benefit of blacks. As she stated on a different occasion, the victims of racial oppression did not struggle merely to have equal or even preferential access to declining mediocrity.

The struggle for racial justice in South Africa has bequeathed to the world an inspiring lesson in courageous, diligent resistance to tyranny. Vice Chancellor Ramphele's paper, reflecting as it does upon insights into the requirements of higher education, promises to bequeath to the world an instructive lesson in righting wrongs while preserving what is best in existing institutions.

# Eight

## PROBLEMATICS OF AFFIRMATIVE ACTION

### A VIEW FROM CALIFORNIA

Neil J. Smelser

### Affirmative Action in Historical Context

FROM COLONIAL TIMES—and consolidated in the moment of constitutional founding—American society has found its legitimacy in four central cultural values: individual liberty and freedom, democracy, progress manifested in mastery of nature and economic expansion, and equality of opportunity. It is a matter of historical fascination that human slavery, an institution that ran contrary to most of these values, persisted for almost a century after the birth of a Republic founded on them. It is also, however, a confirmation of the power of those values that slavery was brought down in their name, and that discriminatory practices established after the Civil War were also curtailed in their name. Yet during World War II Gunner Myrdal could still write of an American dilemma, a society that simultaneously institutionalized those values (Myrdal focused above all on freedom, democracy, and equality of opportunity) and a system of racial inequality that denied those values.

Affirmative action, born officially about two decades after Myrdal wrote, must be regarded as a continuation of the conversation about that dilemma. But it was not simply an extension of past assaults on inequality. It arose in a new historical context and differed qualitatively from past struggles. What was that context, and what was new about it?

The 1960s witnessed a confluence of three historical circumstances that created the facilitating if not necessary conditions for affirmative action:

- A Civil Rights movement, focused mainly on the South but drawing participation from both black leaders and citizens and liberal whites around the country. This movement was named properly, since it concerned above all civil—or public—society and worked to end traditional denials of rights in that arena. The major battlegrounds were the polity, with voting the focus;

public education, with integration the focus; and access to public places, with transportation and businesses such as restaurants the foci. While economic discrimination became the target of some protest, the main emphasis was civil. Furthermore, the battle for civil rights was on *racial* injustices affecting black Americans, and did not extend to disadvantaged groups in general.

- Eight years of political domination by the Democratic party, which, through the leadership of John Kennedy, Robert Kennedy, and Lyndon Johnson, proved to be sympathetic and responsive to the goals of the Civil Rights movement. Moreover, especially under Johnson, the Democrats went beyond civil rights and introduced economic and educational reforms. The war on poverty was couched in general terms linked to the generic problem of poverty, but in practice it encompassed educational programs (such as Head Start) and welfare reforms directed disproportionately toward the poor black population.

- A *generalization* of political protest and alienation, some of it inspired by the goals, methods, and successes of the Civil Rights movement. The new directions included the student movement, targeting the universities and social — including racial — injustices generally; the antiwar movement, which consumed the country from 1965 until the beginning of the 1970s; the mobilization of other disadvantaged racial and ethnic — notably Native American and Hispanic/Latino — groups in protest against injustices specific to them; a mobilization of protest against racial injustice in South Africa; and a revitalization of the feminist movement, with a more explicit emphasis on economic, educational, and other institutional disadvantages than ever before.

These circumstances set the stage for affirmative action. As an institutional innovation it combined ingredients from all of them and added a few new ones. In its essence, affirmative action was a set of policies and procedures intended to give disadvantaged groups differential access to economic and educational opportunities and to their associated rewards. Like the Civil Rights movement, affirmative action aimed to improve the situation of the disadvantaged. Like Johnson's Good Society, it focused on educational and occupational arenas. It was thus a *synthesis* or *convergence* of themes found in the Civil Rights movement and the programs of the Democratic administrations. It remained conscious of civil and political rights, but it focused more on social and economic rights.

In addition, affirmative action involved a number of extensions beyond the themes of the 1960s:

- It included but moved beyond the removal of obstacles to participation in society's institutions. It actively promoted such participation, in the form of preferential treatment in hiring, contracting, and educational admissions.

- It included the rationale that it would redress past as well as present institutional disadvantages, wrongs, and sufferings. This rationale was explicit in the case of African-Americans and Native Americans, but came to pervade the entire logic of affirmative action.
- It involved a generalization of concern beyond the Civil Rights movement focus on race. Affirmative action's initial focus was on American blacks but it soon came to include other racial and ethnic groups—Native Americans, Hispanics/Latinos, Asians, South Sea Island peoples. It initially included gender as well, and subsequently physically disabled persons. What makes affirmative action sociologically interesting is that it generalized in ascriptive directions. Ascription refers to categories that are, by birth or social designation, defined as largely unalterable by personal choice or behavior. Another ascriptive category, age, also entered the picture, but not principally as demands for preferred treatment but as demands to end job discrimination against the elderly and the disadvantages imposed by retirement. Finally, sexual preference, a category that lies ambiguously between ascribed and voluntary, also came on the scene, but this, too, involved protest against discrimination rather than active, preferential treatment.

[Ascription is only an approximate sociological category. In the case of age it is pure, since chronological age, sociologically defined, is unalterable by choice or behavior, even though one might feel or act older or younger than one is. Other areas are less clear. "Passing for white," renouncing ethnic identification, and sex changes give the lie to the adjective "unalterable." At the same time, such changes are regarded as unusual or exceptional, thus confirming the sociological reality of the notion of ascription.]

## SOME ADDITIONAL FEATURES OF AFFIRMATIVE ACTION

### The Cultural Context

No institutional practice exists without explicit or implicit reference to some legitimizing, presumably consensual cultural value that gives meaning and defensibility to that practice. For example, voting procedures, electoral districting, political primaries, and political conventions make sense and gain their institutional desirability by reference to the cultural ideal of representative democracy.

Advocates of affirmative action seek legitimacy in the values of social justice and equality of opportunity. From these values derive the argument that those who have experienced past or experience present disadvantage through some form of oppression have been unjustly treated and deprived of equality of opportunity and merit compensation by preferential treatment. But at the same time, preferential treatment can be regarded as running counter to another connotation of equality of opportunity—namely, meritocracy, or the reward of talent and ability without regard to other considerations. University of California Regent Ward Connerly, for example, who spearheaded the movement to repeal existing affirmative action provisions, said, according to the *San Francisco Chronicle*, 1 December 1995, that the initiative was a way to achieve "an inclusive society in which people of all races, religions, and sexual preference have a right to have our talents considered." And in the immediate wake of the passage of the California Civil Rights Initiative in the November 1996 election, *The New York Times*, 10 November 1996, quoted on page 26 an advocate of the measure as saying, "Equal opportunity is what America is all about—*not* preferences." And in the very next paragraph an opponent of the legislation spoke as follows:

> We believe the vote in California in no way reflects the general public's sentiment on the value and viability of affirmative action programs. Most Americans support preservation of equal opportunity, especially in the workplace.

Because of this circumstance, the nation has been faced with a situation in which both advocates and opponents of affirmative action policies and practices have legitimized their arguments by referring to the same cultural value, equality of opportunity.

This situation, while not unheard of, is not typical. Debates over welfare policies, for example, often invoke conflicting value perspectives: competitive individualism versus humanitarianism or collective responsibility. Furthermore, the simultaneous reference to the same legitimizing context often gives rise to some interesting formulas. For example, one instruction that appears in affirmative-action manuals is the following: If two applicants for a position are equally qualified, but one falls in a preferential treatment category and the other does not, the position should go to the former. This formula attempts to accommodate, through compromise, the tension involved in the simultaneous appeal to equality of opportunity and preferential treatment: to recognize talent and qualification, but to tilt judgments in marginal cases. (It is also true that such a formula creates a difficult if not impossible assignment in practice—how to judge objectively and exactly if two people are equally qualified when such a judgment inevitably involves multiple criteria, some subjective. But when conflicts over meaning and legitimacy are at hand, the closest attention is not always paid to practical issues of workability.)

In addition, when advocates and opponents of affirmative action appeal simultaneously to the same values, this may create a specter of ambiguity and tension for participants. Those who benefit from preferential attention may experience a sense of vindication for past or present wrongs, but they may also experience a sense that they have not "made it" on the basis of their own abilities and achievements. Those who oppose affirmative action may harbor the same suspicion that those who benefited have not really made it on their own, and, on that basis, may resent or tolerate the "less deserving" in their midst — a particularly subtle and evasive form of racism or sexism. Indeed, the argument that affirmative action "demeans" the beneficiaries by elevating them artificially in a merit-based world was one of the principal claims made by those who wished to dismantle affirmative action policies during the debates before the University of California Regents in 1995.

## The Political Context

As noted, affirmative action was born in the context of and sustained by a number of social movements — movements by racial and ethnic groups, different wings of the feminist movement, gay and lesbian movements, and more diffuse sentiments against social injustices of all kinds. The project also gave rise to counter or backlash political movements with varying degrees of articulation, energy, and mobilization. This circumstance, if no other, confirms that affirmative action has been a political phenomenon: an institutional crucible in which social movements and countermovements clash.

The politics of affirmative action is complicated by another political peculiarity. For many social movements, the response of government authorities is to regard them as something "out there," whether they are something to crush, oppose, resist, handle, become divided over, accommodate, or give in to — in other words, to maintain a certain distance from them. Revolutionary political movements, the labor union movement, and the antiwar movement are cases that illustrate this point. In the case of affirmative action, the federal government and some state governments *joined* the movement. For whatever motives, government agencies were often the leaders in promoting affirmative action. Through administrative and judicial pressure the government encouraged if not coerced others to pursue its policies. In higher education, for example, agencies such as the Department of Health, Education and Welfare and the Department of Labor threatened to withhold research funds from universities unless they instituted and followed affirmative-action policies. This government stance not only endowed the relevant social movements for affirmative action with legitimacy, influence, and boldness; it also gave additional momentum to the affirmative-action project as a whole.

Another political dynamic invited the extension and generalization of the affirmative-action project. Two necessary conditions for a group to derive advantage from affirmative-action are for it (1) to identify itself as a tangible group, presumably with a consciousness and identity, and (2) to make a claim — and make that claim stick — that it is suffering or has suffered disadvantage. The government played a role in establishing these conditions by indicating that it was prepared to respond to claims of ascription and disadvantage. The result was to encourage a special kind of politics, called, variously, the politics of ascription, ethnic politics, or the politics of identity. (It is interesting to note that political scientists and sociologists have recently turned their attention to identity-based social movements and identity politics, thereby acknowledging a social reality that had been created for them.)

As a corollary, there is only limited evidence for the salience of social class as a feature of affirmative action. By and large, advocates of affirmative action do not claim to represent class from an economic point of view, even though they often frame their protests and demands in the language of class oppression. Some might regard this as an oddity, given the significance of class in other eras of American politics — for example, the politics of class in the early history of labor unionism and during the Great Depression. In education, too, class has played a major part in the history of preferential treatment. The preferential admission of children of alumni — long a practice of private and some public institutions — can be seen in some cases as affirmative action in favor of the wealthy. Another example is the preferential treatment of able students from backgrounds too modest to afford a college education, which is class-based preference as well. Preferential admission of athletes, while based in the first instance on athletic talent, is in some cases, such as the recruitment of male football players, class preference in practice. (There is, however, great variation among sports and between the sexes with respect to class origins.)

Identity politics, if we may term it that, may turn against the political authorities who acknowledge them. As we will see, identity-based demands tend to develop into claims to entitlement, because advocates of the identity groups often base their arguments on primordial or quasi-sacred considerations — such as common blood or ancestry — which demand dignity and respect. This imparts an uncompromising character to their claims and demands. This circumstance creates difficulties for politicians, because politicians in democracies engage in compromise if nothing else, and, as a rule, are less comfortable with absolute demands than they are with contingent, negotiable ones.

Finally, if demands for entitlement by identity groups come to be translated into quotas for positions, this creates additional difficulties for political resolution. Consider an example from my former university, the University of California at Berkeley. That campus has a deserved reputation of being one of the most aggressive in pressing the project of affirmative action. In noting its achievements, the campus makes public annually the percentages of racial, ethnic, and, in some cases, gender groups admitted. In doing this, the campus encourages (no doubt unconsciously) and finds itself in a political numbers game. If the percentage of one group rises, the percentage of another group must fall. Some groups voice dissatisfaction if their percentage falls, does not rise, or does not rise fast enough. This creates a permanent presence of complaining groups for campus authorities. It has resulted, furthermore, in the slow but steady reduction of students from the white population, who (and whose parents) have not, until recently, been as mobilized or as articulate as minority groups have.

## Points of Ambiguity in Implementing Affirmative Action Programs

While definite phrases (e.g., Equal Opportunity Employer) characterize affirmative action, and while manuals and procedures guide implementation, affirmative action has experienced a certain vagueness and ambiguity about both goals and processes. With respect to goals, the following points of uncertainty can be noted:

- Should affirmative action be defined in terms of specific substantive goals or as a general process aimed at ameliorating present and past disadvantages?
- If the former, how should goals be characterized? Should they be regarded as definite quotas or targets? Should they be regarded as aimed at achieving some proportion of a population, or should they be regarded as efforts to move toward "more" or "better" representation of groups, without further specification?
- Which groups qualify for affirmative action? Certain groups, such as African-Americans, Latino-Americans, and Native Americans come to mind as unambiguous cases, but their recognition has come about at different points in time. Furthermore, different groups within the Latino population have had different salience, with Cuban-Americans being the most ambiguous case. Pacific Island peoples are typically listed officially as qualifying minorities, but figure only little in practice. Asian-Americans constitute another ambiguous case. To take a vivid example at the University of California, Asian-American groups are, de facto, not considered an affirmative-action minority in undergraduate admissions. (Indeed, Asian-American groups have argued that they have been discriminated against, and would fare better under completely meritocratic standards.) At the same time, some academic departments, de facto, consider Asian-Americans as minor-

ities meriting special attention in graduate admissions and faculty hiring. The salience of gender as an object of affirmative action has also varied over time. It has been an insignificant issue in undergraduate admissions, and has diminished in significance in some other arenas. In the end, the effective qualification of different groups has been largely a function of their capacity to make their case and mobilize politically. In practice, finally, there are great regional and institutional differences in the recognition of different groups as qualifying for affirmative action.

- How are members of groups to be identified as belonging to those groups? Recognition by name is a reasonably but not completely accurate way of identifying Latino groups and women. Recognition of African-Americans and Native Americans by name and sometimes by appearance is difficult, sometimes impossible. Asking applicants to identify their group is another measure, but requests of this sort are almost always voluntary, and, as a result, incomplete. In 1975 — when affirmative action was entering into a high gear — I was chairman of my Department at UC Berkeley. I was requested, in the interests of affirmative action, to specify the racial–ethnic and gender distributions of a pool of candidates for academic appointment, but discovered, at the same time, that I was forbidden by administrative rule to request identification from the candidates! The example is extreme, but illustrates the ambiguity.

With respect to procedures for implementing affirmative action, a comparable list of uncertainties emerges:

- Is active discrimination in favor of a group permissible? And does this imply active discrimination against another group? One judicial decision, the *Bakke* case at the medical school of the University of California, Davis, suggested that the answer to the former is negative and the answer to the latter is positive, since the ruling was in favor of a white applicant to medical school, who claimed he was denied admission because places were reserved for minority students. However, such a ruling has not necessarily controlled informal practices in all situations.
- What constitutes a proper search in affirmative-action hiring? Is advertising in a few outlets likely to reach women and minorities sufficient, or should the search be more aggressive? Most institutions have developed definite procedures for searching, but, again, the variation is great.
- What constitutes a proper accounting for affirmative-action efforts? While formulae have emerged (for example, reporting the character of the search, describing the pool of applicants by race/ethnicity and gender, defending why minority candidates were not hired), these have sometimes produced stock, uninformative answers. Some maintain that to require reporting produces positive results; others complain that reporting has little effect and serves mainly to increase paperwork and costs.

- How and in what detail should affirmative-action be policed? Should monitors be satisfied when proper procedures have been carried out, or should they be interested in accounting for and influencing results in hiring and admissions?

To summarize up to this point, affirmative-action policies, while conceptually clear in intent and yielding significant results, have been matters of cultural ambivalence, political conflict, and institutional ambiguity. The origins of this, moreover, lie in the uncertain legitimacy that affirmative action enjoys in the context of American values, the political competition that results, and the practical difficulties in implementation—the last derived in part from the first two. These persistent features of ambivalence, conflict, and ambiguity have contributed in part, but only in part, to the potential for reaction and backlash, which appeared in earnest in the 1990s.

## Three Interrelated Trends

I have been able to discern three irregular trends in affirmative-action practices during the past quarter-century. When viewed together, they may cast some additional light on why a significant opposition to the program has developed. I confess that I have less than full documentation for these trends and have more confidence in some of the following statements than others:

1. We may detect a movement from an emphasis on substantive goals (initiating affirmative-action programs, achieving results in the form of targets) toward an emphasis on procedures. To note this trend is to state the sociologically obvious. It is what Max Weber called routinization. Weber's main illustration was the routinization of charismatic leadership into more stable forms, but his point may be generalized. Any innovation or reform produces an initial period of enthusiasm and vision, but as the innovative becomes the normal, practice comes to be regulated by more explicit and stable norms.

This has been the case with affirmative action. Most employers, both public and private, have sooner or later established modes of searching, evaluating, and monitoring affirmative-action policies. Two additional observations can be made about routinization. The first concerns the general ambiguity, noted earlier, in the project of affirmative action. As a general principle, the more ambiguous the project, the greater the urgency to establish understood ways of administering it. The objective, seldom explicit, of this adaptation, moreover, is to turn the novel and uncertain into the established and certain.

The second observation has to do with the management of conflict.

The substantive goal of affirmative action is to alter practices associated with inequalities in race, ethnic, and gender relations. Such efforts often challenge people's personal beliefs and identities. Resistance to change is invariably strong and conflicts often become bitter and explosive. To focus on the rules of the game — on due process, as it were — often has the effect of diverting conflict away from its hot substantive core and toward more neutral grounds of procedure. In the 1970s, when the University of California and other research universities were under pressure from federal agencies to move forward on affirmative action, UC President Charles Hitch negotiated a kind of truce whereby the agencies would forego insistence on establishing short-term targets if the University would establish procedures designed to further affirmative action. Such a compromise tended to defuse direct conflict and focus attention on the process.

Under such circumstances, discourse and debate tends to move away from substantive conflict and focus on methodological issues. In the early 1980s, as chair of the Berkeley Division of the UC Academic Senate, I was sometimes asked to sit in on visits of representatives of federal agencies to the Berkeley campus to monitor its progress on affirmative action. A fascinating feature of the exchanges in these visits was the focus on methodological points — estimating the size and quality of pools of minority and women in the academic market, disputing the accuracy of measurements, challenging and defending the University's estimates of progress it was making, even arguing about statistical techniques. Some of these discussions became heated. At the same time, they amounted to a way of avoiding confrontations over the substantive rights and wrongs of affirmative action and conflicts between government bureaucrats who were under political pressure to achieve results and the University officials who were pleading for patience and flexibility because of the political exigencies they faced in their own institutions. The substantive conflicts were hidden in the methodological agenda, but, with that agenda, discussion could proceed under the tacit — but possibly mistaken — assumption that the parties agreed on goals and differed only about means. As a result, discussions could proceed with a lower probability of open, bitter, and explosive conflict.

2. Another trend is the movement from preferential treatment to entitlement. The aim of affirmative action was to improve the institutional fortunes of disadvantaged groups. The means were to intervene in the labor and contracting markets and in the admissions policies of educational institutions. Over time tangible results began to appear — in different degrees — in government offices, in colleges and universities, and in business and professional firms. With such progress there often develops a subtle but definite shift in expectations among groups that have benefited: that those gains should be consolidated and protected,

and that further advances should be made. It is only a short step from such expectations to the mentality of entitlement.

Such developments create a difficult political situation. The expectations of all groups simply cannot be met unless positions available in the institutions and organizations involved continue to expand. If those positions expand slowly, remain stable, or decline, then a zero-sum game is at hand. The logic of that game is that if one party gains, the others necessarily lose. This logic conflicts directly with the logic of entitlement to past and future gains. The consequences of that conflict are three: latent or open conflicts among the groups struggling for scarce positions; resistance to further change on the part of those who regard themselves as potential losers; and heightened political pressure on those regarded as responsible for policies — in this case employers, administrators, and government officials. All three consequences have been visible in the history of affirmative action.

3. A final trend is from a focus on economic and institutional justice to a focus on cultural conflict. There is nothing necessary about this trend, but it also expresses a certain logic. Affirmative action promises, above all, an improvement for the groups affected — from second-class citizenship to something better. But the process does not stop there. As Alexis de Tocqueville demonstrated in the cases of the middle classes and the peasantry in eighteenth-century France, advances in one social sphere generated higher levels of dissatisfaction. This is the dynamic of relative deprivation: The wounds of exclusion from spheres not yet improved become all the sorer when advance is attained in one.

That dynamic is evident in the history of affirmative action. One demand that followed the increased admissions of minorities to colleges and universities in the late 1960s and early 1970s was for programs, departments, and schools of ethnic studies. This demand was for equity in educational institutions in which minorities now had greater numbers. Many such academic units were put in place after a period of faculty resistance and political conflict. Despite some successes, most of these units continue to hold a second-class status in the eyes of older and more established academic enterprises in the colleges and universities.

In the 1980s the demand for academic inclusion and respect took a new turn: a call for the reform of long-established curricula. This involved not only a demand for inclusion but also a cultural attack on traditional college and university curricula and on those believed responsible for them. Those who had demanded Third World and ethnic programs were bidding for inclusion as equals. Those who called for ending the traditional "Western Civ" requirement at Stanford and for an "American cultures" requirement at Berkeley were also demanding inclusion, but they combined that with an assault on "Euro-centrism" and a "white male establishment" that exercised its "hegemony" by imposing its Eurocentric views on peoples with different but equally if not more dignified cultures.

The movement for curricular reform in the 1980s — along with related debates on cultural diversity and multiculturalism and the "culture wars" — was a confluence of two major historical forces: first, an escalation of demands to the cultural level by advocates for minority groups and women who still felt disadvantaged on college and university campuses; and second, the postmodernist movement, the appearance of which coincided with the collapse of radical Marxism in the 1980s, and which developed, as a barely beneath the surface agenda, a critique and political protest against those who impose power-as-knowledge on disadvantaged groups.

This escalation to the cultural level has not affected the majority of working people in the country, whose main interest is still in the improvement of their economic and institutional positions and rewards. The cultural debates have been confined largely to spokespersons for social movements, academics, intellectuals, and the sophisticated press. In those circles, however, that escalation poses a deeper and in some respects more difficult political situation than demands for institutional access. The cultural critique is more aggressive than the institutional one. In addition it excites conflicts over cultural values as well as group interests, thus making the conflicts more fundamental and encompassing.

To summarize this section, I would propose a connection among the three trends mentioned: A combination of increased political consciousness of and political pressure by disadvantaged groups and reformers produced a series of economic and educational reforms. The resulting programs and procedures produced a significant incorporation of previously excluded groups. That success generated increased expectations of two kinds: those based on a sense of entitlement and those stemming from a bid for cultural dignity as well as institutional inclusion. These demands, in turn, created a more aggressive and threatening face on the part of the movement, and thus increased the likelihood of backlash and countermovement. This line of analysis may fill in another piece of the puzzle of explaining the backlash of the 1990s. But the story is not yet finished. To complete it I turn to some specifics of the California situation, which reveals some factors not yet considered and helps explain the strength of the backlash in that state.

## THE CALIFORNIA AND THE UNIVERSITY OF CALIFORNIA SITUATIONS

In one respect the situation in California has already been addressed. Most of the general aspects and trends already discussed apply to California, and many illustrations refer to the California scene. That state's situation, however, has been extreme in two senses: Its scene is one of extreme racial and ethnic diversity, and the rollback of affirmative action by the University of California Regents and the voters of California mark two of the most dramatic events in the history of affirmative action.

## Affirmative Action in the University of California

As indicated, the main external pressure for affirmative action in the University came from federal research agencies, the government of California, and demands of minority and women's groups. One should not conclude from this, however, that the University itself was completely passive or resistant. Its campuses — most notably Berkeley and Santa Cruz — have political cultures that welcome reforms to improve disadvantaged populations.

Affirmative action affected every sector of the University, but the effects varied by sector. The major variations are as follows:

- *Administrative staff.* Affirmative-action policies — expressed mainly in the hiring and advancement of women and minority employees — proceeded earlier and further with respect to staff. There are several reasons for this: First, the administration, as direct target of political demands, was most sensitive to pressures to institute affirmative-action policies. Second, the administration can effect changes in personnel policies in its own ranks more easily than it can in areas such as graduate-student admissions and faculty recruitment, which are usually delegated to largely autonomous academic departments. Third, administrative staff, in contrast to faculty, requires a diversity of skill levels among its personnel. While applying criteria of competence and quality in hiring decisions, the administration does not have such an elaborate machinery as faculty recruitment to assure quality and competitive excellence. Finally, employee turnover is higher for administrative staff than for faculty, thus providing greater opportunity for rapid changes in hiring policy.
- *Undergraduate admissions.* Affirmative action proceeded faster and further in undergraduate admissions than in other academic sectors. Admissions at that level is centralized on the campuses and thus more easily affected by central administrative decisions. Furthermore, the characteristics of its recruitment pool — the top one-eighth of graduates from the state's high schools (as required by the California Master Plan for Higher Education) — are well known. Third, a mechanism for preferential treatment of undergraduates was already in place. For years the University had used a "2% rule," instituted mainly in the interest of recruiting athletes, which permitted campuses to extend admission beyond the eligible academic pool for

2% of its entering class. Subsequently, and in the interest of extending affirmative action, this rule was extended to 4%, then to 6%. This afforded campuses greater flexibility in recruiting and greater capacity to bring in minority students.

In practice, the experiences of the different campuses of the University were diverse. They varied according to the aggressiveness of individual administrators and according to the size of minority populations in their respective "catchment areas." The large urban campuses of Berkeley and Los Angeles were most diversified, and by the late 1980s had student bodies with a minority of "Anglo" students. The process went less far on less urban campuses such as Davis and Santa Cruz. In the lore of undergraduate applicants in Southern California—a lore which does not mince words—the Irvine campus was known as the "yellow campus," the Los Angeles campus as the "black and brown campus," and the Santa Barbara campus as the "white campus." Regarded as a whole, however, the University of California carried affirmative-action policies in undergraduate admissions very far in comparison with other educational institutions in the country.

- *Graduate admissions*. Graduate admissions also vary by academic unit and campus, but the general pattern is to evaluate applicants first at the unit level (professional school, academic department), with recommendations going to a central Graduate Division for approval. The latter very seldom challenges the units' judgments, and when it does, it is typically on procedural, not substantive grounds. This decentralization has meant that affirmative action has been pursued variably at the unit level. Some fields, such as engineering and economics, have small pools, and recruitment of qualified women and minorities has been low; others, such as education and sociology, have larger pools. Furthermore, pools cannot be easily expanded, since strong performance in college is a condition for finding a place in them. In addition, disciplinary "cultures" differ along conservative–liberal–radical lines, and these differences affect the degree to which academic units push or resist affirmative-action goals and procedures. Despite these barriers, many schools and departments in the University of California have significantly altered the racial, ethnic, and gender composition of their graduate student bodies.

- *Faculty recruitment*. The factors affecting graduate recruitment apply even more to faculty recruitment. Recruitment pools are even more restricted, since a condition for becoming part of them is to have attained a PhD or advanced professional degree. Furthermore, the campuses of the University of California, like those of all major research institutions, are engaged in a constant and vigorous competitive struggle to hire only "the best." This means that many doctoral and professional graduates are not even considered. Finally, the institution of academic tenure restricts the rate at which the goals of affirmative action can be realized. With an annual turnover rate of 3–5% through retirement and resignation through the 1970s and 1980s (and before the mass exodus of senior faculty via early retirement the 1990s), the opportunities to hire women and minorities were modest. This combination of factors yielded the smallest quantitative results of affirmative action among faculties, compared to other sectors in the University. Once again, however, the University of California was a national leader in implementing affirmative action at the faculty level.

The faculty, however, expressed the strongest political resistance to affirmative-action programs. The basis for this opposition rose mainly from its deep commitment to standards of quality and excellence in recruitment and advancement, and in its highly developed machinery (multiple reviews of faculty members by department faculty, committees on academic personnel, and administrators). Many faculty, themselves politically liberal, shared the belief that hiring and advancement on any standards other than merit was a violation of those standards. Many academic units experienced their bitterest internal conflicts over the hiring of minorities and women. The 1970s and 1980s also witnessed incidents of faculty outrage over administrative reversal of faculty recommendations on minority and women candidates. And on the Berkeley campus, the only really systematic faculty alienation and opposition to I. Michael Heyman, whose tenure as chancellor spanned the 1980s, came from groups of faculty members who believed that he was going "too far, too fast" in pressing affirmative action and compromising standards of academic excellence long embraced on that campus.

Despite the ambivalence, ambiguity, resistance, and conflict associated with affirmative action, by the early 1990s the principles, policies, and procedures of that project were firmly established in the University of California, and were legitimate in the minds — if not entirely in the hearts — of most of its constituencies. The most direct evidence of this is that every constituency — the President and his office, the Chancellors, the faculty through the Academic Senate, and students through their representative institutions — spoke out officially against the initiative of the Board of Regents' resolution of July 1995. This polarization between the Regents and all other constituencies is a remarkable political fact, and will reverberate throughout the University system for a long time.

## THE POLITICS OF THE REGENTAL ACTION

By the end of 1994 the United States confronted a unique historical situation that set the stage for a popular and governmental backlash against affirmative action, especially its racial and ethnic components. Among the factors contributing to this situation were the following:

- Since 1973 the real wages of Americans had remained virtually stagnant, after a period of steady but variable increase in real wages dating back to World War II. In addition, traditionally secure middle-class positions became less secure as firms and other agencies resorted to downsizing as a competitive strategy. For a country historically committed to material progress and the expectation that the next generation will be better off than the last, this economic fact contributed, perhaps more than all others, to the mood of national sourness about its institutions, including its government.

- This stagnation was aggravated, especially from the early 1980s on, by a regressive movement in the distribution of income, accompanied by social problems such as increases in poverty and homelessness. The causes of the stagnation and regression are complex; they include technological change, international wage competition, a weakening of labor unionism, and tax and housing policies of the Reagan administration. But whatever the causes, they were a recipe for dissatisfaction among many groups. The significant economic recession of the early 1990s only exaggerated these economic conditions.

- The combination of stagnation and regression often gives rise to protest from the left. Contrary to this expectation, the electoral politics of the country in the last two decades have been dominated by the right and the Republican party. From the presidency of Richard Nixon to the presidency of Bill Clinton, the country experienced only one episode of Democratic dominance — the unpopular presidency of Jimmy Carter — and the politics of the Reagan and to some extent the Bush administration emanated from ideologies of the right. Clinton's administration promised a reversal, but most of Clinton's liberal initiatives either failed or stalled, and the election of a Republican Congress in 1994 was interpreted by the winners as a mandate against government in general and governmental involvement in domestic policies in particular.

- One reason why difficult economic conditions were expressed in a right-wing mode is that the country experienced, during the same decades, the greatest wave of foreign immigration since the late nineteenth and early twentieth centuries. That fact provided many with an explanation for their economic difficulties: Immigrants compete for jobs, are willing to work for less, and increase expenditures on welfare.

- An early initiative of the Republication Congress of 1994 was an aggressive move on the part of influential Republicans to reverse — by radical revision or even abolition — affirmative action as a governmental policy. That initiative put the Clinton administration on the defensive, and while that administration opposed it, it promised a thoroughgoing review of affirmative-action programs with an eye to correcting excesses.

All these long-term and short-term developments constituted a relevant national environment for California, and, in particular, the national move to weaken or abolish affirmative action was a green light for the state. In addition, some social conditions specific to California intensified those national developments:

- Immigration rates in California were higher than those of the nation. The inflow was mainly Mexicans and Central Americans, but Asians also contributed. It was repeatedly reported in the media and elsewhere that California was becoming a state of minorities, and that by sometime after the year 2000 minority populations would outnumber the Anglo population. Equally common were reports that businesses and wealthier Anglo residents of California were leaving the state and that the overall increase of its population was because of the inflow of immigrants.

- The recession of the early 1990s was more severe in California than it was in the rest of the nation. California's unemployment rates were consistently 2 or 3% higher than the national rate. California's unhappy economic fortunes were generated in part by reductions in government defense spending, concentrated in Southern California, in the wake of events in Eastern Europe and Russia in 1989–90.

- California politics have been dominated since 1982 by Republican governors — George Dukemejian and Pete Wilson. The latter built much of his campaign and political program on antiwelfare and anti-immigration issues, and threw his weight behind Proposition 187, the 1994 action that would deny the state's educational, medical, and other institutions to illegal immigrants. The constitutional status and impact of that proposition are still unclear, but the political message was clear. On 1 June 1995, Wilson issued an executive order to "End Preferential Treatment and to Promote Individual Opportunity Based on Merit." And in the summer of 1995, he exploited the themes of antiwelfare, anti-immigration, and anti-affirmative action in his brief, ill-fated bid for the Republican presidential nomination.

- One consequence of the Republican gubernatorial domination was a radical change in the composition of the University of California's Board of Regents. Regents are appointed by the governor, and those appointments are almost always political supporters of the incumbent governor. Since Regental terms are for 12 years, it transpired that every appointment by Democratic Governor Jerry Brown (who preceded Dukemejian as Governor) left the Regents and no Democrats were appointed to replace them. So, as of the mid-1990s, the entire Board of Regents was composed of Republican appointments by Dukemejian and Wilson. Many of those Regents, moreover, were indebted to Wilson, since appointment to the Board is widely considered to be an important political reward and a source of recognition and prestige for those appointed.

- One Regental appointment was of crucial significance, that of Ward Connerly, an African-American businessman from Sacramento, in 1993. Himself a recipient of contracts under affirmative-action provisions for contracting with minority businessmen, Connerly nevertheless had developed a special antagonism toward affirmative action. This attitude was manifested from the beginning of his term, at which time, he recalled he was "instantly struck by the extent to which group classifications, particularly that of race, were being used in the activities of the University," according to a Connerly news release, 5 July 1995. He began a campaign of criticism of the University's admission policies, but in the early stages this attracted the open support of only a few Regents, though Connerly maintained that many of them "privately shared similar concerns" (*ibid.*) He complained that the university did not take his concern seriously (he spoke of his "Lone Ranger" image), so in January of 1995 he decided "to increase [the issue's] public visibility" (*ibid.*).

Three additional, interrelated contextual features of California politics should be mentioned as background. Those features concern the popular — if not populist — character of its democracy and the public character of its politics. First, dating from its state constitution, California has institutionalized many features of direct democracy, including provisions for initiatives, referenda, and the recall of public officials. These features, especially the referendum, have lent a certain cumbersomeness to California politics, and, from time to time, a certain timidity on the part of politicians, who pass difficult and explosive political issues on to the voting public. Second, California's political parties, in comparison with states to the east, are weak in structure and in capacity to control and discipline their members. The history of California politics has witnessed many unpredictable elections and many political mavericks, which trace in part to this weakness of parties. Third, and derivative in large part from the first two, many political issues are fought out in the public media rather than negotiated in party caucuses and meetings. The advent of the television age has augmented this tendency and, as a result, California politics are conspicuous for their public free-for-alls. The public airing of political conflict during the debate over the affirmative action debate in the UC Regents in the summer of 1995 fit this political style.

## The Affirmative Action Debate of 1995

As of early 1995, and as a result of the contextual factors just reviewed, the political climate in California was ripe for an assault on affirmative action. It began in July in the context of the brief campaign on the part of Governor Wilson for the Republican nomination for the United States Presidency. This campaign included conservative statements on immigration, welfare, and affirmative action.

Regent Connerly's introduction of the rollback motion on 5 July—for consideration at the 20 July Regents' meeting—was clearly an instance of "outside" national and state politics coming into the University. Though Connerly had been pressing the issue for some time within the Regents, and though denials of intervention by the Governor were issued, the Governor's presence was clear. Up to this point there was no significant evidence of initiatives within the University to change the policies and procedures of affirmative action.

Connerly's principal justification for his initiative was that the University, by pursuing its policies, was breaking the law (as manifested in the *Bakke* decision) in its admissions policies. He claimed it was actively discriminating in favor of African-Americans, Latinos, and Native Americans by using race as a criterion for admission (automatically admitting students in those categories on the Davis and Irvine campuses, and giving them special consideration on the Berkeley and Los Angeles campuses). Asian and white students, correspondingly, were being "harmed" because higher standards were being demanded of them. He maintained that the University's standards had been lowered; that the public opinion of California citizens, students, and alumni supported the renunciation of race as an admissions category; that the practices did not promote "racial harmony and integration" but aggravated conflict through practices of racial segregation on the campuses; and that "some of our administrators" were raising the false specter of student protests in opposing his initiative. In the end, Connerly applauded the principle of diversity and argued that his initiative did not mean that the "University is . . . turning its back on affirmative action." He appealed, furthermore, to the principle of equality of opportunity by reminding his audiences that "We need to make clear that there is a difference . . . between providing people with equal opportunity and providing preferences."

Other parties joined the debate in early July. On the date of Connerly's 5 July news release, the University released a statement by the General Counsel, stating that the *Bakke* decision permitted colleges and universities to take race and ethnicity into account so long as it is only one factor and so long as "no places are set aside on this basis." At the same time the release promised that "[changes] will be made at UC Berkeley, UCLA, UC Davis, and UC Irvine to assure that the potential qualifications and experiences of all applicants are reviewed competitively" (*ibid*).

Extended releases by the Office of the President on 10 July also struck a defensive tone. An individual statement by the UC President Jack Peltason, a joint statement by Vice Presidents and Chancellors, and a resolution by the Executive Committee of the systemwide Academic Senate all praised affirmative action for furthering diversity and the American egalitarian tradition. Peltason argued that the July initiative was premature, that the decision should wait until the state election initiative of November 1996, and that, in the meantime, extended review by administrators and faculty should begin. At the same time, he promised investigation and action on the four campuses in question, and promised to modify faculty and employee recruiting away from reliance on minority status. The resolution passed by the faculty leadership argued that affirmative action had made the University "a better institution," and called for it to "continue to act affirmatively to increase the participation of individuals from underrepresented groups, evaluating and modifying these programs in order to strengthen them." The resolution did not, however, take an explicit stand on the use of racial and other group membership as criteria for admission, recruitment, and contracting.

The wording of the resolution adopted by the Regents on 20 July was strong and decisive in several respects, but equivocal in others. On the one hand, it prohibited the University to use "race, religion, sex, color, ethnicity, or national origin as criteria for admission to the University or its programs," either in regular or "exceptional" admission. It also called for admission of between 50 and 75% of any entering class "on the basis of academic achievement" (the previous policies specified 40 and 60%, respectively). On the other hand, it gave until 1997 to put these policies in place, and called upon the administration to consult with faculty with respect to "supplemental criteria," such as giving special consideration to eligible individuals who have shown "character and determination" despite "having suffered disadvantage economically and in terms of their social environment." Furthermore, it ruled out any policies that might conflict with eligibility for receiving funds from any federal or state agency, and did not mention faculty or employee recruitment at all. A final provision contained a statement of principle in favor of diversity but against preferential treatment:

> Because individual members of all of California's diverse races have the intelligence and capacity to succeed at the University of California, this policy will achieve a UC population that reflects this state's diversity through the preparation and empowerment of all in this state to succeed rather than through a system of arbitrary preferences.

[May I digress and point out the general sociological significance of this action? It signalized a shift in the definition of social justice and equality of opportunity—and conflict about these issues—away from race and ethnicity and toward social and economic class, as the reference to "economic disadvantage" suggests. If the Regents' actions were to be carried out, this would mark a dramatic shift in the political, legal, and public definition of social inequality and social divisions. We cannot know the precise consequences of such a shift. On the one hand, it could be argued that it would be healthy, because racial and ethnic divisions have such a primordial, enduring, and bitter quality about them and because class and class conflict are more manageable as permanent divisions in American society. On the other hand, at this moment in history class divisions may have an unappreciated volatility in this country, because of the trends toward income stagnation of a more regressive income distribution. In all events, however, it is difficult to overestimate the profundity of such a shift.]

Several days after the resolution passed, Peltason issued a statement on it. He, too, reaffirmed the principle of diversity, saying that "it is important to make clear . . . that [the resolutions] have to do with means not with goals." He predicted few changes in contracting and employment programs, because these are constrained by federal and state laws. Noting the January 1997 deadline for action on admissions, he promised to consult with Chancellors and faculty on how best to implement admissions policies, "the area in which we expect most change." In the meantime, he promised to set up a multiconstituency task force on improving the preparation of underrepresented minorities and other students for college. He also promised to carry forward on the changes in admissions and appointments promised in his 10 July press release. By late October, four intrauniversity task forces—on contracting, academic and staff employment, undergraduate admissions criteria, and graduate and professional school admissions—had been formed, all with instructions to come back with recommendations for implementing the Regents' resolution.

The peace and calm achieved by these actions, however, is only apparent. Virtually every constituency in the University remains in a state of ambivalence and conflict about the summer actions, and, as a result, very little appears to have been resolved by them. To illustrate:

- *Regents.* Some members of the minority of the Regents who opposed the resolutions made an effort, at the January meeting of the Board of Regents, to reverse the July resolutions. Their efforts failed as the Regents voted to table the motion. The effort to reverse appears to have little short-run hope, particularly in light of the fact that the voters of the state passed an anti-affirmative-action initiative, the California Civil Rights Initiative, similar in wording to the Regents' resolutions, in the election of November

1996. Should that initiative be declared unconstitutional, should California state politics take a turn to the left in the future, and should that reflect itself in an altered composition of the Board of Regents — a process many years in the making — then a reversal or some other modification of the resolutions of July 1995 might appear on the horizon.

In February 1996, a dramatic confrontation between Regents and the President revealed the political salience and volatility of the affirmative action issue. In an administrative act, the new President, Richard Atkinson, delayed the implementation of the Regents resolution on undergraduate admissions from 1997 until 1998. This action prompted a summons to the President to appear in Sacramento for a dressing-down by Governor Wilson, and led Connerly and some other Regents to call a special meeting of the Board of Regents to "review the performance" of Atkinson. (The last time such a meeting was held was in 1967, when Clark Kerr was fired as President of the University.) The meeting was canceled only after a public, written apology by Atkinson. In the wake of that episode, several dozen Democratic Assemblymen and Senators signed a document accusing Regent Connerly of abusing his office and using the incident to stir up support for the California Civil Rights Initiative.

- *Students*. The editorial board of the Berkeley campus student newspaper, *The Daily Californian*, cast a divided vote in favor of the Regents' actions. To those who have followed the editorial preferences of that publication over the years, this was something like hell freezing over. An equally dramatic thunderbolt occurred in November 1996, when the student newspaper came out in favor of the California Civil Rights Initiative. On the other hand, a modest amount of student activity against the resolutions continued to bubble up on the various campuses. In late February 1996, the student newspaper filed a suit against the Board of Regents that charged that the July vote was decided in secret and in advance and should be voided because it violated Regents' policies calling for public meetings.

- *Faculty*. Most of the faculty "establishment" appeared to wish to accept the passage of the summer resolution and work out sensible, informed means of implementing it while working by other means to seek diversity. Another wing of the faculty continued to protest, submitting petitions and seeking faculty expressions of opposition on grounds that the Regents violated the principles of University governance by passing the resolutions. The faculty as a whole, however, appeared to be of mixed mind. A poll of faculty conducted by the Roper organization in December 1995 yielded the finding that about half the faculty favored the renunciation of race and other group criteria (that is, were pro resolution), and half favored their explicit incorporation.

- *Administration*. While campus administrations have no official choice other than to implement the resolutions, matters are not as simple as that.

A difficult atmosphere persists because of the possibility of unofficial subversion of the official nonrecognition of group criteria in the actual work of admitting and recruiting. Regent Connerly issued statements about undermining the Regents' resolutions, and so long as even a small group of Regents continue to be in a policing frame of mind, tension and potential conflict between Regents and administration remain alive.

- *The state political context.* California politics remained embroiled in affirmative-action and other controversies related to the California Civil Rights Initiative, introduced in 1995 as an amendment to the California state constitution. That initiative proposed to end all preferences related to gender, race, national origin, and other related categories. The movement to gain signatures for this met with early difficulties, and late in 1995 Republican supporters of the measure persuaded Regent Connerly to head the campaign to put the measure on the ballot. The movement gained momentum after that time and by the end of February enough signatures had been secured to place the measure on the November 1996 ballot. After a long campaign, which heated as election day appeared, the measure passed by 10 percentage points, thereby generalizing the Regents' action to employment, educational, and contracting activities to the state of California as a whole.

The success of the civil rights initiative is hardly surprising, given the confluence of social and political forces I have outlined. The measure is now bottled up in the courts — with one judge having ordered the state to stay its effects, and a panel of three appeals judges declaring it constitutional — and neither proponents nor opponents will accept defeat until it goes to the United States Supreme Court. Regardless of the ultimate outcome, the measure's passage had one interesting consequence for the University of California. Every constituency in the University, save the Board of Regents, had gone on record as favoring affirmative action for the University, i.e., opposing the initiative. Yet at the same time, its passage at the state level took the University out of the limelight; affirmative action is now at the state and even national political level (with President Clinton and the Department of Justice weighing in against the referendum). If the measure had been defeated, the Regents would have been under enormous pressure to rescind their vote, and the University would have been rocked with internal conflict once again. One can only surmise, therefore, that the University regarded the passage of the Civil Rights referendum with a distinct ambivalence.

In conclusion, the prospect for affirmative action's future may be put as follows. In California, as in the nation as a whole, the advances achieved for both minorities and women have been enormous, and in that respect the affirmative-action project may be considered to have been an institutional success. However, it can be claimed only with greater difficulty that it has been a *political* success. Neither its adoption nor its implementation nor the efforts to reverse it seems to have had — or will have — a calming effect on the racial, ethnic, and gender politics of the country. This suggests that the country's main agenda is not really affirmative action; rather the most important underlying agenda concerns the racial, ethnic, and gender struggles themselves. As a result, any institutional contrivance affecting the terms of this struggle, whether affirmative action or something else, will be bound to generate the ambiguity, ambivalence, conflict, and instability that we have witnessed over the past three decades of affirmative action.

# Nine

## WHAT A UNIVERSITY CAN LEARN AND TEACH ABOUT CONFLICT AND DIFFERENCE

### COMMENTS ON THE ESSAY BY NEIL J. SMELSER

CHANG-LIN TIEN

NEIL SMELSER's stimulating essay provides a very helpful analysis of a fascinating social transformation. In providing a context for response, I will start by pointing out the changes California has experienced, and then discuss their impact on the University of California system as well as Berkeley in particular. In 1967, when I joined the Berkeley faculty, we had only 2% Asians in the state of California. Now we have reached almost 10%. And 30 years ago, Hispanics were less than 10% of the state's population. Now, they comprise 26%. In one generation, the California population has changed dramatically. Within 10 years, no ethnic group will constitute a majority in California.

The question of Asian-American admissions, which has been a major issue in California as well as a number of Ivy League schools, serves as a further social and political challenge. In California right now, 32% of Asian-American high school graduates are eligible to enter the University of California. For whites, the figure is 13%, for blacks 5%, and for Chicano/Latinos 4%. These eligibility numbers are based on what the California master plan for higher education mandated: that the top 12.5% of California high school graduates would be eligible for admission on one of the campuses at the University of California. So California has what we could call disproportional patterns of eligibility. This development poses major dilemmas for the people of California and the missions of the University of California. While I believe that it is in the interest of Asian-Americans to have a socially inclusive student body, the achievement of that objective under present conditions of the "demography" of academic eligibility will mean that we would have to employ measures of capacity and potential in our admission processes that are inconsistent with the trends illustrated by the *Hopwood* decision and Proposition 209.

The question that I want now to pursue is how we can learn from this striking pattern of Asian-American academic success. In this regard I want to reference both the important work of Uri Treisman and my own personal experience. Professor Treisman, in work he initiated at Berkeley, has observed that Asian-American students tend to work together in groups. I agree. Why is this the case? I believe that the underlying issue is that they really value education.

Permit me to be autobiographical. In 1949, my family was one of the major banking forces in Shanghai. We lost everything after the Chinese revolution. We went to Taiwan as refugees, 12 people, living initially in a 15′ by 15′ room. We were virtually homeless. Conditions were terrible; we lacked adequate food. One night as I watched my father sitting there—because with so many people in a 15′ by 15′ room it was hard even to lie down—I said, "Dad, what are you doing? You should sleep." He replied, "I'm worried." I said, "Don't worry. If we run out of food to eat we can all go out and get some part-time work." I was 14 years old and I said, "Don't worry." My father continued, "No, you don't understand. I worry not about food but how to get my children a true education."

That response continues to affect me very deeply. Something we have to think about is the value put on education in Asian-American culture. How do we generate that kind of family support for all students?

Something else we as educators need to consider when thinking about how to continue the diversity at our schools, particularly in California after Proposition 209, is the importance of students' self-perception about their capabilities. I believe very strongly that students do respond, positively or negatively, to what others think about them. That dilemma makes the debate about affirmative action particularly problematic because we cannot have this debate without increasing the vulnerability of underrepresented minority students. Let me share another experience.

Shortly after my arrival in the United States, I worked as a teaching fellow for a professor in Louisville, Kentucky, who refused to call me by name. He referred to me as "Chinaman," a term I originally thought was a friendly nickname. One day the professor told me to adjust some valves on a large laboratory apparatus. I lost my balance on a ladder and grabbed a nearby steam pipe. It was scorchingly hot and produced a jolt of pain that nearly caused me to faint. But I did not scream. I stuffed my throbbing hand into my coat pocket and waited until class was over. Then I ran to the hospital emergency room where I was treated for a burn that had completely singed the skin off my palm.

My response fit the Asian model minority myth: Say nothing and go about your business, but my silence had nothing to do with stoicism. I simply did not want to endure the humiliation of having the professor scold me in front of the class. Some time later, I learned that the term "Chinaman" was a racial epithet. I worried for two days and two nights about what to do. Should I confront him and risk losing my fellowship and my career? Should I ignore it and go about my business? I decided I had to face him. I went to see him and asked him to please stop calling me Chinaman. He agreed, but he never once called me by my name.

Following the 20 July 1995 resolution of the University of California Board of Regents to change the University's affirmative action policy, I visited a public high school to see what impact that decision was having on a group of underrepresented minority students. Many of them had already internalized the message that they were second-class citizens and would be unwelcome at the University of California. "Why should I study? I cannot study," some of them said. That's why I publicly disagreed with the action of the Regents.

We needed to send a different message to the underrepresented and disadvantaged young people: "We need you." This is the American dream; everybody must have opportunity. Minorities are not second-class citizens. That is why, in September 1995, I initiated the "Berkeley Pledge" program, which said "We need you" and creates greater access to Berkeley for those students who will probably be hurt by Proposition 209.

The Berkeley Pledge is based on five goals, each of which is supported by a coordinated campus program. The first is to strengthen Berkeley's partnerships with K–12 schools to increase the numbers of underrepresented and disadvantaged students who will meet UC eligibility requirements and become academically eligible for Berkeley. Second, we want to have the Berkeley Recruitment Corps coordinate all campus recruitment activities in an effort to increase the numbers of students from diverse backgrounds that will apply to the Berkeley Campus. The third goal is to keep Berkeley affordable and therefore accessible for all students, regardless of their income, by raising $60 million by the year 2000 for undergraduate scholarship funds, and identifying campus jobs and designing appropriate financial aid packages for needy students. The fourth goal is to create an environment that will foster success for every student at Berkeley, which we have already begun to do by establishing an Academic Support Team, which will enhance student success from matriculation to graduation and prepare them for graduate study and professional careers. Finally, we want to provide support to students who may be the first in their families to consider applying to graduate school, so that they can continue their education to the next level.

I pledged a substantial amount of money to support this. This was not easy, but I had to take a risk. I did this because I believe that students' perceptions that the University did not welcome them needed to be changed. I referred earlier to the master plan for higher education. What we need is a master plan for K–12 so that we look forward to having a balance of qualified students who better reflect the diversity of California. The Berkeley Pledge is a start toward that goal.

. . . . .

Now to Neil Smelser's very stimulating essay. First, I want to endorse his concluding comment, because I think that's really the central point: Smelser suggests that the country's main agenda is not really affirmative action or any other related kind of program; rather the most important underlying agenda concerns the racial, ethnic, and gender struggles themselves. That's the fundamental problem. If we don't realize that, I do not think we can ever solve the racial division in this country.

Back in 1990, following my appointment as chancellor at Berkeley, several people jokingly called me the affirmative action chancellor. There was no hostility, actually, in these remarks. In fact, some of those who made them are some of my strongest supporters. But I did notice that all those people who joked about that happened to be white. At the same time, many Asian-Pacific-American groups invited me to be the guest of honor at their service clubs, professional associations, and civic organizations. I got so many awards I didn't know what to do. Time and time again they praised my appointment as having shattered the glass ceiling. Many Asian-Americans believed that highly qualified Asian-American professionals encounter impenetrable barriers. This glass ceiling makes it very difficult for Asian-Americans to reach management decision-making levels and assume leadership positions. The problem, these critics say, is that Asian-Americans lack the "right stuff" to be strong leaders. My experience showed me how one action, my appointment as chancellor, could be viewed so differently, depending on the race and ethnicity of the observer. These differing reactions to my appointment did show that, from the beginning of my chancellorship, I could not ignore affirmation action, racial divisions, and campus diversity.

When, a few years later, my colleague, Harry Yen, was appointed chancellor at the University of California at Santa Barbara, interestingly, nobody mentioned the term "affirmative action chancellor," no Asian-American groups gave him awards for shattering glass ceilings. Seriously, that's tremendous progress, tremendous progress. People start to accept it and say, "Yes, this is very common, very normal." So I really feel it is very important to realize the progress. Of course, we are going to have more problems, more conflicts.

What concerns me most about the current debate is that many critics of affirmative action believe that the most democratic and fair way is to be color blind in student admissions, faculty hiring, and even in the outreach to the K–12 schools. Yet, no matter whether we continue or end affirmative action, we must define a way for Americans of diverse backgrounds to overcome racial divisions and to learn to live and work and really produce together for this great country. As Professor Smelser also wisely suggested, this is not a problem that Americans can afford to ignore.

I must confess, though, that I interpret some matters differently from the way Neil Smelser does. (It is not at all unusual for two Berkeley professors to see things differently!) *Where he sees problems and conflict, I tend to see opportunities, and even progress.* First, he described the problems associated with the emergence of identity politics. While I do not deny that that's very important, my view is that if we accept racial division as a key issue in our society, we cannot avoid this development. The best way to confront that issue is in a very positive, direct, open manner. Being direct in this way does facilitate some group-based patterns of association. I think this is progress. I believe that we should not be afraid of this.

My predecessor, Michael Heyman, commissioned a study several years ago, *The Diversity Project.* Led by Troy Duster of the department of sociology, this report delved closely into many patterns of campus life, examining the congruencies between ethnic conflict and learning. One of the recommendations was particularly intriguing: "Give institutional support which appears on the surface to have contradictory aims, i.e., support both a) ethnic 'support groups' and b) groups which explicitly wish to form across ethnic and racial boundaries in behalf of some common purpose" (*The Diversity Project,* p. 60). At Berkeley, as on so many campuses, the emergency of "identity" politics has provided an opportunity both to recognize and to enhance the "cultural competence" of persons who are members of groups who have been excluded. But we have also sought to provide opportunities to work together on behalf of a shared purpose.

One result of this has been the development of the American Cultures Program. Instead of requiring our students to take an ethnic studies class or some similar course, the faculty have designed an entire program with the goal of having students contrast various ethnic groups in America and their experiences. In the American Cultures Program, faculty members are required to teach courses that examine an issue and how it relates to at least three American ethnic groups. Faculty members are offered stipends to transform current courses or research that they might be involved in to fit the guidelines, as most do not. Also arranged are biweekly, two-hour seminars during the month of June and a series of lunches during the school year for professors participating in the program so they can share their work with their colleagues. These meetings allow professors to expand the style as well as the content of their courses, American Cultures as well as their departmental specialties, with different perspectives from other disciplines. An English professor can use history and architecture in relation to a group or concept to flesh out her lecture and make it come alive for students.

Professors can also learn from their students. Due to the nature of the classes, many students can see themselves in the issues discussed in class. This kind of sharing of experiences has provided faculty with new ideas on angles in research questions. Students have responded strongly to the idea of being able to share their experiences and put them in the context of the class, bringing in the diversity of the Berkeley campus to the classroom and helping other students learn. The American Cultures Program is a concrete illustration of my essential belief that taking diversity seriously has enormous intellectual and social benefits.

We must continue to reach for quality and potential among all the citizens of California. I believe that diversity is an educational imperative for a leading public institution and that we must continue to meet the difficult challenge of mediating this imperative with our other central responsibilities and the quest for institutional excellence. Certainly, there will be more disagreements. That likelihood does not mean we should not do a better job in diversifying. It seems to me that the combination of efforts like the Berkeley Pledge and the American Cultures Program provides models that address the double mandate our University faces to pursue both equity and excellence, without shrinking away from facing the ways in which these goals can compete with each other. In an article by Elaine Woo titled "Probe Finds No Bias in Berkeley Admissions," printed in *The Los Angeles Times*, 21 March 1996, I was very gratified to see the figures released by the office of Civil Rights which showed that at Berkeley the student body became more diversified and the quality increased. "That's amazing," people say. "That's impossible."

It is possible if we muster and sustain the will to do it.

EUGENE Y. LOWE, JR.

FROM AN ANALYTICAL perspective, the present South African situation conflates three themes that have developed over a much longer span of time in American experience, where the most vexing racial enigmas also focus on the histories of black and white relations. First, the constitutional reforms that led in October 1996 to the adoption of a nonracially-based constitution definitively signal a new era in political and institutional relationships among the various ethnic groups comprising that country's 41 million people. Second, the apartheid legacy, which until 1990 formally segregated blacks and whites, continues in the post-apartheid period to exercise profound influence on the emergence of a new South Africa. Finally, with respect to higher education, this legacy sets the terms by which higher education institutions mediate the tension between equity and excellence.

The effects of a discriminatory, stigmatizing history—to which the black majority in South Africa and the black minority in the United States have been persistently subjected ideologically and institutionally —have not been obliterated with the ratification of a new constitution. While legal change represents an important positive step, it is not sufficient in and of itself to change the habits of belief and experience that undergird ideologies of discrimination. Stereotypes and racial stigma seem to survive formal institutional repudiation. In both the United States and South Africa, despite important differences of history and culture, the tension between civil rights principles of nondiscrimination and inclusiveness must be reconciled with policies that reasonably respond to the persisting aftereffects of legally sanctioned racism.

The question of immediate concern to those who teach in and oversee our leading educational institutions is how the missions of teaching, research, and service in colleges and universities respond to an inescapable history, while at the same time making judgments that support high standards of excellence—standards that sustain broad support among diverse constituencies. In academic institutions it matters what people believe, particularly in those critical domains of institutional action and teaching and learning that fall outside central administrative oversight. Institutional decisions to become inclusive, effected through administrative action, must also be legitimated by the voluntary adherence of non-administrative constituents before the process of institutional change can become fully effective.

As long as there is estrangement between formally professed beliefs about inclusiveness and diversity and practical habits of thinking and association, the tension of promise and dilemma will persist as a pressure point. In American experience, this tension derives from the foundational tension between individualism and community identified by Alexis de Tocqueville more than 150 years ago in *Democracy in America*. We must recognize that "undoing" the effects of discrimination and racism is a long-term proposition. Policies and practices that reflect this commitment must be grounded in an understanding of the long-term needs of society as a whole. Even with repeated affirmation about the importance of thinking about the long-term political and social interests of the community, these efforts will be subjected to constant criticism in the name of individual fairness.

At the same time, educational institutions must be committed to regular self-examination of policies, programs, and practices that have been adopted to support the goals of racial diversity. The implications of persistently small numbers of qualified underrepresented minority students and the so-called "achievement gap" must be candidly addressed. We cannot fail to be critical about processes and strategies that we have adopted in support of long-term goals of equity. In other words, educational institutions have a responsibility to learn from their experience and improve institutional practices that support racial diversity. Leadership requires both attention to long-term goals and the courage to consider evidence about ways to better do the work that supports those goals (Bowen and Bok 1998).

The decisions taken in American colleges and universities following the civil rights revolution of the 1960s — to become more racially inclusive and to incorporate diversity as an intellectual and moral goal — brought this foundational tension directly into the processes and patterns of institutional life in admissions, campus life, and, finally, faculty and curricular development. This fundamental institutional reorientation, initially stimulated by the imperative of nondiscrimination, has progressed to a point wherein substantive critical reflection can provide the basis for advancing the mission of diversity in ways that also garner the uncoerced support of institutional constituents whose valuations about diversity remain inchoate or uncertain.

The responsible examination of the practices and outcomes in teaching and learning, which both Uri Treisman's and Richard Light's comments enjoin us to consider (though in different ways), provides a platform for engaging the educational meanings of diversity in the experience of students and faculty. Developing an understanding of these effects within and beyond the campus experience itself represents a challenge and an opportunity. Shrinking from this responsibility will substantially constrain us in the pursuit of what is most true and beautiful and good about the promise of diversity, and mire us more deeply in the dilemma that has shaped our historical evolution.

Our purpose in *Promise and Dilemma* has been to provoke and encourage a critical examination of institutional values, practices, and objectives in light of what we have learned and what we must yet accomplish. The distinguished historian John Hope Franklin (Franklin 1989) has argued eloquently about the importance of formulating public and institutional policies that reckon responsibly with the legacy of racial discrimination. While the present time is unquestionably a period of opportunity, we who are stewards of educational institutions have a responsibility to future generations to put in place a foundation for a more encompassing equity and a vision of excellence that does not embody or revive the stigmas of past policies and habits of discrimination.

## REFERENCES

Bowen, William G., and Derek Bok et al. 1998. *The Shape of the River: Long-Term Consequences of Considering Race in College and University Admissions*. Princeton, NJ: Princeton University Press.

Franklin, John Hope. 1989. *Race and History: Selected Essays*. Baton Rouge, LA: Louisiana State University Press.

# INDEX

Academic achievement, non-Asian minorities and:
  between- and within-social-class gaps, 55–58
  cultural differences, role of, 67–70
  discrimination and prejudice, impact of, 63–66
  economic issues, 70–71
  educationally bimodal nature of immigration, 60–63
  parental differences, role of, 66–67
  reasons for gaps, 63–73
  recommendations for increasing, 73–81
  regional variations in, 59–60
  school reform and, 71–73
  size of gaps in, 48–55
Academic identification:
  defined, 98–99
  threats to, 99–103
Academic leadership, diversity and equality and role of, 16–24
ACT (American College Test), 50
Affirmative action:
  ambiguity in implementing programs, 175–77
  backlash against, 183–92
  *Bakke v. Regents of the University of California*, 20, 25–28, 176
  California Civil Rights Initiative (1996), 31–34, 36, 172
  changes in definition of, 4–5, 24–25
  cultural context, 171–73
  debate of 1995, 186–92
  fairness of racial preferences and, 9–11
  historical context, 169–71
  *Hopwood v. University of Texas*, 28–32
  performance differentials and, 5–6
  political context, 173–75
  problem of small numbers, 34–37
  trends, 177–80
  in the University of California, 180–98
African Americans:
  academic achievement test scores, 48–50
  between- and within-social-class performance gaps, 55–58

college dropout rates, 95
grade point averages, 50
SATs, 50–54, 56–58, 61–63
stereotype threat, 107–12
Allport, Gordon, 10
American Cultures Program, 197–98
*American Dilemma: The Negro Problem and Modern Democracy, An* (Myrdal), 10, 92
*American Imperative, An* (Miller), 38–39
Aronson, Joshua, 107, 109, 118
Asian Americans:
  between- and within-social-class performance gaps, 55–58
  grade point averages, 50
  SATs, 50–54, 56–58, 61–63
Atkinson, Richard, 190

*Bakke v. Regents of the University of California*, 20, 25–28, 176
Bandura, A., 119
*Bell Curve, The* (Herrnstein and Murray), 64
Benbow, C. P., 105
Berkeley Pledge, 195–96
Boston public schools, 1970s crisis in, 12–13
Brown, Jerry, 185
*Brown v. Board of Education*, 10

California, affirmative action and assessment of, 193–98
  Civil Rights Initiative (1996), 31–34, 36, 172
  1995 debate, 186–92
  Proposition 187, 32, 185
Canady, Charles T., 33
Carnochan, W. B., 21
Challenge Program, 79
Civil Rights Act (1866), 163
Civil Rights Act (1964), 11
Civil Rights movement, 13–14, 24–25, 170
Clark, K. B., 111
Clark, M. K., 111